Studies Economic Reform and Social Justice

Evaluating Economic Research in a Contested Discipline: Rankings, Pluralism, and the Future of Heterodox Economics

Edited by

Frederic S. Lee and Wolfram Elsner

Studies in Economic Reform and Social Justice

Evaluating Economic Research in a Contested Discipline: Rankings, Pluralism, and the Future of Heterodox Economics

Edited by

Frederic S. Lee and Wolfram Elsner

WILEY-BLACKWELL

This edition first published 2010
© 2010 American Journal of Economics and Sociology, Inc.

Blackwell Publishing was acquired by John Wiley & Sons in February 2007. Blackwell's publishing program has been merged with Wiley's global scientific, technical, and medical business to form Wiley-Blackwell.

Registered Office
John Wiley & Sons Ltd, The Atrium, Southern Gate, Chichester, West Sussex, PO19 8SQ, United Kingdom

Editorial Offices
350 Main Street, Malden, MA 02148-5020, USA
9600 Garsington Road, Oxford, OX4 2DQ, UK
The Atrium, Southern Gate, Chichester, West Sussex, PO19 8SQ, UK

For details of our global editorial offices, for customer services, and for information about how to apply for permission to reuse the copyright material in this book, please see our website at www.wiley.com/wiley-blackwell.

The rights of Frederic S. Lee and Wolfram Elsner to be identified as the author of the editorial material in this work has been asserted in accordance with the Copyright, Designs and Patents Act 1988.

Wiley also publishes its books in a variety of electronic formats. Some content that appears in print may not be available in electronic books.

Designations used by companies to distinguish their products are often claimed as trademarks. All brand names and product names used in this book are trade names, service marks, trademarks, or registered trademarks of their respective owners. The publisher is not associated with any product or vendor mentioned in this book. This publication is designed to provide accurate and authoritative information in regard to the subject matter covered. It is sold on the understanding that the publisher is not engaged in rendering professional services. If professional advice or other expert assistance is required, the services of a competent professional should be sought.

Library of Congress Cataloging-in-Publication Data

Studies in economic reform and social justice : evaluating economic research in a contested discipline : rankings, pluralism, and the future of heterodox economics / edited by Frederic S. Lee and Wolfram Elsner.
     p. cm
  ISBN 978-1-4443-3945-1 (casebound)—ISBN 978-1-4443-3946-8 (pbk.)
  1. Economics—Research—Methodology.   2. Radical economics.   3. Social justice.
I. Lee, Frederic S., 1949–   II. Elsner, Wolfram.
  HB74.5.S88 2010
  330.072—dc22
                                                              2010038215

A catalogue record for this book is available from the Library of Congress.

Set in 10 on 13pt Garamond Light by Toppan Best-set Premedia Limited
Printed in Singapore by Markono Print Media Pte Ltd.

01—2010

Contents

Editors' Introduction*

By Wolfram Elsner and Frederic S. Lee

Evaluating Research and the Ruling Game of Mainstream Economics

Evaluating economic research today is a contested field. This applies
particularly to economics where individual careers of a whole generation of critical young economists are affected. This is because
economics, perhaps more than in any other discipline, is the most
important academic discipline for the ideological legitimization of
capitalism. Hence it is one of the few, if not the only, fundamentally
divided and contested disciplines. What the ruling forces of the
economy, professional politics, administration science, and particularly of economic science have made out of the complex issues and
processes of evaluating research quality is reducing them down to a
simplistic, allegedly exact, objective, and clear, but fundamentally
mistaken procedure of a one-dimensional ranking of quantitative
domination, a cumulative dictatorship of mass. In addition this is
done in surprisingly unprofessional ways, subject to many obvious
misconceptions and failures. For example, the International Mathematical Union, the International Council of Industrial and Applied
Mathematics, and the Institute of Mathematical Statistics have argued
in a joint report released in June 2008 that the belief that citation
statistics are accurate measures of scholarly performance is

*All but one of the articles in this issue were presented at the workshop "Assessing
Economic Research in a European Context: The Future of Heterodox Economics and its
Research in a Non-Pluralist Mainstream Environment," University of Bremen, Germany,
26-27 June 2009. We are grateful to the Hans-Boeckler Foundation of the German trade
unions (DGB) and the Charles-Leopold Mayer Foundation and its International Initiative
for Rethinking the Economy for their financial support of the workshop.

Professor Wolfram Elsner, Faculty of Business Studies and Economics, Institute for
Institutional and Innovation, Economics, University of Bremen, Bremen, Germany,
E-mail: welsner@uni-bremen.de

Professor Frederic S. Lee, Department of Economics, 211 Haag Hall, University of
Missouri–Kansas City, 5100 Rockhill Road, Kansas City, Missouri 64110, United States,
E-mail: leefs@umkc.edu

American Journal of Economics and Sociology, Vol. 69, No. 5 (November, 2010).

unfounded. The use of such statistics is often highly subjective, the validity of these statistics is neither well understood nor well studied, and the sole reliance on citation data provides at best an incomplete and often shallow understanding of research (Adler, Ewing, and Taylor 2008: 2). In the same light, Bruno Frey and Katja Rost (2008: 1) found that publication and citation rankings do not effectively measure research quality and that career decisions based on rankings are dominated by chance.

Not surprisingly, in economics, the problems are quite clear—it is a deeply divided science dominated by mainstream or neoclassical economics. In spite of its dominance, neoclassical economics is not above criticism. Physicist Marc Buchanan (2008) argues in a *New York Times* op-ed piece that economics is the only scientific discipline that is not yet modern, since its mainstream is not complex but simplistic with its dominant market-optimality and equilibrium vision. Moreover, this outmoded mainstream has to be considered responsible—as far as science can be responsible—for the biggest and deepest global financial, economic, food and resources, climate, social, political, and moral crises and catastrophes in the last 60 years. As even *The Times* has stated in February 2009:

> Economists are the forgotten guilty men. Academics—and their mad theories—are to blame for the financial crisis. They too deserve to be hauled into the dock. (Kaletsky 2009a)

Similarly, *The Financial Times* had a lengthy article about the "uselessness of most 'state of the art' academic monetary economics" in March 2009 (Buiter 2009). Also *Scientific American* had an article in April 2008 about mainstream economics with the headline "The Economist Has No Clothes," arguing that mainstream economics has no proper world view to comprehend, articulate, and address the most basic human problems, let alone to tackle and solve them (Nadeau 2008). Countless other critical declarations of economists have appeared since the burst of the giant financial bubble, including an article titled "The Financial Crisis and the Systemic Failure of Academic Economics" published in the so-called *Dahlem Report*, which was launched in February 2009 by David Colander, Hans Foellmer, Alan Kirman, and other well-known complexity and evolutionary economists. However, in spite of the criticisms, mainstream economics is still neatly interwoven with the most powerful ruling forces in big finance, with the big business corporate economy, and with big politics, and still occupies the political and administrative power positions designed for economists.

Despite these severe and fundamental failures, over the last three decades the ruling forces of mainstream economics and their allies in politics, public administration, and in the organizations of big business utilize rankings as a power device to rule, direct research funds to their own ranks, to make or destroy careers of critical economists, up- and downgrade journals and departments, and, particularly, to elbow out of academic research, teaching, and advice their potential competitors of the diverse heterodox approaches (Lee and Elsner 2008; Lee 2009). The dramatic and aggravating real-world problems require an opening up of the neoliberal mythologies that are based on the simplistic core model of the optimal, equilibrating, and stable market economy. A new, broad reflection of the practices of mainstream economics and a motion towards an active pluralism in all leading departments, schools, and journals is overdue in face of the severest crisis the capitalist market economy has experienced since the 1930s. However, on the contrary, it appears that building on its long running current attack, there is a new *offensive of the mainstream* alliance against the heterodox economists to push them out of academia completely. In fact, after some few months of confusion and uncertainty about the disaster caused by their creeds, orders, and advice, mainstream economists are back again developing their own particular narratives of the crisis (Taylor 2009; Meltzer 2009). They argue that it was caused by too much—and inherently deficient—state intervention rather than too little regulation and surveillance in the public interest. After some months of shock and relative retreat and quietness it also remains clear that neoliberal economists are still in power—and some have even newly come into power in the Obama administration or the new German government—and are *back with "more market,"* against real financial market or health insurance reforms, but with hundreds of billions of taxpayer money put into the balances of the gamblers' and desperadoes' banks, financial funds, and insurance companies.

This seems to be exactly what the leading elites require in times of crises: *banning real change*, persecuting critics in the economics profession who want the chance to organize real change in order to realign individual business behavior with the collective requirements of the public. Thus, it seems that the very *economic crisis and depression becomes an additional cause for ideological cleansing* rather than a critical self-reflection and change. In her 2007 "*shock-doctrine*" book Naomi Klein has developed and substantiated the idea that the ruling forces are not, in fact, interested in instrumental problem-solving. Others, such as Marc Lutz, have analyzed economics as the still "*Dismal Science*" that today would accept, if not promote, insecurity, anxiety, turbulence, and pauperization to keep the ruling castes in power and serve their interests (Lutz 2008).

In our introduction of a special issue of *On the Horizon* in 2008, we disagreed with some critical economists like Sheila Dow, John Davis, Tony Lawson, Roger Backhouse, and David Colander who suggested that there is and will be more pluralism emerging in economics and that the mainstream is somehow fragmenting and dissolving (as cited in Lee and Elsner 2008). Our pessimistic view of an ongoing coun-terattack, in contrast, was based on the fact that even a relative dominance of heterodoxy in terms of research questions, approaches, and methodologies over the last, say, 25 years has not spilled over into the areas of funding and recruitment for heterodox economists, of the curricula of mass teaching and the advice business, and has left untouched the mainstream's and its allies' general world view. The theoretical training of mainstream economists and their vested inter-ests continue to dominate the economics profession through their control of the peer review process and the ranking of economic journals and departments, and continue to dominate over economic and societal problem solving. As noted above, the core of the neo-classical paradigm and neoliberal world view remains unshaken. It is of little help that even some prominent economists warn against the destruction of motivations of many young economists and against the obvious "undesired lock-in effects" of the ruling ranking game (Frey and Osterloh 2006). The "Ivory Tower [remains] Unswayed by Crash-ing Economy," as Patricia Cohen has said in the *New York Times* in March 2009, noting that "[t]he basic curriculum will not change."

Although—or because—peer reviewing is essential for stabilizing mainstream economics and the reproduction of mainstream economists in academia, the practices of the ruling peer review process have been under attack for some time. In their book *Peerless Science* (1990) Chubin and Hackett had already reported "that only 8 percent of the members of the Scientific Research Society agreed that peer reviews work well as it is" (Chubin and Hackett 1990: 192). Peer reviewing has come under scrutiny even by the European Union European Science Foundation, which held a conference on peer reviews in October 2006 (European Science Foundation 2007). Frey has a much cited paper titled "Publishing as Prostitution" (2003: 206) where he stated that authors have to slavishly follow the demands of anonymous referees without property rights in the journals they advise, that is, without being committed to the journal and its publication process—or the individual careers of the submitters—let alone to the knowledge impact of the whole procedure. In fact, there are many case studies that have ascertained that "peer review lacks validity, impartiality, and fairness" (Seidl, Schmidt, and Groesche 2005: 506). Moreover, it has been demonstrated that there are straightforward path-dependent effects—or herd behavior one might say—in the *citation culture*: frequently cited papers and authors are cited more often, that is, the fame of papers and authors, once gained, has lasting increasing returns to scale (see Tol 2009). In all, Andrew Oswald has found, in the run-up to the British Research Assessment Exercise (RAE) 2008, that "the publication system is full of error" (Oswald 2006: 9). It would routinely put low-quality papers into the top-ranked journals. He stated that "unless hiring committees, promotion boards and funding bodies are aware of this fact, they are likely to make bad choices about whom to promote and how to allocate resources" (Oswald 2006: 9). Similarly, Frey has stated a "Publication Impossibly Theorem": the publication incentive structure in favor of the top journals (with their few paper slots) is such that the wrong output may be produced in an inefficient way and wrong people may be selected (Frey 2009).

Finally, many have shown that *citation impacts differ considerably across the different bibliographic electronic sources*, such as Econlit, JSTOR, Scopus, and Google Scholar, with major impacts particularly on the ranking positions of heterodox journals and scholars (D'Orlando 2009). This implies that heterodox themes, fields, and authors do vary drastically depending on the databases that are used for the rankings. This will be the subject of several articles in this issue.

From Rankings to the Pluralist Economics of Tomorrow

Time seems to be more than ripe for more pluralism in and pluralist teaching of economics (Raveaud 2009; Groenewegen 2007). As *The Times* has put it in February 2009: "Now is the time for a revolution in economic thought" (Kaletsky 2009b). This would have to be a move towards a culture of *active pluralism*. It implies looking at alternative, enlightened methodologies of evaluating scholarship that do not discriminate, but include and appreciate *any* qualified contribution to the growth of the social knowledge fund. Preparing the ground for this culture is the aim of the articles in this issue of the *American Journal of Economics and Sociology* (*AJES*).

Quality ranking of economic journals and departments is a widespread practice in the United States, Europe, Australia, and elsewhere. In many cases, bibliometric-based scores are created to rank journals and then the scores qua the journal rankings are used to rank departments (Lee 2006). One of the popular bibliometric measures is the Social Science Citation Index (SSCI) impact factor. In a very innovative study, Therese Grijalva and Clifford Nowell (2008) used the SSCI impact factor for economics journals to rank U.S. doctoral programs. However, the SSCI coverage of economic journals omits a number of heterodox economics journals; as a result the impact factor scores for the included heterodox journals are biased downward. So the question is, how would the Grijalva-Nowell rankings of U.S. doctoral programs change if additional heterodox journals with a better bibliometric measure of their research quality were included (with the impact factor scores for the mainstream journals remaining the same). To answer this question, Frederic Lee worked with Grijalva and Nowell to develop a more equitable quality measure for heterodox journals, which is then equated with the SSCI impact scores for mainstream economics journals to produce a quality-equality score for both the heterodox and mainstream journals. This new quality measure or score is applied to the Grijalva-Nowell study augmented with additional heterodox journals. As a result, heterodox doctoral programs have significantly moved up in their rankings, including moving into the top 30 departments. The significance of the Lee-Grijalva-Nowell article is that different measures of research quality produce different journal and department rankings.

This fact is not always acknowledged by heterodox economists. Jakob Kapeller addresses this in his article with a discussion of the inadequacies of the SSCI impact factor in general, and with regard to heterodox economics. He then outlines various options that heterodox economists have to pursue to escape the clutches of the impact factor. Kapeller notes that heterodox economists cite mainstream journals whereas the reverse is not true. Consequently, heterodox economists inflate the impact factor score for mainstream journals, which is in turn used to argue that the research quality of mainstream journals is significantly superior to heterodox journals. Frederic Lee and Bruce Cronin also address this point in their article by first developing an alternative bibliometric peer review research quality measure to rank 62 heterodox journals. They then use the measure in conjunction with the SSCI impact factor to produce a comparative research quality-equality ranking of 62 heterodox and the 192 mainstream journals in the SSCI. The new journal ranking reveals that the research quality of many heterodox journals is comparable to the research quality of many top mainstream journals.

Bibliometric-citation data can be used for purposes other than ranking journals and departments. Martha Starr uses it in her article to examine in a very insightful way the impact of the *Review of Social Economy* (*RoSE*) on heterodox economics. She finds that to increase *RoSE*'s impact on heterodox research, its articles need to be interesting and accessible to broad audiences, to prompt people to change their thinking, and to open up channels of communication between diverse communities of scholars. Similarly, Bruce Cronin uses citation data in conjunction with social network analysis in his article to examine the diffusion of heterodox economic ideas beyond the immediate confines of heterodox and mainstream journals.

Utilizing data from various bibliographic databases, he discovers that heterodox ideas find their way into accounting, sociology, geography, and other areas. Thus, to disseminate heterodox ideas and broaden their academic and economic-political impact, heterodox economists, Cronin suggest, should consider strategies of publishing articles in external but closely aligned journals that are key intermediaries. However, for the strategy to be successful, continual development and strengthening of heterodox economics is necessary. On the other hand, Marcella Corsi, Carlo D'Ippoliti, and Federico Lucidi use bibliometric data in their article to examine the outcome of Italy's recent research evaluation exercise and its possible negative impact on heterodox economics and pluralism. In particular, they argue that by basing the quality of publications on a value scale shared by the mainstream international economics community, the research exercise favored publications in mainstream journals. Consequently, economics departments will discriminate in favor of publications in mainstream journals with negative consequences for heterodox economists.

Since 1986, when the United Kingdom undertook its first research assessment exercise, national evaluation of university research has spread first throughout Europe and then to the rest of the world. When applied to economics, the outcome is quite negative for heterodox economics (Lee 2009: chs. 8–9; Vlachou 2008). In his article, Harry Bloch provides an insider's view of the Australian approach to its national evaluation of university research and its impact on heterodox economics. What Bloch and the abovementioned authors make clear, is that the existence of heterodox economics is dependent in part on how open mainstream is to different economic theories. This point is relevant to Agnieszka Ziomek's article, which deals with the emergence of institutional economics in Poland since 1989. Of particular interest is her discussion of how the ending of the transition period in the late 1990s provided space for both old and new institutional economics to emerge. That is, since 2000, problems of employment, local and regional development, and clientelism have pushed some Polish economists to look for ideas and arguments outside of the more conventional mainstream economics to deal with them.

The last three articles broaden the discussion to what economics, with its two contending factions, should be in the future. In his article, Dieter Bogenhold discusses the methodological and institutional context of heterodox economics and its relationship to mainstream economics. Alan Freeman addresses the question of whether in the United Kingdom a new social contract is needed for economics. He argues that academic economics in the United Kingdom is in a state of regulatory capture by mainstream economists. As a result, there is an enforcement of one way of thinking about economics problems, which resulted in the failure of the economics profession to be able to anticipate and understand the financial crash and recession of 2008. To alter this, a benchmarking for pluralism in economics is needed—economists need to be taught to value pluralism. Drawing from the thrust of the previous two articles, Marco Novarese and Andrea Pozzali ask the question whether academic economics is useful to society and hence deserves to be supported by the state (and society at large). However, they argue, the incentive structure of mainstream economics favors publication in a set of inward looking journals and punishes those economists that do not follow it. This has led to an intellectual stifling of pluralist intellectual debate within the profession, and the inability to contribute to the wider social discussion of important economic issues. This suggests that a new social contract is needed for economics.

Conclusion

Bibliometric analysis, evaluating research quality, and ranking departments are here to stay at least for the foreseeable future. The articles in this issue of the *AJES* accept this and show how they can be used in a positive way for developing and advancing heterodox economics. It is necessary, however, to go beyond them to develop even better ways to evaluate heterodox research and promote its dissemination within and outside of economics. This also requires additional efforts beyond the well-known "Plea for a Pluralistic and Rigorous Economics" published in the *American Economic Review* (McCloskey, Hodgson, and Maki 1992), open letters and petitions against national research and department ranking exercises (Lettera Aperta 2009; La

Defense des Revues 2009; Journals under Threat 2009), and conferences by the International Confederation of Associations for Pluralism
in Economics (Garnett, Olsen, and Starr 2010) to make pluralism a
value that is important to mainstream as well as to heterodox economists. The future of heterodox economics depends on how successful
these efforts are.

References

Adler, R., J. Ewing, and P. Taylor. (2008). "Citation Statistics." A Report from
the International Mathematical Union in Cooperation with the International Council of Industrial and Applied Mathematics and the Institute
of Mathematical Statistics, available at: http://www.mathunion.org/
fileadmin/IMU/Report/CitationStatistics.pdf.

Buchanan, M. (2008). "This Economy Does Not Compute." *New York Times*,
OP-ED, October 1.

Buiter, W. (2009). "The Unfortunate Uselessness of Most 'State of the Art'
Academic Monetary Economics." *Financial Times*, March 3. http://
blogs.ft.com/maverecon/2009/03/the-unfortunate-uselessness-of-most-
state-of-the-art-academic-monetary-economics/.

Chubin, D. E., and E. J. Hackett. (1990). *Peerless Science: Peer Review and U.S.
Science Policy.* New York: State University of New York Press.

Cohen, P. (2009). "Ivory Tower Unswayed by Crashing Economy." *New York
Times*, March 4. http://www.nytimes.com/2009/03/05/books/05deba.
html?_r=1.

Colander, D. et al. (2009). "The Financial Crisis and the Systemic Failure of
Academic Economics." Unpublished. University of Kiel, Germany. http://
debtdeflation.com/blogs/wp-content/uploads/papers/Dahlem_
Report_EconCrisis021809.pdf.

D'Orlando, F. (2009). "Electronic Resources and Heterodox Economists."
University of Cassino. Department of Economics Science Working Paper
2/2009. http://dipse.unicas.it/files/wp200902.pdf.

European Science Foundation. (2007). *Peer Review: Its Present and
Future State.* Strasbourg: ESF. http://www.esf.org/index.php?eID=tx_
nawsecuredl&u=0&file=fileadmin/be_user/publications/Peerreview2006.
pdf&t=1273166789&hash=f9733e225ee15f8f1100cb6cb67cd8ab.

Frey, B. (2003). "Publishing as Prostitution? Choosing Between One's Own
Ideas and Academic Failure." *Public Choice* 116(1–2): 205–223.

———. (2009). "Economists in the PITS?" *International Review of Economics*
56(4): 335–346.

Frey, B., and M. Osterloh. (2006). "Evaluations: Hidden Costs, Questionable
Benefits, and Superior Alternatives." Institute of Empirical Research in

Economics Working Paper No. 302, University of Zurich. http://www.iew.uzh.ch/wp/iewwp302.pdf.

Frey, B., and K. Rost. (2008). "Do Rankings Reflect Research Quality?" Institute for Empirical Research in Economics Working Paper No. 390, University of Zurich. http://www.iew.uzh.ch/wp/iewwp390.pdf.

Garnett, R., E. K. Olsen, and M. Starr. (eds.) (2010). *Economic Pluralism.* London: Routledge.

Grijalva, T., and C. Nowell. (2008). "A Guide to Graduate Study in Economics: Ranking Economics Departments by Fields of Expertise." *Southern Economic Journal* 74(4): 971–996.

Groenewegen, J. (ed.) (2007). *Teaching Pluralism in Economics.* Cheltenham: Edward Elgar.

Kaletsky, A. (2009a). "Economists are the Forgotten Guilty Men." *Times,* TIMESONLINE, February 5. http://www.timesonline.co.uk/tol/comment/columnists/anatole_kaletsky/article5663091.ece.

——. (2009b). "Now is the Time for a Revolution in Economic Thought." *Times,* TIMESONLINE, February 9. http://www.timesonline.co.uk/tol/comment/columnists/article5689642.ece.

Klein, N. (2007). *The Shock Doctrine: The Rise of Disaster Capitalism.* New York: Henry Holt and Co.

La Defense des Revues de Sciences Humaines et Sociales. (2009). http://shesp.lautre.net/spip.php?article46.

Lee, F. S. (2006). "The Ranking Game, Class, and Scholarship in American Economics." *Australasian Journal of Economics Education* 3(1–2): 1–41.

——. (2009). *A History of Heterodox Economics: Challenging the Mainstream in the Twentieth Century.* London: Routledge.

Lee, F. S., and W. Elsner. (2008). "Publishing, Ranking, and the Future of Heterodox Economics." *On the Horizon* 16(4): 176–184.

Lettera Aperta sulla Valutazione della Ricerca nelle Discipline Economiche. (2009). http://www.letteraapertavalutazionericerca.it.

Lutz, M. A. (2008). "The 'Dismal Science'—Still? Economics and Human Flourishing." *Review of Political Economy* 20(2): 163–180.

McCloskey, D., G. Hodgson, and U. Maki. (1992). "A Plea for a Pluralistic and Rigorous Economics." *American Economic Review* 82(2): xxv.

Meltzer, A. H. (2009). "Reflections on the Financial Crisis." *Cato Journal* 29(1): 25–30.

Nadeau, R. (2008). "The Economist Has No Clothes." *Scientific American* 298(4): 42.

Oswald, A. (2006). "Prestige Labels." *Royal Economic Society Newsletter* 135(October): 7–10.

Raveaud, G. (2009). "A Pluralist Teaching of Economics: Why and How." In *Economic Pluralism.* Eds. R. F. Garnett, E. Olsen, and M. Starr, pp. 250–61. London: Routledge.

Seidl, C., U. Schmidt, and P. Groesche. (2005). "The Performance of Peer Review and a Beauty Contest of Referee Processes of Economics Journals." *Estudios De Economia Aplicada* 23(3): 505–551.

Taylor, J. B. (2009). *Getting Off Track: How Government Actions and Interventions Caused Prolonged, and Worsened the Financial Crisis.* Stanford: Hoover Institution Press.

Tol, R. S. J. (2009). "The Matthew Effect Defined and Tested for the 100 Most Prolific Economists." *Journal of the American Society for Information Science and Technology* 60(2): 420–426.

Vlachou, A. (2008). "Ranking and the Prospects of Heterodox Economics in Greece." *On the Horizon* 16(4): 293–297.

Ranking Economics Departments in a Contested Discipline: A Bibliometric Approach to Quality Equality Between Theoretically Distinct Subdisciplines

By Frederic S. Lee, Therese C. Grijalva and Clifford Nowell

ABSTRACT. Quality ranking of economic journals and departments is a widespread practice in the United States. The methods used are peer review and bibliometric measures. In a divided discipline such as economics scientific knowledge is contested. So knowing which journals and departments are the best in terms of research is somewhat muddied. If the methods used to measure the production of quality scientific knowledge are tilted towards one of the contested approaches, the resulting quality rankings of journals and departments are tilted as well. So if the objective is the open-minded pursuit of the production of scientific knowledge, then it is important to have measures of quality that treat the different contested approaches equally. Our article explores this issue by examining the impact that a quality-equality bibliometric measure can have on the quality rankings of doctoral economic programs in the United States.

Introduction

Quality ranking of economic journals and departments is a widespread practice in the United States, Europe, Australia, and elsewhere. The methods used are peer review, bibliometric[1] measures, or (in a few cases) an ill-defined combination of the two.[2] Although the

Professor Frederic S. Lee, Department of Economics, UM—Kansas City, Kansas City, MO 64110, E-mail: leefs@umkc.edu

Professor Therese C. Grijalva, Department of Economics, Weber State University, Ogden, UT 84408-3807, E-mail: tgrijalva@weber.edu

Professor Clifford Nowell, Department of Economics, Weber State University, Ogden, UT 84408-3807, E-mail: cnowell@weber.edu

American Journal of Economics and Sociology, Vol. 69, No. 5 (November, 2010).

methods are subject to various criticisms, they continue to be used because they provide answers of sorts to questions that are continually asked by economists, undergraduate advisors and students, and university administrators, as well as government officials when the disbursement of large sums of monies to universities are involved (Lee 2006, 2009; Moed 2005; Weingart 2005).

The questions take the general form of "which journals and departments are most effective in producing scientific economic knowledge regarding the provisioning process." Since understanding, explaining, and suggesting ways to alter the provisioning process in light of particular political agendas and social policies is what economics and economists are all about, knowing the degree to which a journal or a department contributes to the production of scientific economic knowledge is important. However, in a divided discipline where scientific knowledge is contested, knowing which journals and departments are the best in doing so is somewhat muddied. If the methods used to judge or "measure" the production of quality scientific knowledge are tilted towards one of the contested approaches, the resulting quality rankings of journals and departments are tilted as well. So if the objective is the open-minded pursuit of the production of scientific knowledge of the provisioning process, then it is important to have measures of quality that treat the different contested approaches equally. Our article explores this issue by examining the impact that a quality-equality bibliometric measure can have on the quality rankings of doctoral economic programs in the United States.

In a recent article on ranking the 129 U.S. economic department programs existing in 2004, Grijalva and Nowell (2008) took a rather unusual bibliometric approach. That is, they first identified the tenure-track or tenure faculty of each department and then secondly identified the journal publications for each faculty member of each department for the period 1985 to 2004 if the journal was listed in the *Journal of Economic Literature* database Econlit.[3] Next, they selected the impact factors published in the 2004 Social Science Citation Index (SSCI scores) as the quality measure (Q) for each journal.[4] For each article, a weighting (W) was calculated that consisted of the number of pages divided by the number of authors, giving the number of pages per author, which was then divided by the average page length of all the articles in the journal for the period 1985 to 2004.[5] The quality measure was then multiplied by the weighting to yield a productivity value (P)–Q x W = P—which indicated the weighted quality assigned to each article assigned to each author. These weighted productivity values were summed by individual and then by department. The overall productivity values were used to rank the 129 departments in terms of absolute scores and by their average productivity (see Table 2, columns 2 and 4, pages 976–980). Finally, each article was assigned a JEL classification code from which it was possible to rank each department in each JEL "field" by summing the productivity values (see Table 3, pages 981–985 and Table 4, pages 987–994).[6]

Grijalva and Nowell acknowledged that SSCI impact factor based rankings are open to criticisms, such as the accuracy of the article-author-department combination, that they favor North American, Western European, and English language journals, and others (see Nisonger 2004).[7] However, given the domain of their study and the method of collecting the article-author-department data, these usual criticisms are minimized if not irrelevant. Instead our concerns are with two interrelated issues: the assumption that in economics, scientific knowledge is homogeneous to which any quality measure can be unambiguously applied and the limited coverage and partiality of the SSCI impact factor scores even when restricted to North American, Western European, and English language journals.

Economics is about explaining the provisioning process, the real economic activities that connect the individual with goods and services, or more succinctly, economics is defined as the science of the provisioning process.[8] As a field or discipline of scientific study, it consists of two distinctly different theoretical approaches to analyzing and delineating the provisioning process: neoclassical or mainstream economics and heterodox economics (Lee 2009, forthcoming). Although they contest each other's theoretical analysis, both mainstream and heterodox economics adhere to the discipline's goal of producing scientific knowledge regarding the provisioning process. But what constitutes scientific knowledge and its quality is determined by the scientific practices within the two subdisciplines in economics. Therefore, a quality metric utilized for mainstream economics is not appropriate for identifying quality research in heterodox economics.[9]

Consequently, for a quality metric to be used in an even handed way to rank departments in terms of the quality of research, it needs to be a synthesis of the different measures used in the two subdisciplines.

Secondly, the SSCI includes five heterodox economics journals: *Cambridge Journal of Economics, Feminist Economics, Journal of Economic Issues, Journal of Post Keynesian Economics*, and *Science and Society*;[10] and it does not include six well-known and established heterodox economic journals: *International Review of Applied Economics, Metroeconomica, Review of Black Political Economy, Review of Political Economy, Review of Radical Political Economics*, and *Review of Social Economy*.[11] By not including the latter six journals, the SSCI impact factor underreports the impact of the five heterodox journals it includes since the six excluded journals cite the five included journals (Lee 2008a, 2009); and implicitly assigns a zero impact to the journals it does not include. In terms of the Grijalva and Nowell study, articles appearing in the five SSCI heterodox journals possibly had lower impact factor scores than if the six excluded journals had been included in their determination, and articles that appeared in heterodox journals not covered by the SSCI were not counted. Both of these results reduced the overall productivity values for departments whose faculty publish in these journals.[12]

The SSCI impact factor has two additional shortcomings, the first being that it is a global measure and thus not restricted to a specific subdiscipline (Nisonger 2004). That is, the impact factor for a journal is based on citations made to it by other journals. If the population of other journals and articles that are prone to cite it is very large, then that journal has the possibility of a large impact factor score. On the other hand, if a journal is likely to be cited by a much smaller population of journals and articles, then it is likely that its impact factor score would be smaller (Moed 2005). This is the situation in economics where the population of mainstream journals and articles is quite large compared to heterodox journals and articles, with the outcome that many mainstream journals have impact factor scores four or five times that of any heterodox journal.[13] The situation is further skewed in that articles in heterodox journals cite mainstream journals whereas articles in mainstream journals do not cite heterodox journals.[14] Thus population size combined with the one-sided academic engagement between mainstream and heterodox economics pushes the SSCI impact factor scores towards mainstream journals.[15]

The second shortcoming is that because impact factor scores are implicitly based on the assumption that a discipline is engaged in normal science and scientific knowledge is homogeneous, they cannot deal with a situation, as in heterodox economics, where scientific knowledge is somewhat fractionalized and is in the process of becoming more interdependent and homogeneous. In this situation something more is needed in addition to impact factor scores to evaluate the quality of research and the scientific knowledge being produced.

In light of the above comments, the rest of the article is structured as follows. The next section briefly delineates the nature of citation-based quality measures, outlines a citation-based heterodox quality measure and compares it to the SSCI impact factor, and finally integrates both quality measures into a single overall heterodox *quality-equality measure*. The third section applies the measure to the data in the Grijalva and Nowell study augmented by publications from the six heterodox journals not included to examine the impact the heterodox-adjusted ranking of departments in terms of a overall productivity, average productivity, and fields. Since it is possible to identify and isolate the "heterodox presence" in economic departments qua doctoral programs, they can as a result also be ranked, which is carried out in the fourth section. The final section of the article discusses the implications that emerge from the previous sections for department rankings.

Methods

It is often argued that peer review is the only way to judge the quality (which is often not clearly defined) of an article, while the citations of the article are only an indirect and perhaps imperfect measure of its quality. However, there is enough evidence to suggest that peer review is also a very imperfect method of determining quality. The issue here is that quality is seen as something intrinsic to the piece of research and embodied in the article. This notion of quality has more to do with whether the article followed the protocols of accepted scientific practices; thus as long as such practices are followed, then an article has achieved acceptable *scholarly quality*. But this does not mean the article will be useful or of interest to its intended research community.

Given this, the *research quality* (as opposed to the scholarly quality) of an article can be identified in terms of its usefulness to and influence on the research community to which it is directed. In this case, citations are a very good way to quantitatively measure quality qua usefulness. Hence citation-based quality approaches measure the relative usefulness of an article qua journal to the community of scientists to which the article or journal is directed (Moed 2005; Lee 2006). However, the particular citation-based approach used to measure the research quality of a journal to a community of scholars depends on what research issue is being addressed.

As noted above, in economics the research goal of both mainstream and heterodox economists is to produce scientific knowledge about the provisioning process that is useful to their colleagues in teaching, research, and engagement in economic policy (and also to the wider public). In mainstream economics, with its normal science and homogeneous knowledge, the SSCI impact factor scores are a widely accepted measure of the usefulness of a journal and its articles to the community of mainstream economists, but this is not the case for heterodox economics where its scientific knowledge is relatively more heterogeneous, resulting in a lower degree of research dependency.

As argued in Lee (2008b), one purpose of heterodox economic journals is to publish peer-evaluated scientific knowledge, since it is through peer review, with the attention it pays to ensuring that papers follow the scientific practices and conventions of the heterodox community and subsequent discussion by the heterodox community, that the scholarly quality of journals publication is maintained. Because peer review is practiced by heterodox journals, it is assumed that articles published by them are similar in overall scholarly quality in terms of being adequately researched and written, of competently utilizing research methodologies and techniques, and of addressing topics of relevance to heterodox economists.

A second purpose is to build up an integrated body of heterodox scientific knowledge. This is achieved in two ways, the first being to build up a body of specific knowledge associated with a particular heterodox approach(s) and the second being to promote the development of an integrated heterodox economic theory through increasing the research dependency among heterodox economists. It is this second purpose—building specific economic knowledge and integrated heterodox theory through research dependency—that is the basis for determining the research quality of heterodox economic journals. Thus the research quality associated with a journal and its articles is in terms of the usefulness, importance, and relevance they have to building heterodox theory and research dependency; and this is the same kind of research quality that is associated with the SSCI impact factor, but measured differently.

The heterodox measure of research quality of a journal identifies the building of specific economic knowledge with its self-citations and the development of research dependency with its citations of current and past research published in many different heterodox journals. Hence a heterodox journal that is a significant builder of scientific knowledge through research dependency imports citations from and exports citations to most heterodox journals, has an overall balance of trade, and generates domestic production of citations equal to its imports and exports; in addition, its domestic production and import of citations include citations from recent (within the last five years) and distant publications. The maximum research quality score for a journal is seven, which means that it has fulfilled all the conditions for building both specialized and integrative heterodox scientific knowledge through research dependency; and a score of less than seven indicates that not all conditions have been met and therefore the extent that the journal can improve its contribution. The research quality scores for the heterodox journals (HEQ) used in this article are derived from Lee (2008b) and found in Table 1, column 2.[16]

Since both the SSCI impact factor and the HEQ measure the same kind of research quality, it is possible to develop a overall quality measure that coherently combines and integrates them both. However, there is one difference between them. The HEQ measure has a maximum score of seven, which is the benchmark that all heterodox journals could aim to achieve while the SSCI impact factor does not have such a benchmark that mainstream journals could aim

Table 1

The Research Quality Scores of Heterdox and Mainstream
Economics Journals

Journals	HEQ (out of 7)	HEQ*	SSCI Impact Factor	HEQSSCI
Cambridge Journal of Economics	3.11	0.444	0.217	1.412
Feminist Economics	2.84	0.406	0.250	1.290
International Review of Applied Economics	2.43	0.347		1.103
Journal of Economic Issues	2.52	0.360	0.373	1.144
Journal of Post Keynesian Economics	3.98	0.569	0.236	1.807
Metroeconomica	1.92	0.274		0.872
Review of Black Political Economy	1.17	0.167		0.531
Review of Political Economy	1.70	0.243		0.772
Review of Radical Political Economics	4.14	0.591		1.880
Review of Social Economy	1.97	0.281		0.894
Science and Society	2.76	0.394	0.263	1.267
American Economic Review			1.938	1.938
Econometrica			2.215	2.215
Journal of Economic Literature			5.243	5.243
Journal of Financial Economics			2.723	2.723
Journal of Political Economy			2.196	2.196
Quarterly Journal of Economics			4.756	4.756

HEQ—heterodox economics quality, derived from Lee (2008b, Table 1, column 10, p. 247).
HEQ*—the degree to which a journal has achieved the benchmark standard of research quality.
SSCI Impact Factor—the 2004 SSCI impact factor scores.
HEQSSCI—the HEQ SSCI impact factor equivalent scores.

for. But it is possible to establish one by taking an impact factor score as a benchmark (IFBS). To equate the HEQ to the IFBS, we first calculate HEQ*, which equals HEQ/7 and represents the extent to which the heterodox journals achieve the goals outline by Lee (2008b). Next the research quality scores of the heterodox journals are made equivalent to the impact scores by multiplying HEQ* by IFBS:

$$HEQSSCI = HEQ^* \times IFBS. \tag{1}$$

While HEQSSCI is the common denominator that lets us compare heterodox and nonheterodox journals, the comparison is sensitive to the value of the IFBS. For example, if the impact factor score of the *Journal of Economic Literature* (5.243) is taken as the benchmark, then the HEQSSCI score for the *Review of Radical Political Economics* would be 3.10, which is greater than the impact factor scores of the *Journal of Political Economy* (*JPE*), *Econometrica*, and the *American Economic Review* (*AER*). This is clearly implausible to most economists, whether mainstream or not. On the other hand, if the impact factor score of the *AER* (1.928) is taken as the benchmark, then the *Cambridge Journal of Economics* would have a research quality score equivalent to less than half of the *AER*, which heterodox economists would find implausible. To avoid these extremes, we take the IFBS as the average of the top six mainstream journals' impact factor scores, which means that the impact of the top six mainstream journals on mainstream economics is the benchmark impact that mainstream journals should aim for with regard to mainstream economics.[17] The six journals, *AER, Econometrica, Journal of Economic Literature, Journal of Financial Economics, JPE,* and *Quarterly Journal of Economics,* have been identified as blue-ribbon journals or otherwise as high quality journals and their average 2004 SSCI impact factor score is 3.1785 (Lee 2006, 2009). As a result, all the HEQSSCI scores are below the *AER*'s impact factor score, but not so much as to be seen as implausible by heterodox economists (see Table 1, column 5).

What is noticeable is that in comparison to the SSCI impact factor scores, the HEQSSCI scores are three to six times higher, suggesting that the former has a built-in undervaluation of heterodox journals. This relative increase in the importance of the heterodox journals results from the assumption that a heterodox journal achieving all goals outlined in Lee (2008b) is equivalent to the average of the six mainstream journals listed above. When the HEQSSCI scores are included in the SSCI impact factor, either in place of the existing SSCI impact factor scores or as a net addition to them, a heterodox quality-equality measure (HQEI) is created that can be used to evaluate the research quality of all journal articles on an equal basis. In the next section, the HQEI is used to reevaluate the Grijalva and Nowell rankings of the 128 economic departments with doctoral programs.[18]

Grijalva and Nowell Results Reexamined

The results of applying the HQEI to the Grijalva and Nowell data (which affects 492 or 1.5 percent of the 33,068 references) plus the 270 references from the heterodox journals noted above is shown in Table 2.

Using the new index, total productivity of the 128 departments increases by 685 points or by 3 percent and average productivity of all 2,673 publishing faculty increases by almost 0.3 percent. However, 10 departments account for 69.5 percent of the increase in total productivity. Because the increase in productivity is concentrated in relatively few departments, only 21 of the 75 departments with increased productivity had an increase in their total productivity ranking. The largest change in total productivity is for the University of Missouri, Kansas City. Column 3 of Table 2 indicates its rank increased 54 places, from 121 to 67. Only 23 departments show an increase in their average productivity ranking, with the University of Missouri, Kansas City showing the largest change, from 105 to 9.

Although the global impact of the HQEI and the additional 270 articles is small, their concentration in specific qua "heterodox" departments generates "significant" changes in the Grijalva and Nowell rankings. The changes in rankings are shown in the third column of Table 2. This column shows heterodox-adjusted rankings along with the rankings given by Grijalva and Nowell. As can be seen, the differences between the two rankings is quite small (Spearman rank

Table 2

Overall Heterodox-Adjusted Rankings for Ph.D.-Granting
Institutions in Economics

School	Number of Faculty	Overall Productivity Rank (Grijalva-Nowell Rank)	Z-Score	Per Faculty Rank (Grijalva-Nowell Rank)
Harvard U	43	1 (1)	5.47	1 (1)
UC Berkeley	56	2 (2)	4.08	4 (4)
Princeton U	49	3 (3)	3.96	3 (3)
MIT	34	4 (4)	3.50	2 (2)
Yale U	43	5 (5)	1.89	12 (11)
U Michigan	49	6 (6)	1.85	19 (18)
New York U	37	7 (7)	1.76	7 (8)
UCLA	45	8 (8)	1.64	18 (16)
Stanford U	40	9 (9)	1.54	14 (13)
Columbia U	35	10 (11)	1.47	5 (9)
U Chicago	31	11 (10)	1.47	10 (5)
Northwestern U	34	12 (12)	1.27	13 (12)
UC San Diego	29	13 (13)	1.23	6 (6)
U Wisconsin, Madison	29	14 (14)	1.06	11 (10)
Boston U	34	15 (15)	0.87	23 (22)
U Pennsylvania	27	16 (16)	0.68	17 (15)
Ohio State U	34	17 (17)	0.68	31 (28)
Michigan State U	43	18 (18)	0.62	49 (49)
Cornell U	29	19 (19)	0.56	24 (23)
U Virginia	25	20 (20)	0.54	20 (17)
U Maryland, College Park	29	21 (21)	0.49	28 (27)
U Illinois, Urbana	35	22 (22)	0.47	41 (38)
Carnegie Mellon U	35	23 (23)	0.46	43 (41)
Duke U	30	24 (24)	0.40	34 (31)
UC Davis	26	25 (25)	0.38	26 (25)
U Southern California	22	26 (26)	0.35	15 (19)
U Texas, Austin	25	27 (27)	0.33	25 (24)

Table 2   *Continued*

School	Number of Faculty	Overall Productivity Rank (Grijalva-Nowell Rank)	Z-Score	Per Faculty Rank (Grijalva-Nowell Rank)
Brown U	27	28 (28)	0.31	32 (29)
North Carolina State U	39	29 (30)	0.28	63 (58)
U Minnesota	22	30 (29)	0.28	21 (20)
Vanderbilt U	28	31 (32)	0.27	36 (35)
Johns Hopkins U	19	32 (33)	0.26	16 (14)
Iowa State U	39	33 (31)	0.26	64 (59)
City U of New York	51	34 (44)	0.19	85 (98)
Pennsylvania State U	27	35 (35)	0.19	39 (43)
Syracuse U	31	36 (34)	0.18	53 (53)
U Massachusetts, Amherst	21	37 (70)	0.11	30 (85)
Boston College	20	38 (37)	0.09	27 (26)
Georgetown U	25	39 (36)	0.08	44 (40)
California Inst Tech	13	40 (38)	0.08	8 (7)
U Rochester	17	41 (39)	0.02	22 (21)
UNC, Chapel Hill	25	42 (40)	0.01	50 (48)
George Mason U	27	43 (41)	0.00	56 (55)
UC Santa Cruz	19	44 (43)	−0.03	33 (30)
U Colorado, Boulder	27	45 (42)	−0.03	59 (56)
U Washington	24	46 (45)	−0.04	51 (50)
U Illinois, Chicago	20	47 (46)	−0.04	35 (34)
Arizona State U	27	48 (47)	−0.05	61 (57)
Rice U	19	49 (48)	−0.10	38 (36)
Florida State U	24	50 (52)	−0.10	58 (61)
Texas A&M U	26	51 (49)	−0.11	66 (60)
Georgia State U	28	52 (50)	−0.14	74 (69)
UC Santa Barbara	26	53 (51)	−0.15	67 (63)
Indiana U	18	54 (53)	−0.20	46 (46)
George Washington U	27	55 (54)	−0.23	81 (75)
Rutgers U	24	56 (55)	−0.26	76 (70)
UC Irvine	16	57 (56)	−0.27	60 (44)

Table 2   *Continued*

School	Number of Faculty	Overall Productivity Rank (Grijalva-Nowell Rank)	Z-Score	Per Faculty Rank (Grijalva-Nowell Rank)
U Oregon	18	58 (57)	−0.28	57 (54)
U Houston	23	59 (58)	−0.28	75 (72)
UC Riverside[a]	19	60 (72)	−0.29	62 (81)
U of Iowa	16	61 (60)	−0.32	54 (52)
U Pittsburgh	21	62 (59)	−0.32	73 (68)
U Wyoming	13	63 (61)	−0.32	37 (32)
U Arizona	15	64 (62)	−0.34	52 (51)
U Kentucky	14	65 (63)	−0.35	47 (45)
U Florida	18	66 (64)	−0.35	70 (64)
U Missouri, Kansas City	7	67 (121)	−0.36	9 (105)
American U	20	68 (81)	−0.37	79 (102)
Southern Methodist U	17	69 (65)	−0.37	68 (62)
Washington U, St. Louis	16	70 (69)	−0.39	65 (67)
U Connecticut	24	71 (68)	−0.39	92 (89)
Clemson U	19	72 (66)	−0.39	78 (73)
Purdue U	20	73 (67)	−0.40	83 (76)
Emory U	15	74 (71)	−0.45	72 (66)
U Nebraska, Lincoln	14	75 (86)	−0.46	69 (84)
U South Carolina	10	76 (73)	−0.46	42 (39)
U Wisconsin, Milwaukee	18	77 (79)	−0.48	90 (95)
U Georgia	13	78 (74)	−0.49	71 (65)
Virginia Tech	15	79 (75)	−0.49	80 (74)
U Albany	14	80 (76)	−0.50	77 (71)
SUNY Binghamton	16	81 (77)	−0.51	82 (77)
Colorado State U	17	82 (105)	−0.51	91 (116)
New School U	10	83 (98)	−0.52	55 (87)
Rensselaer Polytechnic I.	7	84 (84)	−0.52	29 (33)
Wayne State U	9	85 (78)	−0.53	48 (47)
U Utah	20	86 (108)	−0.53	104 (123)
U Delaware	20	87 (80)	−0.54	106 (101)

Table 2   *Continued*

School	Number of Faculty	Overall Productivity Rank (Grijalva-Nowell Rank)	Z-Score	Per Faculty Rank (Grijalva-Nowell Rank)
U Missouri, Columbia	14	88 (82)	−0.55	84 (78)
U Kansas	17	89 (83)	−0.55	100 (93)
SUNY Buffalo	14	90 (85)	−0.55	86 (83)
U Alabama	15	91 (89)	−0.57	95 (96)
U Notre Dame	7	92 (88)	−0.58	45 (42)
Florida International U	15	93 (87)	−0.58	98 (92)
U Oklahoma	14	94 (90)	−0.60	99 (97)
Brandeis U	6	95 (91)	−0.61	40 (37)
Louisiana State U	11	96 (92)	−0.62	89 (80)
SUNY Stony Brook	12	97 (93)	−0.62	97 (91)
Oregon State U	11	98 (94)	−0.63	93 (86)
Lehigh U	13	99 (95)	−0.63	103 (99)
U Miami	10	100 (96)	−0.63	87 (79)
Auburn U	11	101 (97)	−0.64	96 (90)
Temple U	19	102 (111)	−0.65	121 (124)
Washington State U	10	103 (99)	−0.66	94 (88)
U New Hampshire	14	104 (117)	−0.66	110 (121)
Oklahoma State U	13	105 (100)	−0.66	108 (104)
Northern Illinois U	11	106 (102)	−0.67	105 (100)
Southern Ill U, Carbondale	10	107 (101)	−0.67	101 (94)
West Virginia U	16	108 (103)	−0.67	116 (111)
Portland State U	10	109 (123)	−0.67	102 (120)
U New Orleans	16	110 (104)	−0.67	117 (113)
Western Michigan U	17	111 (110)	−0.68	122 (119)
U Tennessee, Knoxville	12	112 (106)	−0.68	109 (106)
U Hawaii, Manoa	16	113 (107)	−0.68	120 (115)
Northeastern U	12	114 (119)	−0.69	111 (117)
U Arkansas	12	115 (109)	V0.69	112 (107)
U Mississippi	12	116 (113)	−0.70	115 (110)
Kansas State U	13	117 (114)	−0.70	118 (114)

Table 2   *Continued*

School	Number of Faculty	Overall Productivity Rank (Grijalva-Nowell Rank)	Z-Score	Per Faculty Rank (Grijalva-Nowell Rank)
U New Mexico	13	118 (112)	−0.70	119 (112)
Fordham U	10	119 (115)	−0.72	113 (108)
U Rhode Island	8	120 (116)	−0.72	107 (103)
Utah State U	20	121 (118)	−0.73	127 (127)
Claremont Graduate U	5	122 (120)	−0.73	88 (82)
Middle Tennessee State	12	123 (124)	−0.74	124 (125)
Clark U	8	124 (122)	−0.75	114 (109)
Colorado School of Mines	9	125 (125)	−0.77	125 (122)
Texas Tech U	7	126 (126)	−0.77	123 (118)
Suffolk U	8	127 (127)	−0.79	126 (126)
Howard U	9	128 (128)	−0.80	128 (128)

[a]U California, Riverside and U California, Irvine rankings were switched in Grijalva and Nowell (2008). The rankings are corrected this table.

correlation is $R_s = 0.979$), with the first "significant" change occurring with the City University of New York whose ranking increases from 44 to 34 quickly followed by the University of Massachusetts, Amherst whose ranking increases from 70 to 37. The other major changes involved departments moving from the bottom 25 percent of departments to the bottom third of departments—advances to be sure but not that significant. The exception is the University of Missouri, Kansas City, which moves from the bottom 6 percent of the departments to almost the top half of departments. So while there is movement in the overall productivity rankings, they generally involve the movement of "heterodox" departments from the lower to the middle ranks, thus making them look more like the "average" mainstream department, although the differences in the aggregate productivity is fairly small, as indicated by the z-score in column 4 of Table 2.[19]

The fifth column of Table 2, "Per Faculty Rank," shows how each department ranks when its heterodox-adjusted total productivity sum is divided by the number of publishing faculty within the department; it represents the average productivity of publishing faculty in a department. First, in comparison to the overall productivity ranking, the difference between heterodox-adjusted average productivity ranking and the Grijalva and Nowell ranking (which are in parentheses) is a bit more pronounced (rank correlation is 0.949 vs. 0.979). Moreover, the correlation between overall productivity rank and per faculty rank is lower ($R_s = 0.903$). This is because many of the departments that publish a significant part of their scholarly work in "heterodox" journals are relatively small.[20] Departments such as University of Missouri, Kansas City, New School University, Portland State, University of New Hampshire, and University of Nebraska, Lincoln all have fewer than 15 members and increase their average productivity ranking by at least 10 places when using the HQEI. If highly productive faculty is one characteristic of a quality department, as Grijalva and Nowell suggest, then departments with relatively high total or average HQEI rankings are potentially high quality doctoral programs.

Table 3 lists the 37 departments that are ranked in the top 30 based on total or average productivity. Of these, all but five appeared as top ranked departments in six recent bibliometric and peer-review department ranking studies (Tschirhart 1989; Conroy and Dusansky 1995; Goldberger, Maher, and Flattau 1995; Scott and Mitias 1996; Dusansky and Vernon 1998; Kalaitzidakis, Mamuneas, and Stengos 2003; also see Lee 2006). When using the HQEI, three heterodox departments join this group of acknowledged top departments. Thus heterodox departments can provide a high quality doctoral education, albeit on a smaller scale.[21]

As expected, using a heterodox weighted quality index, the schools known for their strengths in heterodox economics achieve the largest gains. Table 4 shows departments that gain at least 10 percentage points in their total productivity ranking, and is perhaps a clear indication of the strength and importance of departments with an emphasis in heterodox economics. For instance, University Missouri, Kansas City shows a large gain in productivity and rank; thus, heterodox is an important area of research for this department. Departments near the bottom of the table show fairly large gains in productivity, but overall ranks and faculty dedicated to the area are

Table 3

Top 30 Departments Based on Heterodox-Adjusted Total or Average Productivity

Harvard U	U Wisconsin–Madison	U Southern California
UC Berkeley	Boston U	U Texas, Austin
Princeton U	U Pennsylvania	Brown U
MIT	Ohio State U	North Carolina State U
Yale U	Michigan State U	U Minnesota
U Michigan	Cornell U	Johns Hopkins U
New York U	U Virginia	California Inst Tech
UCLA	U Maryland, College Park	U Massachusetts, Amherst
Stanford U	U Illinois, Urbana	Boston College
Columbia U	Carnegie Mellon U	U Rochester
U Chicago	Duke U	U Missouri, Kansas City
Northwestern U	UC Davis	Rensselaer Polytechnic I.
UC San Diego		

not as large. This suggests that there are a couple of fairly productive heterodox faculty members within the department, but heterodox economics may not be as significant as other areas in economics (see Table 6, columns 2 and 3).

The heterodox-adjusted productivity does not, for the most part, significantly change Grijalva and Nowell JEL field rankings in that where a "heterodox" department increases its ranking by 34 places, its actual ranking goes from 102 to 68, as in the case of Portland State University in the field of labor and demographic economics. But there are exceptions, noted below, because the distribution of the 590 JEL field classified heterodox references[22] are unevenly distributed across the 16 JEL fields: methodology and history of economic thought (21 percent), macroeconomics and monetary policy (18 percent), economic systems (9 percent), and economic development (6 percent).[23] If, however, a "new field" of heterodox economics is introduced, the top departments, as measured by the total productivity

Table 4

Departments Impacted the Most by Additional Heterodox Articles[a]

Department	Grijalva and Nowell	HEQI	Percent change in total productivity
U Missouri, Kansas City	121	67	426%
U Massachusetts, Amherst	70	37	143%
U Utah	108	86	115%
Colorado State U	105	82	112%
Portland State U	123	109	105%
New School U	98	84	73%
American U	81	68	64%
U New Hampshire	117	104	59%
U California, Riverside	72	60	48%
Howard U	128	128	42%
U Nebraska, Lincoln	86	75	42%
Northeastern U	119	114	39%
Temple U	111	102	38%
City U of New York	44	34	28%
U Wisconsin–Milwaukee	79	77	19%
Middle Tennessee State	124	123	16%
Rensselaer Polytechnic Institute	84	83	16%
Florida State U	52	50	12%
Western Michigan U	110	111	11%

[a]Represents any school with at least a 10 percent increase in total productivity.

sum of articles published in heterodox journals, include none of the prestigious, highly ranked departments identified in the ranking studies noted above—see Table 5. What is noticeable is that the top 10 heterodox departments essentially dominate the field of methodology and history of economics thought, with five of the top 10 departments, eight of the top 14 departments, and the University of Missouri–Kansas City being the top department replacing Princeton.

Table 5

Impact of the Heterodox-Adjusted Productivity on Field Rankings

Heterdox Economics, Top 10 Departments	Top 20 Ranking in JEL Fields			
U of Massachusetts, Amherst	B(11)*	E(18)*	O(15)	P(9)*
U of Missouri, Kansas City	B(1)	E(11)*		
City U of New York[+]	B(5)*	J(15)	P(6)	
Colorado State U	B(8)	P(15)*		
American U	B(18)*	P(17)*		
UC Riverside	B(14)*			
U of Utah	B(12)*			
U of Nebraska, Lincoln	B(10)	A(2)	Q(17)*	
New School U	B(9)*			
Portland State U				

A—General economics and teaching.
B—Methodology and history of economic thought.
E—Macroeconomics and monetary policy.
J—Labor and demographic economics.
O—Economic development, technological change, and growth.
P—Economic systems.
Q—Agricultural and natural resources economics.
( )—Field rank.
*—Not in the top 20 departments in the Grijalva and Nowell study.
[+]—In the JEL fields of financial economics and health, education, and welfare, City is ranked in the top 20 departments, but none of its total productivity comes from publishing in heterodox journals.

In addition, the University of Massachusetts–Amherst advances into the top 20 ranking in the fields of macroeconomics and monetary policy and economic development, technological change, and growth; while the University of Missouri–Kansas City advances into the top 20 ranking of macroeconomics and monetary policy, Colorado State University and American University advance into the top 20 ranking of economic systems, and University of Nebraska–Lincoln advances into the top 20 ranking of agricultural and natural resources economics.

Ranking Heterodox Economics Departments

Mainstream economists would most likely view heterodox economics as a particular field. Heterodox economists, on the other hand, would reject this view since, for them, heterodox economics includes microeconomics, macroeconomics and monetary policy, mathematical and quantitative methods, and the other JEL fields. Consequently, for prospective doctoral students interested in heterodox economics and its many fields, the identification and ranking of doctoral programs according to the number of faculty who publish in heterodox journals, the importance of heterodox productivity in the department's overall productivity, overall heterodox productivity, average productivity, and fields of expertise would enable them to make an informed decisions about which departments to apply to and attend.

The first step for identifying "heterodox" doctoral programs is to identify the articles that are associated with heterodox economics. This is done by including all the articles that were published in the heterodox journals listed in Table 1 plus two additional heterodox journals that are not carried in the Econlit data base: *Capital and Class* (which adds eight additional references) and *Contributions to Political Economy* (which adds five additional references) (see Table 1A).[24] The second step is to calculate the overall heterodox productivity values and the average productivity values for each of the 75 economics departments. Because we are interested in viable heterodox programs, the 48 departments that have only one publication in a heterodox journal, a total productivity of less than four, and/or no clearly recognizable heterodox economists are discarded, leaving 27 departments whose doctoral programs have a *heterodox presence*.[25]

Table 6 shows the 27 departments with doctoral programs that have a viable heterodox presence. The departments have from one to 17 faculty engaged in publishing in heterodox journals (column 2) and the importance of heterodox economics in the departments' research productivity ranges from 99 percent down to nearly zero (column 3).[26] The variation between the rankings of overall productivity (column 4) and average productivity (column 5) generates a low rank correlation ($R_s = 0.57$). Thus, there is a partial tradeoff between the size and the

Table 6

Rankings of Ph.D.-Granting Institutions in Heterodox Economics

School	Number of Faculty	Importance Index[a]	Overall Productivity Rank	Per Faculty Rank	Average Ph.D. Graduates (2002–2007)[b]
U Massachusetts, Amherst	17	0.67	1	6	8
U Missouri, Kansas City	7	0.99	2	1	4
City U of New York	5	0.27	3	3	9
Colorado State U	11	0.70	4	15	4
American U	9	0.46	5	11	7
UC Riverside	5	0.35	6	5	10
U Utah	12	0.61	7	22	10
U Nebraska, Lincoln	3	0.44	8	2	2
New School U	8	0.47	9	18	12
Portland State U	5	0.67	10	14	0[c]
Florida State U	4	0.13	11	12	4
Pennsylvania State U	2	0.09	12	4	12
U New Hampshire	4	0.41	13	19	2
U Wisconsin, Milwaukee	4	0.19	14	21	6
Temple U	3	0.31	15	17	3
Northeastern U	2	0.36	16	9	New Program
U Michigan	2	0.02	17	10	9
Rensselaer Polytechnic I.	3	0.16	18	20	2
Washington U, St. Louis	2	0.10	19	13	8
New York U	2	0.02	20	16	10
Michigan State U	5	0.03	21	25	12
U Connecticut	5	0.06	22	26	5
U Houston	1	0.05	23	7	6
U Alabama	1	0.10	24	8	5
UC Berkeley	2	0.00[d]	25	23	23
George Mason U	4	0.03	26	27	15
Western Michigan U	2	0.13	27	24	4

[a]The Importance Index is the ratio of the department's heterodox productivity value to its overall productivity value.
[b]Taken from Grijalva and Nowell (2008, Table 2, column 9, pp. 977–980).
[c]Portland State U does not offer a Ph.D. in economics. The university offers degrees in urban studies and systems science, both of which offer an emphasis in economics.
[d]The ratio is less than 0.005.

average productivity. The final column of Table 6, "Average Ph.D. Graduates (2002–2007)," as well as columns 2 and 3, provides additional information on the viability, importance, and size of the heterodox presence.

Concentrating on the top 10 heterodox departments ranked by total productivity, they have 74 percent of the heterodox references and 76 percent of the total productivity.[27] Hence they represent the academic face of heterodox economics. Utilizing the 590 JEL classified heterodox references, Table 7 identifies the various fields in which they publish.[28] What is noticeable is that, while all the JEL fields are covered by one or more heterodox department, all the departments do not cover all the fields. Some fields are represented by many departments and others by just a few. In particular, heterodox economics concentrates its research activity, not unexpectedly, in five fields— micro-macro theory, history of thought, labor, and industrial organization—and has significant presence in four others; on the other hand, there is relatively very little heterodox activity in eight JEL fields. This shows the uneven development of heterodox economics. Still, if an undergraduate desires to go to graduate school to study heterodox economics, there are clearly 10 departments to choose from, each offering a good to excellent broadly comprehensive doctoral education with faculty and fields of study that compare favorably to education in heterodox economics offered by many of the highly regarded mainstream departments.

Conclusion

In March 2003, the Provost of Academic Affairs, the Dean of the College of Arts and Letters, and the Chair of the Economics Department at the University of Notre Dame argued that the heterodox component of the Notre Dame economic graduate program combined with the heterodox economic research and publications in unranked heterodox journals by many of its professors had resulted in a low department ranking among American economic programs at research-doctorate universities. More specifically, they (and others) argued that publishing in top neoclassical journals was necessary if the economics department was to achieve a ranking that was better than its ranking

Table 7

Field Rankings
(based on first-listed JEL code for publications)

School	A	B	C	D	E	F	G	H	I	J	K	L	N	O	P	Q	R
			JEL Classification System for Journal Articles														
U Massachusetts, Amherst	X	X	X	X	X	X	X	X		X		X		X	X		
U Missouri, Kansas City		X	X	X	X		X	X		X		X			X		
City U of New York	X	X		X	X	X				X		X			X		
Colorado State U		X		X	X	X	X	X	X	X	X	X	X	X	X		X
American U		X		X	X					X		X		X	X		
UC Riverside		X		X	X		X			X					X		X
U Utah		X		X	X					X		X	X	X	X		
U Nebraska, Lincoln	X	X		X	X		X	X		X	X	X				X	
New School U		X		X	X	X	X			X				X			
Portland State U	X	X		X	X	X	X			X		X		X			

A—General economics and teaching.
B—Methodology and history of economic thought.
C—Mathematics and quantitative methods.
D—Microeconomics.
E—Macroeconomics and monetary policy.
F—International economics.
G—Financial economics.
H—Public economics.
I—Health, education, and welfare.
J—Labor and demographic economics.
K—Law and economics.
L—Industrial organization.
N—Economic history.
O—Economic development, technological change, and growth.
P—Economic systems.
Q—Agricultural and natural resources economics.
R—Urban, rural, and regional economics.

of 81 out of 107 research-doctorate programs that appeared in the well-known National Research Council publication, *Research-Doctorate Programs in the United States: Continuity and Change* (Goldberger, Maher, and Flattau 1995). In addition, they argued that only neoclassical economics was real scientific knowledge and hence the only kind of knowledge that appears in top journals, policymakers and the business community listen to, should be taught to undergraduates, and should be used to really train graduate students. Thus, their solution, which the university acted upon, was to exile the heterodox economists to a specially created undergraduate Department of Economics and Policy Studies (which is now dissolved) and create a new Department of Economics and Econometrics founded on the basis that only "the very best neoclassical economists whose research . . . is routinely published in the leading economic journals" would be recruited.

The leading journals were defined as "the premier economics journals, or at least the top 20 journals, in the last decade." Using the data and SSCI quality weighting from the Grijalva and Nowell study and adding in the journal publication data for nine members[29] of the exiled department, the overall productivity and average productivity ranks for the economics department are 88 and 42 (see Table 3), while the respective ranks of the exiled department are equivalent to 102 and 94. Thus, the claims of the Dean and the department chair appear to be supported. However, if the HQEI is applied to the same data augmented with publications from the heterodox journals noted in Table 1, the ranking results change dramatically, with the overall productivity and average productivity ranks of the Notre Dame department being 92 and 45 (see Table 3) while the respective ranks of the exiled department are equivalent to 74 and 25. In this case, the claims of the Dean and the chair are not at all supported and their decision to exile the heterodox economists essentially dismantled a better department and replaced it with one of a lesser rank (Fosmoe 2003a, 2003b; Gresik 2003; University of Notre Dame, Academic Council meeting, March 20, 2003—http://provost.nd.edu/academic-resources-and-information/ac_minutes/documents/3-20-03.pdf; Donovan 2004; "Proposal About Economics at Notre Dame," 17 March 2003).

The Notre Dame case dramatically illustrates how bibliometric (and peer review) based methods can be used to silence dissenting voices and to render invisible heterodox ideas and departments in a contested discipline such as economics. This article does not disagree with the use of bibliometric methods to rank departments (and journals);[30] but what is objected to is their misuse in the name of science and objectivity.

We recognize that other quality rankings exist. One could certainly create a health, education, and welfare (HEW) weighted index, where the most desirable standards for HEW journals are considered comparable to the top mainstream economic journals and additional HEW journals are entered into the analysis. In fact, such an index has been developed to rank economic departments in terms of their contributions to econometrics (Hall 1987; Baltagi 1998). Ultimately, different weighting schemes value the contributions of different research groups differently (as noted in note 19). Yet this does not mean that the research of a specific group is necessarily devalued, although this could be the case. But whatever the weighting scheme, the scheme itself is constructed for particular social purposes—that is to say, it is socially constructed as opposed to "naturally given." Hence any scheme must be argued for each time it is used instead of being assumed as unquestionably valid.

What we show with this article is that with the introduction of a heterodox weighted quality-equality index (while keeping all other factors the same) combined with the use of good bibliometric practices regarding contending subdisciplines, doctoral programs that appear ordinary or extremely weak advance into the ranks of ordinary and even the acknowledged excellent programs.[31] It is not that doctoral programs with a heterodox presence are better than programs without, but they are also not inferior to them—just different but equal. Rather, the programs of the same general ranking provide the same quality of doctoral education in heterodox economics as taught by the same equally research-capable professors. Another way of saying this is that a properly carried out bibliometric study of department rankings reduces the impact that peer-based biases have in affecting the outcome—what is silent and invisible now has a voice and recognition and the ranking of departments truly becomes sensitive to the changes in their faculty's performance over time (Tombazos 2005).

Notes

1. Bibliometric is defined as applying quantitative and statistical analysis to citations and other kinds of bibliographic information.
2. See Lee (2006, 2007, 2009), King and Kriesler (2008), and Vlachou (2008) for references to the literature.

3. Econlit does not include all heterodox economics journals, such as *Capital and Class* and *Contributions to Political Economy*.

4. While the Web of Science SSCI impact factor scores are widely accepted by economists, reasons for this are never clearly articulated. In particular, the SSCI includes only a portion of the journals included in the Econlit database and its impact factor is based on two lagged years (although in recent years it has produced a five-year impact factor). However, for many disciplines, including economics, a three- to five-year lag is more appropriate and generates higher impact scores; but, at least in economics, the two-year impact factor is still preferred (Moed 2005; Adler, Ewing, and Taylor 2008; Nederhof 2008; Engemann and Wall 2009).

5. This weighting of "page productivity" does not take into account the size of pages for different journals; and this will have an impact on productivity of authors; but the impact on department ranking may be nil because the Spearman rank correlation between the "adjusted" and "raw" page count is almost one (Tombazos 2005; Hall 1987: 174).

6. For a similar study, see Sternberg and Litzenberger (2005).

7. Impact factor scores can change significantly from one year to the next. Grijalva and Nowell could have strengthened their findings if they had carried out a "sensitivity analysis" by utilizing SSCI impact factor scores for 2003 and 2005.

8. Science is being understood as a systematic approach to a sphere of knowledge (the provisioning process) guided by methods of investigation that are accepted by a community of scholars.

9. The issue of subdisciplines/subfields or different paradigms or approaches in the same discipline/field having quite different publication and referencing practices and characteristics that generate quite different impact factors as measures of research quality is well-known in the bibliometric literature. This specifically means that it cannot be taken for granted that the SSCI is a valid research quality indicator for either mainstream or heterodox economics; and, moreover, the appropriate research quality indicator for mainstream and heterodox journals may be different, so making comparisons of journals from the different subdisciplines difficult (van Raan 1996; Thomas and Watkins 1998; Glanzel and Moed 2002; Vinkler 2002; Nisonger 2004; Moed 2005; Nederhof 2006).

10. The SSCI also includes the *American Journal of Economics and Sociology*, which is a pluralistic and interdisciplinary economics journal. For this article, it is not included as a heterodox journal, although it could claim to be one.

11. Since the five SSCI heterodox journals cite, to a significant degree, these non-SSCI heterodox journals, it is good bibliometric practice to expand the group of journals to include them (Lee 2008b, 2009; Moed 2005: 140–142).

12. In their study, Grijalva and Nowell collected references that appeared in journals included in the Econlit database—which include *International Review of Applied Economics* (21), *Metroeconomics* (23), *Review of Black Political Economy* (54), *Review of Political Economy* (37), *Review of Radical Political Economics* (84), and *Review of Social Economy* (51) for a total of 270. (A reference is a single article in a journal but can have multiple authors; hence, for example, there can be two references to a single article when the article has two authors, both of whom have tenure lines in a doctoral program.)

13. This argument can also be applied to impact factors of mainstream journals associated with fields that have relatively few practitioners.

14. For evidence, see Lee (2008b, 2009: Appendix A.10, pp. 52–54 (http://www.heterodoxnews.com/APPENDIX--formatted.pdf), 2010).

15. Such an outcome is well-known in the bibliometric literature: " 'Top' journals in large subfields tend to have a higher citation impact than top journals in smaller ones" (Moed 2005: 40).

16. This is an example of good practice in bibliometric research where the bibliometric investigator measures what the evaluator delineates as the measure of research quality of a journal (Moed 2005: 30–31).

17. For the importance of benchmarking in bibliometric research, see Moed (2005: 305–307).

18. Tulane University has been dropped from the initial data set because it no longer has a doctoral program; this reduces the total number of departments in the article to 128.

19. As suggested above, the robustness of the productivity rankings in column 3 (as well as column 5) are sensitive to the choice of values of IFBS. When a higher benchmark is used, then each of the heterodox journals' relative impact increases, and hence, faculty publications in these journals will increase the productivity in their respective departments. If the *AER* IFBS is used, the rankings of heterodox departments fall an average of 5 ranking positions, with the greatest decline of 17 in the rank of the University of Missouri, Kansas City; but this decline is not as large as the differences between Grijalva and Nowell's rank for it. When using the *Journal of Economic Literature* IFBS, the rankings increase an average of 7 rank positions, with the greatest gains in rank going to University of Missouri, Kansas City (up 17) and University of Massachusetts, Amherst (up 16). The Spearman rank correlations among the various measures of productivity are all greater than 0.99. From a methods standpoint, it seems reasonable to use the average, given the spread of rankings for the University of Missouri, Kansas City and other heterodox departments.

20. See Baltagi (1998: 13) for a discussion of this problem in the ranking of economics departments in terms of their contributions to econometrics.

21. For the period 2002–2007, these 37 departments awarded nearly 50 percent of the Ph.D.s in economics.

22. The difference between 762 vs. 590 is that not all heterodox references had JEL codes and the references in the JEL field of "other special topics" is not included.

23. On the other hand, the seven fields of mathematical and quantitative methods, law and economics, economic history, urban, rural, and regional economics, general economics, financial economics, and public economics have in total only 9 percent of the heterodox references.

24. The research quality scores of the two journals are as follows:

Table 1A

The Research Quality Scores of Heterodox
Economics Journals

Heterdox Journals	HEQ (out of 7)	HEQ*	SSCI Impact Factor	HEQSSCI
Capital and Class	4.10	0.586		1.862
Contributions to Political Economy	2.47	0.353		1.122

25. With regard to the cut-off of 4 for total productivity, when dealing with all 128 departments, the lowest productivity for a department is above 6. It is hard to conceive of a viable heterodox presence in a doctoral program that has an overall productivity of less than 4.

26. For the portion of a department's faculty that has published in heterodox journals, compare Table 2 column 2 to Table 6 column 2.

27. This degree of concentration is not dissimilar to other studies reporting on the degree of department concentration in publications in economics (Hall 1987; Baltagi 1998).

28. *Capital and Class* and *Contributions to Political Economy* did not assign JEL classification codes to their articles; hence their articles are not included when determining the heterodox field rankings.

29. The exiled department had a tenth member that published, Teresa Ghilarducci; but it was not possible to get a list of her publications.

30. However, ranking departments solely on the basis of bibliometric methods applied only to journals is inadequate; it should also include data on books, book chapters, working papers, and other published material; on teaching; and on the work environment (Lee 2009: ch. 11; Cronin, Snyder, and Atkins 1997).

31. Tombazos (2005) reaches a similar conclusion regarding the construction of W, "page productivity."

References

Adler, R., J. Ewing, and P. Taylor. (2008). "Citation Statistics." A Report from the International Mathematical Union in Cooperation with the International Council of Industrial and Applied Mathematics and the Institute of Mathematical Statistics, available at: http://www.mathunion.org/fileadmin/IMU/Report/CitationStatistics.pdf.

Baltagi, B. H. (1998). "Worldwide Institutional Rankings in Econometrics: 1989–1995." *Econometric Theory* 14(1): 1–43.

Conroy, M. E., and R. Dusansky. (1995). "The Productivity of Economic Departments in the U.S.: Publications in Core Journals." *Journal of Economic Literature* 33(4): 1966–1971.

Cronin, B., H. Snyder, and H. Atkins. (1997). "Comparative Citation Rankings of Authors in Monographic and Journal Literature: A Study of Sociology." *Journal of Documentation* 53(3): 263–273.

Donovan, G. (2004). "Economics Split Divides Notre Dame." *National Catholic Reporter* 9 April, http://www.natcath.com/NCR_Online/archives2/2004b/040904/040904c.php.

Dusansky, R., and C. J. Vernon. (1998). "Rankings of U.S. Economics Departments." *Journal of Economic Perspectives* 12(1): 157–170.

Engemann, K. M., and H. J. Wall. (2009). "A Journal Ranking for the Ambitious Economist." *Federal Reserve Bank of St. Louis Review* 91(3): 127–139.

Fosmoe, M. (2003a). "The Great Divide." *South Bend Tribune* 3 March.

———. (2003b). "Views on Economics Split Polarize ND Faculty." *South Bend Tribune* 4 March.

Glanzel, W., and H. F. Moed. (2002). "Journal Impact Measures in Bibliometric Research." *Scientometrics* 53(2): 171–193.

Goldberger, M. L., B. A. Maher, and P. E. Flattau. (eds.) (1995). *Research-Doctorate Programs in the United States: Continuity and Change.* Washington, DC: National Academy Press.

Gresik, T. A. (2003). "The Economics Department Needs Reform." *Observer* 37.91, http://www.nd.edu/~observer/02112003/Viewpoint/3.html.

Grijalva, T. C., and C. Nowell. (2008). "A Guide to Graduate Study in Economics: Ranking Economics Departments by Fields of Expertise." *Southern Economic Journal* 74(4): 971–996.

Hall, A. D. (1987). "Worldwide Rankings of Research Activity in Econometrics: 1980–1985." *Econometric Theory* 3(2): 171–194.

Kalaitzidakis, P., T. P. Mamuneas, and T. Stengos. (2003). "Rankings of Academic Journals and Institutions in Economics." *Journal of the European Economic Association* 1(6): 1346–1366.

King, J. E., and P. Kriesler. (2008). "News from Down Under." *On the Horizon* 16(4): 289–292.

Lee, F. S. (2006). "The Ranking Game, Class, and Scholarship in American Economics." *Australasian Journal of Economics Education* 3(1–2): 1–41.

———. (2007). "The Research Assessment Exercise, the State and the Dominance of Mainstream Economics in British Universities." *Cambridge Journal of Economics* 31(2): 309–324.

———. (2008a). "A Comment on 'The Citation Impact of Feminist Economics'." *Feminist Economics* 14(1): 137–142.

———. (2008b). "A Case for Ranking Heterodox Journals and Departments." *On the Horizon* 16(4): 241–251.

———. (2009). *A History of Heterodox Economics: Challenging the Mainstream in the Twentieth Century.* Routledge: London.

———. (2010). "Who Talks to Whom: Pluralism and Identity of Heterodox Economic Journals." Unpublished.

———. (Forthcoming). "The Pluralism Debate in Heterodox Economics." *Review of Radical Political Economics.*

Moed, H. F. (2005). *Citation Analysis in Research Evaluation.* Dordrecht: Springer.

Nederhof, A. J. (2006). "Bibliometric Monitoring of Research Performance in the Social Sciences and the Humanities: A Review." *Scientometrics* 66(1): 81–100.

———. (2008). "Policy Impact of Bibliometric Rankings of Research Performance of Departments and Individual in Economics." *Scientometrics* 74(1): 163–174.

Nisonger, T. E. (2004). "The Benefits and Drawbacks of Impact Factor for Journal Collection Management in Libraries." *Serial Librarian* 47(1/2): 57–75.

Scott, L. C., and P. M. Mitias. (1996). "Trends in Ranking of Economics Departments in the U.S.: An Update." *Economic Inquiry* 34: 378–400.

Sternberg, R., and T. Litzenberger. (2005). "The Publication and Citation Output of German Facilities of Economics and Social Sciences—A Comparison of Faculties and Disciplines Based upon SSCI Data." *Scientometrics* 65(1): 29–53.

Thomas, P. R., and D. S. Watkins. (1998). "Institutional Research Rankings via Bibliometric Analysis and Direct Peer Review: A Comparative Case Study with Policy Implications." *Scientometrics* 41(3): 335–355.

Tombazos, C. G. (2005). "A Revisionist Perspective of European Research in Economics." *European Economic Review* 49: 251–277.

Tschirhart, J. (1989). "Ranking Economics Departments in Areas of Expertise." *Journal of Economic Education* 20(2): 199–222.

Van Raan, A. F. J. (1996). "Advanced Bibliometric Methods as Quantitative Core of Peer Review Based Evaluation and Foresight Exercises." *Scientometrics* 36(3): 397–420.

Vinkler, P. (2002). "Subfield Problems in Applying the Garfield (Impact) Factors in Practice." *Scientometrics* 53(2): 267–279.

Vlachou, A. (2008). "Ranking and the Prospects of Heterodox Economics in Greece." *On the Horizon* 16(4): 293–297.

Weingart, P. (2005). "Impact of Bibliometrics upon the Science System: Inadvertent Consequences?" *Scientometrics* 62(1): 117–131.

Citation Metrics: Serious Drawbacks, Perverse Incentives, and Strategic Options for Heterodox Economics

By Jakob Kapeller*

ABSTRACT. This article reviews strategic suggestions for heterodox economic journals and heterodox economists relating to quantitative indexing. It contains a critique of Thomson Scientifics "Journal Impact Factor" as well as an integrated discussion of general strategic guidelines and specific strategic suggestions accounting for the special paradigmatic position of heterodox economics.

Introduction

Quantitative indexing and evaluation is more and more being taken for granted within the scientific community. Meanwhile, it is an established practice to evaluate researchers, departments, or proposals for research grants by relying on the "Journal Impact Factor" of their publication outlets. Consequently, also the European Commission (directly[1]) and the British Research Assessment Exercise (indirectly[2]) rely on quantitative indexing to measure the quality of research output in economics. Individual academic careers, proposals for research grants, or the future of specific departments thus depend on the impact factors gathered by the particular researchers (cf. Lee and Elsner 2008). This standard procedure, somehow surprisingly, doesn't lead to skepticism of researchers. On the contrary, many scientists seem to internalize the rules of the "ranking game" and try to succeed within a given set of institutional mechanisms:

*University of Linz, Department of Philosophy and Theory of Science, Freistädterstraße 315, 4040 Linz/Austria, +43/732/2468-7196, jakob.kapeller@jku.at. I would like to thank Leonhard Dobusch, Carlo D'Ippoliti, Gerhard Fröhlich, Volker Gadenne, Frederic S. Lee, and the participants of the workshops in Bremen (June 2009) and Atlanta (January 2010), as well as two anonymous reviewers for their helpful comments on earlier drafts of this article.

American Journal of Economics and Sociology, Vol. 69, No. 5 (November, 2010).
© 2010 American Journal of Economics and Sociology, Inc.

That scientists . . . try to achieve as much impact-factor-capital as possible has, from my point of view, to be understood as a fundamental law . . . ." (Statement from an anonymous German medical scientist, cited according to Dobusch (2009), translation JK)

This attitude is surprising for various reasons: First, it principally accepts the separation of content from the evaluation of academic texts, since the impact-factor calculations or the rankings based upon these calculations only count citations and are not directly concerned with the "intrinsic" quality of a certain contribution. Second, there are various biases incorporated in and numerous problems associated with the standard approaches of quantitative indexing, such as the indices provided by Thomson Scientific (TS), constituting a general problem rarely discussed in the economic community. The relative discrimination of heterodox economics within such an evaluation process is on the contrary a specific problem, only partially related to the general biases incorporated in the TS indices.

These mere technical problems have to be understood as part of a larger discussion aimed at the journal culture in economics and other scientific disciplines. Since these topics are obviously related, a few remarks on this debate seem to be helpful to contextualize the arguments presented in this article. Generally, the journal culture in mainstream economics often relies on informal channels: "Top" authors often do not even "submit" their "submissions" but hand them in privately (cf. Shepherd 1995). Many authors anticipate criticism and a priori withhold or change arguments to please the editors or referees ("preference falsification"; see: Davis 2004; Bedeian 2003). Heterodox submissions seem to be, at last partially, rejected due to their meth-odological or political orientation (Reardon 2008). It is for these reasons that 60 percent of North-American economists agree in a survey that "a 'good-old-boy' network in the profession influences the probability of article acceptance, expressing the same strength and consensus of opinion as for school or business affiliation" (Davis 2007). "Old-*boy*" hits the point in this context since women are massively underrepresented in mainstream's editorial boards (Green 1998).

Moreover, there are documented cases of uncorrected errors in mainstream economic journals (cf. Jong-a-Pin and de Haan 2008), strengthening the impression that review processes and editorial decisions are arbitrary to some extent. This is also evidenced by the noteworthy amount of hot papers in economics that were rejected by the peer reviewers at their first attempt to get published (cf. Gans and Shepherd 1994).

Based on these considerations, the structure of this article is the following: First, I review and discuss several drawbacks of the most important quantitative indexing and evaluation standard—Thomson Scientifics "Journal Impact Factor" (JIF) and the often perverse incentives related to this method of quality measurement (second and third sections). This illustrates that quantitative evaluation encourages the production of specifically framed articles (from the perspective of the individual author) as well as the emergence of specific citation patterns (from a paradigmatical perspective). Second, I sketch general strategic options for heterodox economists (fourth section). Based on these and other findings, related to different aspects of the scientific publication process, I try to develop a handful of specific suggestions for conscious strategic behavior of heterodox economists (fifth section). As a last step I merge the general strategic options from the fourth section with the specific and more concrete suggestions from the fifth section to develop a well-structured picture of potentially useful strategies for heterodox economists.

The Drawbacks of the Journal Impact Factor (JIF)

> Impact factors, as one citation measure, are useful in establishing the influence journals have within the literature of a discipline. Nevertheless, they are not a direct measure of quality and must be used with considerable care. (Amin and Mabe 2000: 6)

Most research assessments based on quantitative evaluation refer to Thomson Scientifics impact factor. This section provides an overview about the general problems and specific methodological biases of this mode of measurement. This critique can be used in three ways, namely, (1) to challenge the authority of the TS data and their implications, (2) to exploit the biases to improve one's performance in the ranking game, and (3) to consider the failures when designing an alternative indicator.

The standard calculation of the impact factor is relatively simple (Garfield 1994): The export citations of a certain journal in one year referring to articles published in the two preceding years is divided through the number of (citable) articles published in the two preceding years. The calculation of some impact factor in 2009 is thus equal to:

$$JIF_{2009} = \frac{Citations_{2009} \; to \; articles_{2007-2008}}{(citable) \; articles_{2007-2008}}.$$

A general reflection of this evaluation procedure can be based on the question whether such a method is a reliable and valid measure of scientific quality. The fact that citations do not only depend on the quality of the cited items but on other factors, like trends in the scientific discourse, the influence of the "Matthew Effect in Science" (Merton 1968), citations set to criticize an article or argument, or the convention to cite "standard references" generally question the validity of the JIF. For example, the introductory quotation above suggests that the JIF measures the relative power ("influence") of outlets, not their quality. A provocative but highly significant example of missing validity is provided by Woo Suk Hwang's papers on stem cell research published in *Science*. While these papers are the source of the biggest recent scandal relating to fraud in the scientific community and, thus, surely hit rock bottom of scientific quality, these papers have been highly cited (over 450 times within the TS database) and pushing the JIF of its publication outlet (*Science*). Moreover, the JIF is not a nonreactive measurement procedure, since authors and editors may anticipate the rules and biases incorporated in the calculation of the JIF and therefore change their publication behavior in order to improve their performance in the ranking game. Authors, for example, face the incentive to split their contributions in as many articles as possible in order to maximize their impact-factor capital subject to the "least publishable unit" in a particular discipline.[3] In other words, the reliability and validity of the JIF, which are understood as basic criterion of any scientific research, are highly questionable.

A more detailed critique of the JIF could focus on four different dimensions: (1) missing control variables in the JIF formula, (2) selection problems and other data-related biases, (3) problems regarding the application of the JIF as an instrument for evaluation, and (4) a lack of transparency in combination with irreproducible results provided by Thomson Scientific.

Missing Variables

The formula shown above lacks some important control variables like the number of authors (how many people contributed to the cited articles[4]), the circulation of a certain outlet (how many people will read it or have access to the publication), the length of individual articles, or the number of self-citations. These missing variables are even more problematic when the JIF is used to compare the performance of individual researchers.

Technically, it would also seem necessary to correct for article type, since review articles or "data-rich" empirical analysis naturally attract more citations than methodological or theoretical articles (Garfield 1994; Amin and Mabe 2000: 3).

Sample Selection Biases

Scientific literature consists of different modes of publication, like books, journal articles, research reports, working papers, and so on. Thomson Scientific primarily includes international journals in its database, thereby excluding the vast majority of scientific publications. While the total number of academic journals is estimated between 50,000 and 500,000 (cf. Fröhlich 2008) only about 11,700[5] journals (along with very few books and some book series) are covered in the TS database, thereby neglecting that books are normally the publication mode with the highest citation impact (Hooydonk and Milis-Proost 1998; Cronin et al. 1997). Moreover, research reports or similar "grey literature" are not included at all. This is decisive since a "full-option-method," implying the usage of a sample of publications as big as possible, delivers results completely different from Thomson's (Hooydonk and Milis-Proost 1998).

In addition to this selection bias there are several technical problems related to the automated citation filtering process, which is based on scanned reference lists of the included publications.[6] Generally, the whole TS system has a language bias, which discriminates against non-English publications (Adler et al. 2008: 8). Furthermore, typos in reference lists appear very often[7]—especially in names or a title stemming from languages different from the author's—and distract the automated citation filtering process. The software used by TS in this case seems not very flexible: Neither authors nor journals should change their names—otherwise all the credits gathered before the change would not be considered in the TS evaluation system.[8] For journals changing the name of the publication is comparable to a sentence of death since the impact factor of such a journal will drop down to zero for at least two years.

Another problem is the short time-span considered when computing the JIF of a certain journal: In economics this two-year time-span on average covers less than 10 percent of all citations to a certain article (Adler et al. 2008: 7). However, the alternative five-year impact factor, which covers roughly 25 percent of citations per article in economics, has recently received a slightly more prominent role within TS' Journal Citation Reports. While TS rightly points out that the five-year impact factor on average correlates well with the standard two-year impact factor (see also Garfield 1998), the differences for the individual journal might be substantial. Especially journals publishing relatively few articles per year have a higher short term volatility of citations.

Problems Regarding the Application of the JIF in Evaluation Processes

One of the most significant problems is the inappropriate usage of the JIF in comparing individual articles or researchers. This is highly problematic because the JIF gives absolutely no information about the success of a single article: JIF values are mostly driven by a few articles, which are cited very often, while most articles receive a much smaller amount of citations than one would expect when solely looking at the JIF (Seglen 1997; Adler et al. 2008). In other words: Citations per article are far from equally distributed, but exhibit a power-law distribution, indicating that equating the quality of an individual article with the JIF of its outlet is highly misleading. This is well known and even acknowledged by TS (Thomson Scientific 2008). More precisely, TS even appeals to the scientific community to abandon the practice of interpersonal comparisons based on the JIF, but these postulates remain unheard by those using the JIF of an individual article's outlet in order to determine its quality.

It is of course particularly problematic in this context to compare different disciplines by using the JIF, since different disciplines also exhibit different citation cultures, which make comparisons across disciplines totally senseless (cf. Adler et al. 2008: S. 9–12).

Lack of Transparency and Irreproducible Results

While TS offers the Web of Science database for individual usage, JIFs cannot be reproduced using the data delivered by Web of Science. This unpleasant feature led to the case reported by Rossner et al. (2007, 2008), where a publisher (Rockefeller Press) bought citation data from TS and still failed to replicate the JIF calculations even by using the bought data. In standard scientific discourse no irreproducible quantitative result could be accepted, since intersubjectivity is a necessary precondition for any kind of scientific statement. This raises the question why scientists accept a criterion for scientific evaluation that does not fulfill scientific standards by itself. It seems to be a problem of transparency highly critical not only for the scientific community but also for the public, which is often relying on the exactness of scientific propositions.

Another matter of transparency is related to the classification of "citable" and "notcitable" articles as apparent in the formula stated above. The idea is that only "substantial articles" (Garfield 2005) should be considered in the JIF calculation, implying that the TS staff has to categorize all articles appearing in a certain journal into "substantial" (and thus "citable") and "unsubstantial" articles. This indexation is in turn affecting the denominator of the JIF calculation and may have drastic implications for the JIF of a certain journal; a phenomenon best illustrated by the high JIFs but low numbers of "substantial" articles of journals such as *Science, The Lancet,* or *Nature.* Here are two aspects of transparency at stake: First, we do not know the guidelines for differentiating "substantial" and "unsubstantial" articles, and thus we may only hope that this kind of separation follows reliable and valid criterions. Second, we do not know whether it is possible for individual editors and publishers to successfully complain about a certain routine of indexing. Such complaints may be motivated by an incentive to cheat or by sound and respectable arguments regarding content, but in any case we do not know and can again only hope that TS is honestly trying to separate the careful editors from the venturous cheaters. Rossner et al. (2007: 1091) give the following example for such an odd case: "*Current Biology* had an impact factor of 7.00 in 2002 and 11.91 in 2003. The denominator somehow dropped from 1032 in 2002 to 634 in 2003, even though the overall number of articles published in the journal increased."

Heterodox Discrimination?

Summing up the drawbacks of the JIF is thus leading to quite a long list, which includes missing variables, serious selection biases, wrong interpretations and applications, and, eventually, a disputable practice in terms of the usual scientific standards of data handling and integrity. On the whole, it seems that the JIF is an evaluation instrument that is at best slightly misleading but in most cases applied (especially in cases where grants, tenure, or hiring are discussed) highly arbitrary and completely unrelated to the questions at hand.

What are the implications of these arguments for heterodox economics? The answer to this question is threefold: First, the general insight that the JIF is invalid as an evaluation instrument seems to be valuable for every scientist—if any scientist was aware of this fact, the JIF might soon lose its institutional power. Second, one may speculate whether the outlined biases could be exploited in a Machiavellian sense, a question asked in the following section. Third the biases already discussed seem not to be responsible for the relative discrimination of heterodox economics—a problem demanding a more specific answer relating to the network effects of paradigms in terms of citation networks. One main determinant of this asserted discrimination is of course related to the sample selection problem sketched above, implying that many important heterodox economics journals are simply not included in Thomson's Social Science Citation Index

(SSCI) (cf. Lee 2008a).[9] Thus the heterodox community is weakened, since its network is split in two parts—those included in the SSCI and those not included—implying a significant reduction of heterodox JIFs when compared to a "full-option-method," that is, a calculation including a sample of publications "as big as possible." The other main source of discrimination is that big and dominant paradigms obviously exhibit positive network effects in terms of citations: more outlets for orthodox or mainstream economics lead to a higher number of (potentially citable and potentially citing) articles, which in turn lead to a higher number of citations. The JIF thus favors a dominant paradigm in any case, since it has a much bigger citation network at hand, thereby further strengthening the discrimination of heterodox journals.

Perverse Incentives Associated with the Journal Impact Factor

As has been mentioned already, the JIF is a reactive measurement procedure, meaning that the units of analysis—the researchers—may adapt their behavior in order to maximize their results. Of course, this kind of adaptation to the rules of the game—relating to the incentives created by the JIF—can across the board be understood as a "manipulation" of the JIF, that is, as a serious violation of the moral standards of the scientific endeavor (as in Reedijk and Moed 2006). While in most cases we cannot observe whether individual scientists yield to the perverse incentives embodied in the ranking game, there seems to be consensus on a more general level. Most scientists probably would agree that in theory the only incentive science should follow is its curiosity related to observable phenomena. But in practice, as it is the case here, most things look different. The examples given in the following paragraphs are, thus, not to blame the individual's "manipulating" the JIF, but to show its working routine. I hereby simply follow an economic tradition, which is not to blame the selfishness of the agent, but the structural defects of the principal's rules.

In this case we find incentives on three different levels: the individual scientist's, the editor's, and the general paradigm's level. The following table is based on the preceding section and gives an overview of the variety of perverse incentives associated with the JIF.

Table 1

Perverse Incentives Associated with the Journal Impact Factor

Drawback	Incentive	Level	Perversity[10]
Missing variable: length of articles	Publish articles as short as possible.	Individual	++
Missing variable: number of authors	Publish articles with as many authors as possible.	Individual	+
Missing variable: article type	Publish primarily review or "data-heavy" articles.	Individual	+
Missing variable: circulation	Publish only in outlets with high circulation.	Individual	+
Sample selection bias: mainly journals	Publish only in SSCI-listed journals (no books or book chapters!).	Individual	+
Sample selection bias: language	Publish only in English.	Individual	−
"noncitable articles"	Cite your journal articles heavily in editorials.	Editor	++
Missing variable: self-citations	Encourage submitting authors to cite your journal (as a condition for publishing).	Editor	−(++)
"noncitable articles"	Introduce noncitable commentary sections in your journal(s) to increase citations.	Editor	−
Lack of transparency (coding of articles)	Intervene at TS to change the coding of your articles related to "citable" and "notcitable."	Editor	?[11]
Automated scanning process	Cite only working paper versions of articles from a rival paradigm or abstain from such citations.	Paradigm	++
Lack of transparency (journal inclusion)	Try to "anticipate the rules" and cite a related journal heavily before it applies for inclusion in TS Web of Science.	Paradigm	+

On the individual level there is a series of clear-cut incentives, namely, to publish articles that (a) are review or "data-rich" *articles* (no books or book chapters, never!), (b) as short as possible with (c) as many authors as possible (d) written in English only and (e) in SSCI-listed journals with a high circulation. These are certainly somehow perverse imperatives for researchers who want to completely adapt to the rules of the "JIF game."

Also, editors of journals face noteworthy incentives mostly related to the word "citable" in the denominator of the JIF calculation. Since "unsubstantial" and, thus, "noncitable" contributions are not counted in the denominator, this is obviously one possibility to influence the JIF. Moreover, since citations in such "noncitable" texts are also counted in the enumerator of the JIF calculation, it is possible to manipulate the JIF by heavily citing own articles in editorials and commentaries. The *Journal of Gerontology: Medical Sciences* constitutes an example of excessive self-citing in editorials, gaining more than one impact factor point in 2003 (4.1 instead of 2.9) due to such self-citations (cf. Reedijk and Moed 2006: 188–189). Another, more obvious and much less corrupt, way to increase the number of (journal-)self-citations is of course to simply encourage authors to cite articles from the journal they are submitting to (in sharp contrast to imposing journal self-citations as a *condition* for publishing).

Another incentive editors face is to include "noncitable" commentary sections in their journals: While contributions to such a section are "free," that is, not counted in the denominator, citations to such articles are still counted in the enumerator. Since commentary sections are often very inspiring to read this incentive does not seem as perverse as most other incentives associated with the impact factor mechanics. However, generally speaking, there is always a potential to manipulate the JIF by influencing the coding of articles conducted by Thomson Scientific. In the individual case this may be justified ("hey, you coded all our book reviews as full articles!") or not, but eventually the whole process is a black box.

Furthermore, incentives can also be identified from a paradigmatical perspective: One may abstain from citing articles from a paradigmatic rival at all[12] or only refer to working paper versions as substitutes for the original articles so not to strengthen one's paradigmatic competitor in terms of citation metrics. Moreover, as a reactive measurement procedure the Thomson's impact factor game invites to anticipate its rules. According to various sources (Garfield 1990; Testa 1998; Dolfsma and Leydesdorff 2008; Testa 2009) the entry of a certain journal is, aside from other criteria such as internationality, timeliness, availability of English titles and abstracts, or the use of a peer review system, based on a "quasi-IF," which is calculated by filtering out citations from journals already included in the SSCI to the "applicant" that is the applying journal. The calculation procedure follows the same routine as defined in the second section. So journals already included in the SSCI could cite applying journals associated with the same paradigm more frequently within the year(s) their application will be based on.[13] They could initiate this secretly (by requesting authors to cite this or that journal), openly (by encouraging contributions from this or that field), or really subtly (by providing special issues devoted to the pet subjects of other journals associated with the same paradigm).

Most of the incentives discussed in this section clearly exhibit a tendency towards bad scientific practice. One could argue that by discussing these incentives one, therefore, also encourages the bad scientific practice. While I would agree that the whole ranking game rests on a doubtful logic, I think a transparent and accurate description of the current situation is a precondition for developing reasonable alternatives. Thus, the bad scientific practice is clearly on the side of the JIF and its adherents.

General Strategic Options for Heterodox Economists

Hirschman (1970) identifies three main possibilities of action in the context of a social conflict, that is, a state of affairs not acceptable to a certain group or individual. Basically he differentiates between exit and voice, where the former indicates the possibility to "stop buying the firm's products or [to] leave the organization" (Hirschman 1970: 4), whereas the latter option emphasizes "any attempt at all to change, rather than to escape from, an objectionable state of affairs" (Hirschman 1970: 30). These two mechanisms, based on economic competition (exit) and political discourse (voice), do not work in isolation, but in a complex dynamic interplay allowing for a complementary or substitutive relationship between these two modes. Loyalty, on the contrary, is introduced as a relevant variable influencing the decision between exit and voice prolonging the former and intensifying the latter. However, Hirschman also develops a concept of "unconscious loyalist behavior," which is "by definition free from felt discontent, it will not lead to voice"[14] (Hirschman 1970: 91) but still prolongs a potential exit. Therefore, the three broad categories introduced have a lively interplay mutually influencing each other. In relation to the matter in hand, systems of quantitative evaluation will be interpreted as the referential product. The basic modes of action suggested by Hirschmann provide a conceptual framework for discussing the specific suggestions introduced in the subsequent sections. In this context, compatibility, not origin, is the main criterion for assigning suggestions to the different strategic levels. In this context, the non-exclusiveness of exit, voice, and loyalty favors such an approach. Thus, reinterpreting this framework for addressing the specific problem of the relative discrimination of heterodox economics within the TS standard leads to the following three general options:

- EXIT: Heterodox economists completely refuse to accept quantitative indices, especially the TS standard, as a measure of quality (nevertheless anticipating that *others will do*).
- VOICE: Heterodox economists try to alter the status quo by designing *and establishing* their own (quantitative) indicators or criterions of research quality.
- LOYALTY: Heterodox economists accept the TS standard as a measure of quality and try to compete at the best in the given evaluation system.

These three categories broadly illustrate the scope of action available to heterodox economists. Thus it seems reasonable to consider the compatibility of all the specific suggestions discussed later in the article with these three general categories. Some suggestions will fit into all categories—heterodox economists can adhere to them without even agreeing on a general orientation towards quantitative indices (which is, eventually, an individual decision). Other suggestions will fit into only one or two categories and, thus, could be interesting for discussing the general strategic orientation. Such a discussion seems necessary to realize the potential network benefits associated with a situation, where heterodox economists could agree on this point in terms of a certain commitment.

Specific Strategic Suggestions

A Methodological Note

In order to give a clearly arranged account on all the specific suggestions I will code them according to the following scheme: #Number—Topic, for example #1-NET is indicating the first suggestion related to the citation behavior of heterodox economists. All suggestions coded this way will be incorporated in a common framework showing which of the specific suggestions go along with the different general strategic orientations introduced in the preceding section.

Establish Stronger Networks

Citation networks are an important factor in discussing the performance of heterodox economics as measured by the JIF. We can view citation dynamics in terms of network effects and ask how the disciplinary citation behavior is distributing citations among different journals. The following table, which analyzes the top-10 orthodox and top-10 heterodox journals according to the TS Journal Citation Report 2007, might help to focus on problems associated with this perspective.

Table 2 is based on a 20-year sample (1989–2008) of all citations between 20 economics journals. The sample selection rests upon the Journal Citation Report (JCR) 2007; it includes the top 10 journals of the JCR (=top 10 orthodox[15]) and the top 10 heterodox[16] journals identified in accordance with Frederic S. Lee's heterodox directory (Lee 2009a).[17] Two important properties or restrictions of the sample utilized above are noteworthy: First, all the citations related to *articles published between 1989 and 2008* have been counted (i.e., citations to articles published before 1989 have been excluded) and second—due to the idiosyncratic operating of the Web of Science database, which does not precisely show the references but only the citing articles—an article that cites two or more articles from another journal counts only as one citation ("citing article"). Nonetheless the above comparison clearly demonstrates that the neoclassical citation network is much tighter, since heterodox journals cite each other less frequently—they import relatively more citations from orthodox journals than vice versa and have a much higher amount of self-citations.

The same conclusions apply when relying on a different sample of heterodox journals provided by Lee. The following table, a modified version of one of Lee's tables (Lee 2009b: 53, 153–154) based on the years 1993–2003, includes 11 heterodox journals. On grounds of the content-oriented selection of journals in this sample emphasizing radical, post-Keynesian, and socioeconomic approaches, only one of these journals, the *Cambridge Journal of Economics*, is also part of the above sample of the "JCR top 10 heterodox." Interestingly, while the sample used in Table 2 is much more diverse in terms of paradigmatical viewpoints (Marxist, post-Keynesian, ecological, evolutionary, feminist journals, and a journal very close to the mainstream are included), the results derived from Lee's much more coherent sample are very similar.[18] Moreover, it gives an intuition about the structural reasons for the loose heterodox citation network.

Table 2

Orthodox vs. Heterodox Citation Networks

	Average percentage of citations from top 10 heterodox journals	Average percentage of citations from top 10 orthodox journals	Average intra-network (heterodox/ orthodox) citation percentage excluding self citations
in top 10 heterodox	60.35% (intra-network)	39.65% (inter-network)	**19.3% (intra-network)**
in top 10 orthodox	4.89% (inter-network)	95.11% (intra-network)	**64.22% (intra-network)**

Taken from Dobusch and Kapeller (2009); see also Cronin (2008).

Table 3 gives a more precise picture of what has basically been already said: A stereotypical heterodox economist publishing in the journals depicted in Table 3 follows a rather standardized citation routine, which can be summarized as follows:

(1) First: Cite your enemies, that is, mainstream economic journals.
(2) Second: Cite yourself, that is, the journal you are submitting to.
(3) Third: Cite your buddies, that is, the two journals with the strongest connection to the journal you are submitting to.
(4) Lastly: Cite your allies, that is, heterodox economic journals except the three already mentioned (that is, the 17 remaining journals within this sample).

This fatal routine is subtly, but not in full detail, also present in Table 2 and can be (roughly) read as 40 percent mainstream citations, 40 percent self-citations, 20 percent citations of allies for heterodoxy compared to 65 percent citations of allies, 30 percent self-citations and 5 percent heterodox citations for orthodoxy. These differences in network density are striking especially when remembering that the sample of *orthodox* journals used in Table 2 is less homogenous in terms of content than the *heterodox* sample used in Table 3 (the orthodox sample in Table 2 includes the *Journal of Accounting and Economics* or the *Journal of Economic Geography*). In a nutshell: The orthodox citation network is much tighter—consequentially also heterodox journals have relatively more journal self-citations and import more citations from orthodox journals than vice versa.[21]

From a pluralist perspective this leads to a rather surprising result: Under the assumption that a pluralist attitude, as heterodox economists often invoke it, implies *talking to each other* (otherwise it would not be pluralism, but some kind of careless ignorance), which in a scientific context implies *citing each other*, we find that heterodox economics—as compared to its paradigmatic rival—is actually very pluralistic (according to Table 2, roughly 40 percent of the citations in heterodox journals stem from mainstream journals). On the contrary, the analysis suggests that the economic mainstream is theoretically closed, that is, not open for alternative theoretical approaches and thus not pluralistic (according to Table 2, only about 5 percent of the citations in mainstream journals stem from heterodoxy).[22] While this

Table 3

Citation Behavior Among a Content-Oriented Selection of Heterodox Economic Journals

Journal	Total Citations	% Mainstream[19]	% Self	% Buddies	% Allies[20]
Cambridge Journal of Economics	21,363	9.7%	2.6%	1.6%	1.7%
Contributions to Political Economy	2,204	9.1%	1.4%	2.3%	1.0%
International Papers in Political Economy	2,164	7.1%	0.3%	2.9%	3.0%
Journal of Economic Issues	22,917	4.9%	7.1%	1.0%	1.2%
Journal of Post Keynesian Economics	10,918	13.1%	7.6%	2.7%	1.6%
New Left Review	10,451	0.0%	3.2%	0.2%	0.1%
Review of Black Political Economy	3,886	6.1%	3.2%	0.6%	0.1%
Review of Political Economy	9,580	9.3%	1.5%	3.0%	2.6%
Review of Social Economy	9,067	5.5%	2.3%	2.4%	1.9%
Review of Radical Political Economics	9,391	4.2%	4.1%	1.8%	2.9%
Science & Society	7,735	0.2%	3.2%	2.1%	1.4%
Average:		**6.29%**	**3.32%**	**1.87%**	**1.59%**

The categories "self" and "buddies" have been added by the author.

observation goes well along with a series of complaints about the discrimination of heterodox ideas within the mainstream journal culture it only holds from bird's eye view interpreting heterodox economics as a single paradigmatical alternative to mainstream economics. If we remove the tendency to paint opposing paradigmatical fractions by using a "broad brush" (Backhouse 2004: 268) and focus on intra-fractional citation behavior it comes clear that heterodoxy is more pluralistic in its relation to the mainstream than in its internal discourse: Only about 20 percent of citations in heterodox journals stem from the *other* heterodox journals in the same sample (that is, the sample Table 2 is based on). Thus heterodoxy imports twice as many citations from mainstream literature as it produces domestically, that is, within the heterodox paradigm. This indicates that heterodox economists should try to partially reorient their pluralist attitude from mainstream journals to other heterodox branches, not at least to intensify the theoretical discourse between different heterodox journals and schools of thought, potentially leading to a "Win-Win-Situation." While an intensified discourse on theoretical or methodological questions between different heterodox schools of thought might improve the theoretical and empirical standards as well as the applicability of heterodox economics in general, it would probably also lead to a significant improvement in terms of the ranking-game (#1-NET).

Practically speaking, heterodox scholars should always check 15–20 heterodox journals for potentially useful sources before submitting an article (the idea to rank journals according to their contribution to pluralism as presented in Lee (2008b) is in fact a kind of carrot to pursue this task). Under the assumption that citations are a reciprocal phenomenon the same argument applies to related disciplines such as economic sociology, management studies, political science, economic geography, and women's or development studies (#2-NET; cf. Reardon 2008). If mainstream economists are not willing to cite their heterodox counterparts maybe "neutral" researchers from other fields might well do so if the heterodox economists' work proves to be interesting. Again a potential "Win-Win-Situation" with characteristics very similar to those described above might arise between heterodox economists and economics' neighboring disciplines.

In any case it seems necessary to alter the current situation, which is characterized by the fact that heterodoxy comparatively strengthens the orthodox position in the content-avoiding JIF logic, as is evident from the following table based on the same sample as Table 2.

Table 4 examines the "cross-paradigmatical-border" citation behavior between the heterodox and the orthodox citation community. To fully clarify this situation it should be mentioned that the majority of the 385 citations that are exported from heterodoxy to orthodoxy are created by the respective "outliers" of each side: While 201 are exported by the *Journal of Economic Behavior and Organization*, another 111 are imported by the *Journal of Economic Geography* (excluding those from the former to the latter journal). Thus only 73 export citations within 20 years remain for the nine "nonoutliers" on each side. Technically, this implies that heterodox economists strengthen the neoclassical paradigm in terms of citation metrics (Factor 10 in this sample!), since they import many more citations from orthodoxy than vice versa. This is somehow paradoxical since heterodox economists often cite mainstream journals to criticize neoclassical theory or to demarcate themselves. It's a wonderful example of the content-blind "logic" of simple citation counting. Consequentially this analysis implies that heterodox journals should decrease their presence in the TS database, which is a rather radical and potentially self-damaging option mainly compatible with a strong rejection of any quantitative quality measurement (#3-NET). Tables 2 and 3 and the argument that the relative discrimination of heterodox journals regarding the JIF rests partially on the exclusion of some heterodox journals, on the other hand, would imply to try to increase the presence of heterodox journals in the SSCI (#4-NET).

Disseminate Your Papers

As already mentioned in above, circulation is an important criterion influencing the presence and availability and, thus, also the citation frequency of a certain article. Hence the following section is devoted to the question how to increase the visibility and circulation of heterodox articles to increase citations and impact factors of heterodox articles and journals.

Table 4

Citation Imports and Exports Between Top 10 Orthodox and Top 10 Heterodox Journals

Top 10 heterodox journals	Citations in top 10 orthodox (export)	Citations of top 10 orthodox (import)	Difference	Proportional Factor
Economy and Society	16	49	−33	3.06
Ecological Economics	10	681	−671	68.10
Work, Employment and Society	5	29	−24	5.80
Review of International Political Economy	26	70	−44	2.69
Journal of Economic Behaviour and Organization	201	1,884	−1,683	9.37
New Political Economy	1	38	−37	38.00
Cambridge Journal of Economics	47	463	−416	9.85
Journal of Development Studies	43	487	−444	11.33
Journal of Evolutionary Economics	31	395	−364	12.74
Feminist Economics	5	133	−128	26.60
Total	385	4,229	−3,844	10.98

Taken from Dobusch and Kapeller (2009).

Looking, for example, at the two-year time-span used to calculate the JIF, it is obvious that the availability of articles is crucial for the development of one's JIF—preprint publication is thus simply a must (#1-DIS), otherwise the outlet is "hurting itself" in terms of the JIF calculation. The reason for this is very simple: An article published in December (say, 2009) will be counted in the denominator for the 2010 JIF and citations to this article in 2010 will be counted in the enumerator. But most articles being published in 2010 will already be under review at the end of 2009. So most articles appearing 2010 could not even consider an article published in December 2009, if it was not accessible earlier via preprint channels.

Another aspect of this perspective refers to the amount of heterodox journals in total and the number of journals included in the SSCI. These data combined with some knowledge about the rejection rates in different heterodox outlets should make it possible to consciously found new journals in order to fully utilize the capacities of the heterodox economic community. In the case of founding new journals, the possibility of online open access journals should be taken into account, since this kind of publication is accessible all over the world and thus combines low costs with high circulation. For example, an open access journal for good heterodox review articles on topics relevant for developing countries might achieve quite a popularity, since most of the classical heterodox journals are simply not accessible in many universities of developing countries, while heterodox approaches might prove very useful for their students and staff (#2-DIS).

A further feature of the digital sphere is that research that is freely available on the Internet, for example, by downloading from the author's homepage, or disseminated along digital research platforms (like RePEc or SSRN) or mailing lists, gathers significantly more citations (Bergstrom and Lavaty 2007). A simple conclusion is therefore that heterodox economists should be allowed to post their scholarly articles as working papers on the web—a short reminder on the title page (published in this or that journal Vol. x(y); pp. a–b) could guarantee that the relevant Journal also gathers the citation, if the particular working paper is cited by someone (#3-DIS). This observation may also serve as a further incentive to create new journals as open access journals, which should suffer from the same "positively distorting" bias. Furthermore, this suggestion is strengthened by the observation of Novarese and Zimmermann (2008) that heterodox articles posted on the RePEc platform and distributed via the "New Economic Papers" (NEP) mailing lists are on average downloaded more often than mainstream articles. Thus it seems reasonable to consciously improve the dissemination of heterodox work through digital channels as research platforms or mailing-lists (#4-DIS; for example, there are still no heterodox research networks within the SSRN[23]).

Lastly, heterodox economists should consider some general network effects influencing citation behavior. A general effect well known is that scientific publications, which appear (prominently) in the media, are cited more often than other papers (Fröhlich 2008: 73). So the imperative is: be interesting (to get cited)! Another "back-door option" to get on the citation lists is to enter the political debate. Publicly well known persons also tend to be cited more often and heterodox economists may act politically as commentators, experts, advisers, or advocates related to some topic, politician, or postulate. There are also mutual network effects between these societal fields: Political activities tend to be reported more often in the media than scientific results, but citations still grow through presence in the media. Thus another and related imperative is: be political (to get cited)! (#5-DIS) By the way, being political often goes along with good scientific practice: Since value judgments are hardly avoidable in social science, especially in economics (Myrdal 1963), one should treat them with the greatest transparency possible instead of hiding them behind (more or less) complex battlefields of algebra.

Advocate for Alternatives

Another perspective on this complex of problems is related to the general question of the validity of the JIF. It basically asks if we can find more valid instruments or proxies for measuring the quality of an outlet or an article. A possibility for heterodox journals to differentiate themselves in terms of associated quality and influence from the "old-boys-network" could be the introduction of a so-called triple blind review system as a nonquantitative argument in a discourse on quality. "Triple blind" is in this context referring to the fact that not only authors and reviewers do not know each others name, but also editors do not know the identity of the authors. The German *Zeitschrift für Soziologie* has introduced triple blind review and consequentially it also rejected manuscripts from "star authors" (Fröhlich 2008: 68). This system could represent some kind of discursive Unique Selling Proposition, especially since some TS journals are not even peer reviewed, not to speak of triple blind reviewed (#1-ALT). Another, quite different, possibility to achieve a qualitative difference from mainstream journal review practices would be to make review processes more transparent, e.g., by posting submissions and reviews on the web and allowing visitors to comment on both—the submission and the respective reviews (something similar is proposed by Earl 2008; #2-ALT). If submissions and reviews are posted on the web this could also induce authors to be even more careful in their manuscript preparations.

A further important advice referring to a better estimation of the quality of a specific scientific piece of work is to analyze the absolute impact of a certain publication in terms of total citations. Different databases or instruments can be used to measure the volume of citations to a certain publication, from Google Scholar over Scopus to TS Web of Science.[24] One should, thus, always calculate the concrete publication impact if an individual's work is evaluated in quantitative terms, no matter whether it concerns hiring or promotion decisions or the application for diverse grants. Especially for heterodox economists concrete and substantial "article impacts" are important since they represent an instrument less invalid and less unreliable as compared to the standard JIFs; moreover article impacts needn't suffer from the implicit discrimination embodied in the JIF (#3-ALT).

Lastly, of course, the various problems related to the exclusion of potentially relevant variables and the sample-selection bias associated with the JIF highlight avoidable problems, which could be eliminated by design through the creation of a new, alternative quantitative index for evaluating economic research (#4-ALT). The relevant biases in this context are mainly the small sample size and the two-year time-span for calculating the JIF, as well as the missing control variables for the number of authors, the length of articles, the circulation of the outlet, article type, and the number of self-citations. Of course, the weight of these variables has to be interpreted with respect to the task at hand: When evaluating journals the length of the article seems to be a less crucial variable as compared to the evaluation of single authors. However, in the long run it seems necessary to establish alternative and superior measures of scholarly quality and visibility and, thus, new standards in research evaluation (see also Frederic Lee's contribution to this special issue). In this spirit alternative indicators could also be based on different "basic principles" instead of mere citation counting. For example, these could include the building of specific knowledge (journal self-citations), the ability to combine insights from various fields of research within a certain discipline (network centrality) resp. to connect different schools of thought (pluralism) or the interdisciplinary openness of a given outlet (citation trails to other disciplines). Moreover, the introduction of peer review or the inclusion of download statistics for individual articles (if accessible) could broaden the horizon of quantitative evaluation. More generally speaking, this would imply to reform the methodology of quantitative evaluation in favor of a multi-method approach. Thereby the related and potentially allied neighboring disciplines, already mentioned, could operate as international and interdisciplinary partners in a project applying for official funding to create a better alternative index (#5-ALT).

Another preliminary suggestion to compensate for the relative discrimination of heterodox economics within the SSCI is to develop a complementary index, which is correcting for some factor of pluralism (#6-ALT; as suggested by Lee 2008b).

Conclusion: Putting the Pieces Together

Why is it interesting for a philosopher of science to discuss the impact of citation metrics on heterodox economics? First, the scientific community's institutions are often a blind spot in theory of science, which thus seems all too detached from the practical process of science in many cases; this is the *theoretical* motivation. Second, philosophers of various epistemological camps agree that critique is a basic prerequisite of scientific discourse (Popper 1934). This is the reason why many of them are skeptical regarding dominating paradigms in the social sciences and constitutes the *normative* motivation for writing this article. Third, citation ranking in philosophy is even more disastrous since the English-speaking bias is a much more serious problem when compared to economics (cf. Stekeler-Weithofer 2009), which constitutes the *affective* motivation. Fourth, I think that hetero-dox economics has great things to offer for improving the understand-ing of our economic environment, which is my *personal* motivation. It is for these reasons that I give a pragmatic outlook here mainly by providing an overview and discussing some general implications.

As a first step, the following table evaluates the above suggestions along the lines of the three general strategic criterions exit, voice, and loyalty. Thereby an "X" signifies the compatibility of a certain sugges-tion with the respective general strategic criterion. Suggestions printed in *italics* are signaling that the relevant suggestion has, from the author's point of view, a serious strategic drawback.

It is immediately observable that most suggestions are compatible with all three general strategic orientations. This is good news, since it implies a kind of flexibility for heterodox economists: Most activities listed above can be pursued without a general strategic consensus. Of course, there is still a high demand for further coordination and cooperation between different heterodox journals and schools of thought, but it is not primarily necessary to go for a "great debate on strategy." The differences between the broad strategic orientations consequently concentrate on a few points: Exit asks the fundamental question of boycotting the whole system in suggestion #3-NET. But this option seems to exhibit self-damaging properties and thus renders suggestion #3-NET more or less invalid. This observation illustrates that the quasi-monopoly power of TS is rendering this strategy obso-lete, since exit relies on competitive mechanisms simply not available in the light of TS' dominance. Thus, without an alternative or competitive product to choose, exit is hardly justifiable. Lastly, the exclusive characteristic of voice is the creation of competitive (or complementary) indices for evaluating (economic) research.

An important observation embodied in the first suggestions depicted in Table 5 is that the different heterodox schools of thought

Table 5

A matrix of suggestions

Dimension	Suggestion	Exit	Voice	Loyalty
Etablish stronger networks	#1-NET: Reorienting Pluralism I: Consciously increase (current) citations of other heterodox communities, journals and scholars.	X	X	X
	#2-NET: Reorienting Pluralism II: Increase citations of related and maybe "allied" disciplines as economic sociology, political science, development studies, social/economic geography, organization/management science . . .	X	X	X
	#3-NET: *Decrease presence of heterodox journals in the SSCI.*	X		
	#4-NET: Increase presence of heterodox journals in the SSCI.		X	X
Disseminate your papers	#1-DIS: Pre-print publication is a strategical 'must' in order to succeed in the ranking game.	X	X	X
	#2-DIS: Fully utilize the capabilities of the heterodox economic community: Found new (Open Access) heterodox journals if rejection rates are considered too high.	X	X	X
	#3-DIS: Allow heterodox economists to distribute working paper versions of their publications via digital channels.	X	X	X
	#4-DIS: Access and create mailing-lists and online communities; disseminate research via RePEc, NEP, SSRN . . .	X	X	X
	#5-DIS: Enter the non-economic discourse (media, politics).	X	X	X
Advocate for Alternatives	#1-ALT: Introduce triple blind review as stand-alone criterion for objectivity.	X	X	X
	#2-ALT: Increase transparency in review processes as a stand-alone criterion	X	X	X
	#3-ALT: Calculate concrete 'publication impacts' if you are – directly or indirectly – affected by an evaluation process (partially) relying on data from TS.	X	X	X
	#4-ALT: Create an alternative and superior index to Thomson's JIF.		X	
	#5-ALT: Try to forge an alliance between heterodox economists and potential allies from other disciplines and apply for funding to create a better index.		X	
	#6-ALT: Create an index of heterodox journals complementarity to the SSCI correcting for pluralism (cf. Lee 2008b).	X		X

should consciously try to implement a common heterodox paradigm. More work should be devoted to discuss theoretical and empirical connections and complementarities between these different schools in order to tighten the theoretical and citation-related network of heterodox economics. Discussing each other's theoretical and empirical results—i.e., talking with each other—naturally leads to reading and citing each other.

In terms of a general strategy a concrete suggestion could be based on Heinz von Förster's famous two imperatives concerning smart behavior in complex, nondeterministic situations (Förster 1993: 49). While the *aesthetical imperative* ("if you are eager for knowledge, learn how to act") leads, as in most cases, to a merely trivial conclusion, namely, "do something, just do," the *ethical* imperative ("if you act, act in a way which increases your options!") gives a deeper advice: Choose the strategy with the most options. In the collection of suggestions above this strategy would be voice. Moreover, voice has also a substantial net advantage when compared to the other strategic orientations: While the institutions of scientific evaluation do not seem to be very responsive to the exit option and the possibility of influencing the system postexit is probably even smaller, unconscious loyalty on the contrary has another severe drawback as it would lead to basically accepting what is essentially wrong, namely, the JIF system. Therefore, in the given context, voice is the most promising route to change in the spirit of Hirschmann, since the creation of a rival system offers the possibility to empower the other options associated with exit and voice (cf. Hirschmann 1970: 55–56, 120–126).

Notes

1. Based on EconLit and the Social Science Citation Index (SSCI); see European Commission (2004).

2. The evaluation process of the Research Assessment Exercise is based on the Diamond List, which is again based on the SSCI; cf. Diamond (1989), Lee (2007).

3. These "perverse incentives" resemble the effects of governmental specifications in centrally planned economies: For example, the specifications regarding Christmas trees in the former Soviet Union were communicated in tons, which led to the production of massive and oversized trees,

These were very heavy and thus helped to fulfill the relevant specifications, but surely did not meet the standards expected by the consumers (cf. Fröhlich 2008).

4. The more people contribute to an article the higher is its probability of being cited, either by the authors themselves or by their related networks.

5. Roughly 2,700 of these are included in the SSCI. see: http://science.thomsonreuters.com/cgi-bin/jrnlst/jlresults.cgi?PC=SS (dl. 17-06-09).

6. If a journal contains no reference lists, but only footnotes, TS seems to count citations within the footnotes, i.e., the automated scanning system counts every single citation set to a certain publication and not only its appearance in the reference list (cf. Klein and Chiang 2004).

7. Typos appear in roughly 10 percent of all references according to Opthof (1997), while Evans et al. (1990) report that 48 percent of the references in their sample, consisting of three medical journals, were incorrect.

8. Individual researchers can register at the platform www.researcherid.com, where they can mark their articles within Web of Science, giving the opportunity to manually correct this bias.

9. Some examples of important heterodox journals not included in the SSCI are: *Journal of Institutional Economics, Review of Radical Political Economics, Contributions to Political Economy, Review of Social Economy, Journal of Socio-Economics, and Review of Political Economy.*

10. This column shows a proxy for the "degree of perversity" embodied in the given incentives, based on the way I see the relation between the incentive and what one might call "good scientific practice" (++: very perverse incentive, +: perverse incentive, −: perversity hinges on the context of the JIF—while the action as such might be reasonable, the fact that it is based on the anticipation of an evaluation mechanism still causes some headache; this of course resembles the well-known area of tension between deontological and consequentialist ethics).

11. As outlined in the preceeding section this depends heavily on the editor's concrete motivation.

12. As exemplified by mainstream economics.

13. According to the TS homepage, journals applying for inclusion have to submit three consecutive issues of their journal to TS (http://science.thomsonreuters.com/info/journalsubmission/; dl. 04-05-09). So if some journal applies in 2011 by sending three 2011 issues to TS, the calculation of the quasi-IF will most probably be based on the years 2010 and/or 2009. This implies that other paradigmatically allied journals should cite the applying journal more frequently in 2009 and 2010 and these citations should relate to articles from 2007–2009 (most interesting are of course citations relating to articles published 2008, since they are relevant in any case). However, this outline is still quite speculative as the journal inclusion process is eventually a black box as rightly argued by Klein and Chiang (2004).

14. Very similar to this point is the notion of passive loyalty described in Hirschmann (1970: 78).

15. *Journal of Political Economy, Journal of Economic Literature, Quarterly Journal of Economics, Journal of Accounting and Economics, Journal of Financial Economics, Econometrica, Journal of Economic Perspectives, Journal of Economic Geography, Review of Economic Studies, Journal of Economic Growth.*

16. *Economy and Society, Ecological Economics, Work, Employment and Society, Review of International Political Economy, Journal of Economic Behaviour and Organization, New Political Economy, Cambridge Journal of Economics, Journal of Development Studies, Journal of Evolutionary Economics, Feminist Economics.*

17. The acquired dataset is accessible via http://www.dobusch.net/pub/uni/citation-data.xls.

18. A stronger content-oriented selection would intuitively imply stronger relationships in terms of citations.

19. All citations to 12 different mainstream journals have been counted: *American Economic Review, Economic Journal, Economica, Econometrica, International Economic Review, Journal of Labor Economics, Journal of Political Economy, Journal of Monetary Economics, Oxford Economics Papers, Quarterly Journal of Economics, Review of Economics and Statistics, Review of Economics Studies.*

20. All citations to 20 different heterodox journals have been counted (see Lee 2009b: 153–154).

21. Journal-specific evaluations help to precisely analyze the citation routines of a certain outlet in order to provide journal-specific suggestions for possible improvements from this perspective. See Starr (2010) or Kapeller (2010) for two recent examples.

22. This is clearly an epistemological fallacy of mainstream economics, since the standard epistemological routine suggests to be highly interested in and concerned with critical articles or asserted falsifications relating to an established theory.

23. See http://ssrn.com/ern/index.html (dl. 04-05-09).

24. See Neuhaus and Daniel (2006) for an overview of different data sources for citation analysis. Ann-Wil Harzing's Software "Publish or Perish" is a small and useful tool for counting citations based on GoogleScholar; see http://www.harzing.com/pop.htm (dl. 06-07-09).

References

Adler, R., J. Ewing, and P. Taylor. (2008). "Citation Statistics." URL: http://www.mathunion.org/fileadmin/IMU/Report/CitationStatistics.pdf (dl. 01-04-09).

Amin, M., and M. Mabe. (2000). "Impact Factors: Use and Abuse." *Perspectives in Publishing*, October 2000: 1–6.

Backhouse, R. E. (2004). "A Suggestion for Clarifying the Study of Dissent in Economics." *Journal of the History of Economic Thought* 26: 261–271.

Bedeian, A. G. (2003). "The Manuscript Review Process: The Proper Roles of Authors, Referees, and Editors" *Journal of Management Inquiry* 12: 331–338.

Bergstrom, T. C., and R. Lavaty. (2007). "How Often Do Economists Self-Archive?" eScholarshipRepository, University of California Santa Barbara, Department of Economics. URL: http://repositories.cdlib.org/cgi/viewcontent.cgi?article=1203&context=ucsbecon (dl. 15-05-09).

Cronin, B. (2008). "Journal Citation Among Heterodox Economists 1995–2007: Dynamics of Community Emergence." *On the Horizon* 16: 226–240.

Cronin, B., H. Snyder, and H. Atkins. (1997). "Comparative Citation Rankings of Authors in Monographic and Journal Literature: A Study of Sociology." *Journal of Documentation* 53: 263–273.

Davis, W. L. (2004). "Preference Falsification in the Economics Profession." *Econ Journal Watch* 1: 359–367.

——. (2007). "Economists' Opinion of Economists' Work." *American Journal for Economics and Sociology* 66: 267–288.

Diamond, A. M. (1989). "The Core Journals of Economics." *Current Contents* 12: 3–9.

Dobusch, L. (2009). "Von Open Access zu Free Knowledge." In *Gerechtigkeit*. Eds. B. Blaha and J. Weidenholzer. Wien: Braumüller.

Dobusch, L., and J. Kapeller. (2009). "Why is Economics Not an Evolutionary Science? New Answers to Veblen's Old Question." *Journal of Economic Issues* 43(4): 867–898.

Dolfsma, W., and L. Leydesdorff. (2008). "Journals as Constituents of Scientific Discourse: Economic Heterodoxy." *On the Horizon* 16: 214–225.

Earl, P. E. (2008). "Heterodox Economics and the Future of Academic Publishing." *On the Horizon* 16: 205–213.

European Commission (2004). *Mapping of Excellence in Economics.* Luxemburg.

Evans, J. T., H. I. Nadjari, and S. A. Burchell. (1990). "Quotational and Reference Accuracy in Surgical Journals—A Continuing Peer-Review Problem." *Journal of the American Medical Association* 263: 1353–4.

Förster, H. v. (1993). *Wissen und Gewissen—Versuch einer Brücke.* Frankfurt: Suhrkamp.

Fröhlich, G. (2008). "Wissenschaftskommunikation und ihre Dysfunktionen: Wissenschafts-journale, Peer Review, Impact Faktoren." In

WissensWelten. Eds. H. Hettwer, M. Lehmkuhl, H. Wormer, and F. Zotta. Gütersloh: Bertelsmann.

Gans, J., and G. B. Shepherd. (1994). "How are the Mighty Fallen: Rejected Classical Articles by Leading Economists." *Journal of Economic Perspectives* 8: 165–180.

Garfield, E. (1990). "How ISI Selects Journals for Coverage: Quantitative and Qualitative Considerations." *Current Contents* 22: 5–13.

——. (1994). "The Thomson Scientific Impact Factor." URL: http://thomsonreuters.com/business_units/scientific/free/essays/impactfactor/ (dl. 24-03-09).

——. (1998). "Long-Term vs. Short-Term Journal Impact (Part II)." *Scientist* 12: 12–13. URL: http://garfield.library.upenn.edu/commentaries/tsv12(14) p12y19980706.pdf (dl. 15-04-09).

——. (2005). "The Agony and the Ecstasy—The History and Meaning of the Journal Impact Factor." Presentation at the International Congress on Peer Review and Biomedical Publication, Chicago, September 16, 2005. URL: http://www.garfield.library.upenn.edu/papers/jifchicago2005.pdf (dl. 17-05-09).

Green, K. (1998). "The Gender Composition of Editorial Boards in Economics." Royal Economic Society's Committee on Women in Economics. URL: www.res.org.uk/society/pdfs/editoria.pdf (dl. 22-03-09).

Hirschman, A. O. (1970). *Exit, Voice, and Loyalty: Responses to Decline in Firms, Organizations, and States.* Cambridge, MA: Harvard University Press.

Hooydonk, G. v., and G. Milis-Proost. (1998). "Measuring Impact by a Full Option Method and the Notion of Bibliometric Spectra." *Scientometrics* 41: 169–183.

Jong-a-Pin, R., and J. de Haan. (2008). "Growth Accelerations and Regime Changes: A Correction." *Econ Journal Watch* 5: 51–58.

Kapeller, J. (2010). "Some Critical Notes on Citation Metrics and Heterodox Economics." *Review of Radical Political Economics* 42: 330–337.

Klein, D. B., and E. Chiang. (2004). "The Social Science Citation Index: A Black Box—With an Ideological Bias?" *Econ Journal Watch* 1: 134–165.

Lee, F. S. (2007). "The Research Assessment Exercise, the State and the Dominance of Mainstream Economics in British Universities." *Cambridge Journal of Economics* 31: 309–325.

——. (2008a). "A Comment on the Citation Impact of Feminist Economics." *Feminist Economics* 14: 137–142.

——. (2008b). "A Case for Ranking Heterodox Journals and Departments." *On the Horizon* 16: 241–251.

——. (2009a). "Informational Directory for Heterodox Economists: Graduate and Undergraduate Programs, Journals, Publishers and Book Series,

Associations, Blogs, and Institutes and other Websites." URL: http://www.heterodoxnews.com/directory/heterodox-directory.pdf (dl. 20-01-09).

——. (2009b). "Challenging the Mainstream: Essays on the History of Heterodox Economics in the Twentieth Century—The Appendix." URL: http://www.heterodoxnews.com/APPENDIX=formatted.pdf (dl. 14-05-09).

Lee, F. S., and W. Elsner. (2008). "Publishing, Ranking and the Future of Heterodox Economics." *On the Horizon* 16: 176–184.

Merton, R. K. (1968). "The Matthew Effect in Science. The Reward and Communication Systems of Science are Considered." *Science* 159: 56–63.

Myrdal, G. (1963). *Das politische Element in der nationalökonomischen Doktrinbildung.* Köln: Junker & Dünnhaupt.

Neuhaus, D., and H. D. Daniel. (2006) "Data Sources for Performing Citation Analysis: An Overview." *Journal of Documentation* 64: 193–210.

Novarese, M., and C. Zimmermann. (2008). "Heterodox Economics and the Dissemination of Research Through the Internet: The Experience of RePEc and NEP" *On the Horizon* 16: 198–204.

Opthof, T. (1997). "Sense and Nonsense About the Impact Factor." *Cardiovascular Research* 33: 1–7.

Popper, K. R. (1934). *Logik der Forschung.* 3rd Edition. Tübingen: Mohr.

Reardon, J. (2008). "Barriers to Entry: Heterodox Publishing in Mainstream Journals." *On the Horizon* 16: 185–197.

Reedijk, J., and H. F. Moed. (2006). "Is the Impact of Journal Impact Factors Decreasing?" *Journal of Documentation* 64: 183–192.

Rossner, M., H. van Epps, and E. Hill. (2007). "Show Me the Data." *Journal of Cell Biology* 179: 1091–1092.

——. (2008). "Irreproducible Results: A Response to Thomson Scientific." *Journal of Experimental Medicine* 205: 260.

Seglen, P. O. (1997). "Why the Impact Factor of Journals Should Not be Used for Evaluating Research." *British Medical Journal* 314: 498–502.

Shepherd, G. B. (1995). *Rejected. Leading Economists Ponder the Publication Process.* Sun Lakes.

Starr, M. (2010). "Increasing the Impact of Heterodox Work: Insights from RoSE." Paper presented at the 2010 ASSA-conference (Atlanta, January 3 2010).

Stekeler-Weithofer, P. (2009). "Das Problem der Evaluation von Beiträgen zur Philosophie—Ein streitbarer Zwischenruf." *Deutsche Zeitschrift für Philosophie* 57: 149–158.

Testa, J. (1998). "The ISI-Database: The Journal Selection Process." URL: http://cs.nju.edu.cn/~gchen/isi/help/HowToSelectJournals.html (dl. 15-04-09).

——. (2009). "The Thomson Reuters Journal Selection Process." URL: http://thomsonreuters.com/business_units/scientific/free/essays/journal selection (dl. 15-04-09).

Thomson Scientific (2008): "Preserving the Integrity of the Journal Impact Factor: Guidelines from the Scientific Business of Thomson Reuters." URL: http://forums.thomsonscientific.com/t5/Citation-Impact-Center/ Preserving-the-Integrity-of-The-Journal-Impact-Factor-Guidelines/bc-p/ 1243#C16 (dl. 24-03-09).

Research Quality Rankings of Heterodox Economic Journals in a Contested Discipline*

By Frederic S. Lee[†] and Bruce C. Cronin[‡]

assisted by Scott McConnell[†] and Erik Dean[†]

ABSTRACT. This article argues that the discipline of economics consists of two subdisciplines: heterodox and mainstream economics. Being distinct bodies of knowledge, it is possible that the processes of building scientific knowledge are different enough so to generate distinctly different referencing and citation practices. Therefore, a specific impact contribution score is necessary for ranking heterodox journals in terms of their contribution to building heterodox economics. If properly developed such a metric could also be used to produce a single overall quality-equality ranking of mainstream and heterodox journals. Utilizing citation data and peer evaluations of 62 heterodox economics journals, a research quality measure is developed and then used to rank the journals. The measure is then used in conjunction with the SSCI five-year impact factor to produce a comparative research quality-equality rankings of the 62 heterodox and the 192 mainstream journals in the SSCI.

The bibliometric[1] literature frequently addresses the issue of discipline ranking of journals. This is because the widely used impact factor approach to ranking journals does not necessarily capture the impact

*The article was made possible by the financial support from the Charles Leopold Mayer Foundation for the Progress of Humankind.

[†]Department of Economics, 211 Haag Hall, University of Missouri–Kansas City, 5100 Rockhill Road, Kansas City, Missouri 64110, United States, E-mail: leefs@umkc.edu

[‡]Department of International Business, University of Greenwich Business School, University of Greenwich, Park Row, London SE10 9LS, United Kingdom, E-mail: c.b.cronin@greenwich.ac.uk

American Journal of Economics and Sociology, Vol. 69, No. 5 (November, 2010).

a journal has on its discipline since many of its citations may come from journals not at all connected with it.[2] Consequently, a discipline-contribution score has been developed. To calculate the score, it is necessary to identify the relevant discipline-specific journals. One way is to adopt a third party's, such as the Web of Science-Social Science Citation Index (SSCI) or Scopus, classification of journals; another way is to make an informed selection of the appropriate journals. A third way is to combined the previous two methods and utilize an iterative approach based on an informed, predetermined set of core journals, the journals they cite, a discipline impact factor, and a poll of relevant researchers. The approach of the discipline-contribution score can also be used to investigate more specialized areas of research within a discipline, where the subdiscipline research areas are viewed as significantly distinct from each other as measured in terms of citation flows and impact factor scores among the relevant subset of journals. As a result, a subdiscipline "specific impact contribution" score has been developed (Hirst 1978; Schubert and Braun 1993; van Raan 1996; Thomas and Watkins 1998; DuBois and Reeb 2000; Glanzel and Moed 2002; Vinkler 2002; Nisonger 2004; Moed 2005; Kodrzycki and Yu 2006; Azar 2007).[3]

Although the subdiscipline approach presumes that a common body of scientific knowledge binds the subdisciplines together into a single discipline, this need not be the case. Mainstream and heterodox economics are distinct alternative subdisciplines within economics, based on having distinct bodies of theoretical knowledge and problems and puzzles to investigate (Lee 2009, forthcoming). Moreover, being distinct bodies of knowledge, it is quite possible that the processes of building scientific knowledge are different enough so to generate distinctly different referencing and citation practices. Therefore, a "heterodox" subdiscipline or a specific impact contribution score is necessary for ranking heterodox journals in terms of their contribution to building heterodox economics and for evaluating their research qualityrelative to mainstream journals. That is, journal rankings are used to evaluate economists for hiring, tenure, and promotion and rank economic departments (Lee 2006). Because department rankings have financial and reputational impacts, it is important that journals are fairly ranked. As Lee, Grijalva, and Nowell (2010) show, a more equitable journal ranking produces a significant change in the ranking of heterodox departments. Thus, equitable ranking of heterodox journals relative to mainstream journals is important for the working lives of heterodox economists and the viability of their workplace.[4]

In Lee (2008a, 2009) and Lee, Grijalva, and Nowell (2010) a case is made for ranking heterodox economic journals, a ranking methodology developed, and a select group of 17 and 20 heterodox journals ranked. Dolfsma and Leydesdorff (2008) and Cronin (2008) examined the same heterodox journals to explore their network relationships relative to the formation of a community of heterodox economists that engaged in common theoretical and applied pursuits and utilized a common theoretical language. In addition, Lee, Grijalva, and Nowell (2010) argue that the research quality measures used to rank mainstream and heterodox journals can be combined to produce a single overall *quality-equality* ranking of economic journals. This article draws on this bibliometric literature and combines it with a larger citation data set to further develop these contributions. First, it constructs a research quality ranking for 62 heterodox journals based on their contribution to building a more integrated heterodox economics. The construction of the ranking takes place in three steps. The initial one is to develop a comprehensive or total citation-based ranking of the journals that combines a bibliometric ranking based on the methodology in Lee (2008a) with a social network ranking. The next step is to develop a peer evaluation ranking of the heterodox journals, and the final step is to combine the total citation and peer evaluation rankings to arrive at a overall final research quality ranking of the heterodox journals.[5] Secondly, drawing on the previous results, a overall "comparative" research quality-equality rankings of the 62 heterodox and the 192 mainstream journals in the SSCI is developed. The final section concludes the article.

Research Quality Ranking of Heterodox Journals

Methodology

Journals can be ranked according to any evaluative criterion that differentiates between them. And any methodology used to rank journals is derived from the purpose for engaging in the ranking exercise. In the case of heterodox journals, the evaluative criterion is research quality, that is, the relative effectiveness, measured against a benchmark, for promoting the development of a coherent, integrated heterodox economic theory that explains the social provisioning process. Given the criterion for ranking, the appropriate methodology has three components. The first uses journal-specific citation data to determine in a piece-meal additive fashion the degree a heterodox journal builds journal-specific knowledge and promotes research dependency with other heterodox journals through importing and exporting citations. To overcome the limited evaluation of the interdependent relationship among heterodox journals, the second component utilizes social network analysis to evaluate the same citation data. Bibliometric methods are good at distinguishing between journals that make a significant contribution to research discourse and those that do not; but they are not very good for making refined distinctions. To do that, peer evaluation of journals is needed, which is the third component of the methodology. Together, the bibliometric measure, social network analysis, and peer evaluation produce an informed, citation-grounded ranking of heterodox journals based on their relative contribution to building an integrated heterodox economic theory.

Heterodox economic journals are established to publish peer-reviewed, community evaluated scientific knowledge, since it is through peer review and subsequent discussion by the heterodox community that the scholarly quality of journal publications is maintained. Because peer review is practiced by heterodox journals and buttressed by community discussion and the following of acceptable scientific practices is ubiquitous among heterodox economists, the articles, notes, and conference papers published in heterodox journals are similar in overall *scholarly quality* in terms of being adequately researched and written, competently utilizing research methodologies and techniques deemed relevant by heterodox economists; and address topics of relevance at least to some heterodox economists. In addition, heterodox journals are used to build up a body of heterodox scientific knowledge through publishing articles, notes, and conference papers that have *research quality*, that is, whose contents are useful to other heterodox economists. While scholarly quality is attached to an individual article, research quality is a community generated attribute that is attached not to a single article but to a collection of articles, such as represented by a heterodox journal or more generally to a collection of heterodox journals. Thus, citations quantitatively represent the links between journal articles that build and bind together heterodox knowledge; in other words, they show "who talks to whom." Therefore, citations can be used to evaluate how effective heterodox journals are in this regard (Borgman and Furner 2002; Moed 2005; Lockett and McWilliams 2005; Pieters and Baumgartner 2002).

There are two ways to achieve *research quality*, the first being to build up a body of specific knowledge associated with a particular heterodox approach(es), a specific area or topic of research, or a general body of knowledge that is important to all heterodox economists. Although they have the common goal of explaining the social provisioning process in its many aspects, heterodox economists have only gone part of the way of melding and synthesizing their different theoretical approaches and arguments. Hence not all heterodox scientific knowledge can be drawn upon by all heterodox economists. This makes for research and teaching uncertainty as well as hindering the overall development of heterodox economics. Therefore, the second way for heterodox journals to build heterodox knowledge is to promote the development of an integrated heterodox economic theory through increasing the research dependency among heterodox economists. *It is research quality—building specific economic knowledge and integrated heterodox theory through research dependency— that is the basis for evaluating and ranking heterodox economic journals.* Moreover, this process of building specific knowledge and research dependency results in the emergence of a heterodox normal science comparable with the mainstream normal "science," complete with its acceptable scientific practices, relevant topics and puzzles to explore, and variety of research programs that push and remold the boundaries of heterodox economics (Aliseda and Gillies 2007).

Bibliometric Measure of Research Quality

One way for a journal to contribute to the building of heterodox economics is to build a journal-specific body of scientific knowledge.

This is done by publishing articles that draw upon scientific knowledge previously published in the journal. Such *domestic production* of scientific knowledge is manifested in terms of journal *self-citations*. In the economics ranking literature, journal self-citations are often dismissed because they have little impact on the profession at large. This view, which is rejected here and in the bibliometric literature (Moed 2005: 133), is predicated on the assumption that the journal is not a location of a body of specialized knowledge. In particular, journals in specific research areas and journals associated with specific theoretical approaches and interests build an integrative body of knowledge that is represented in terms of self-citations. This is what makes the journal interesting and relevant to the authors and readers in the first place. Journals that do not build an identifiable body of knowledge become marginal to all researchers since there is no reason to take the time to examine their content.

A second way for a journal to contribute is to promote the development of integrative theory through enhancing *research dependency* among heterodox economists. This is done by having them engage in their research with different heterodox approaches and draw upon different areas of research. This engagement is concretely manifested in terms of citations. Thus, a heterodox economist is building research dependency, hence integrative knowledge, when he/she cites articles from the recent and not-so-recent past from many different heterodox journals associated with different heterodox approaches and research areas. For a heterodox economist's research to contribute to research dependency it must also be utilized, hence cited, by other heterodox economists in their journal publications. Therefore, the significance of an article for developing heterodox theory is the degree to which it contributes to research dependency through its drawing upon and utilizing a wide range of heterodox research. Similarly, a journal is promoting research dependency when it publishes articles that cite journals associated with different heterodox approaches and research areas. In this way, the cited journals can be viewed as *imports* and increasing imports is a way to increase research dependency. Moreover, imported citations also represent *exported* citations from other heterodox journals; thus a journal's exported citations also contribute to research dependency. In short, the extent to which a heterodox journal imports and exports recent and distance citations indicates the degree to which it promotes the development of heterodox economic theory through research dependency (Moed 2005; Lockett and McWilliams 2005).

A journal that is a significant builder of scientific knowledge through domestic production and research dependency generates domestic production of citations equal to its citation imports and exports, imports citations from and exports citations to most heterodox journals, and has an overall balance of trade; in addition, its domestic production and export citations include citations from recent (within the past five years) and distant publications. In contrast, a surplus trade balance indicates that a journal is not, relatively speaking, promoting research dependency because it is not drawing upon and engaging with other heterodox journals; a deficit trade balance implies that the journal's production of scientific knowledge is not readily usable by other journals and hence indicates a lack of contribution to research dependency; and a journal with significant domestic production relative to imports and exports is engaging in an inward production of scientific knowledge and not engaging in promoting the development of an integrative heterodox theory through research dependency and hence building a community of heterodox economists. *Therefore a journal's bibliometric research quality "score" and hence research quality ranking relative to other heterodox journals is a summary evaluation of its contribution to building both specialized and integrative scientific knowledge.*

The score itself is independent of the absolute number of citations but depends on the journal's domestic production of citations, the ratio of its imports and exports to its domestic production, its balance of trade, and the extent of its imports and exports. The overall intent of the research quality rankings qua evaluation is to indicate the extent that a journal needs to improve its building of specialized and/or integrative heterodox knowledge so that ultimately *all heterodox journals can achieve the same highest score or ranking* (Stigler 1994; Stigler, Stigler, and Friedland 1995; Liner and Amin 2004).

The criteria for scoring the research quality of a journal that emphasizes the building of specific knowledge and promoting research dependency are the following:

(1) maximize domestic production (DP), citation exports (E), and citation imports (I);

(2) maximize the number of journals to which citations are exported, subject to a threshold of 1 percent of domestic production;

(3) maximize the number of journals to which citations are imported, subject to a threshold of 1 percent of domestic production;

(4) maximize research dependency impact factor (RDIF);[6]

(5) subject to the following constraints:

    (i) ratio of domestic production to total citations (DP/TC)– defined as domestic production plus import and export citations–tends towards 0.33;

    (ii) ratio of export citations to domestic production (E/DP), ratio of import citations to domestic production (I/DP), and ratio of imports to exports (I/E) all tending towards one;

    (iii) ratio of the number of actual export journals (AEJ) to the total number of possible export journals (TEJ), which is 61 and tends towards one;

    (iv) the ratio of the number of actual import journals (AIJ) to the total number of import journals (TIJ), which is also 61 and tends towards one; and

    (v) RDIF tending towards 0.50.[7]

From the criteria, an algorithm for scoring the research quality of heterodox journals in terms of building specialized economic knowledge and promoting research dependency is derived. It consists of seven components, (DP/TC), (E/DP), (I/DP), (I/E), (AEJ/TEJ), (AIJ/TIJ), and (RDIF). Since each component has an equal say in the overall score, DP/TC is multiplied by three and RDIF is multiplied by two. Thus we have the following:

$$\text{Journal Bibliometric Quality Score (JBQS)} =$$
$$(3)[\text{DP/TC}] + [\text{E/DP}] + [\text{I/DP}] + [\text{I/E}] + [\text{AEJ/TEJ}] + \qquad (1)$$
$$[\text{AIJ/TIJ}] + (2)[\text{RDIF}].$$

The closer each component score is to one, the more effective is the journal in building specialized knowledge and promoting research dependency, thus the greater its research quality. Hence the scores of the components are based on minimizing their distance from one, except for (3)[DP/TC], [E/DP], [I/DP], [I/E], and (2)[RDIF] when their distance from one are greater than one, then their score is zero.[8] Therefore, the maximum JBQS a journal can receive is seven, which is the benchmark for assessing a journal's contribution to building both specialized and integrative scientific knowledge. Consequently, if a journal receives a score of five, it has achieved a 71 percent success in reaching the benchmark; and in comparison to a second journal with a score of 2.5, it is twice as successful in attaining the benchmark score.[9]

Social Network Analysis and Research Quality

The bibliometric approach produces heterodox journals" research quality scores that provide only a partial insight into the contributions a journal can make to building specific economic knowledge and integrated heterodox theory through research dependency. In particular, the relationship between journal self-citation and the import and export of citations, while clearly evident in the citation data in Table A1 in Appendix II, remains obscure because it is dealt with in a piece-meal fashion. A journal's significance may also derive in part from its position in the flow of knowledge among a research community, in the way that an entrepôt brokers international trade.

To make the specific nature of the interdependent relationships among the heterodox journals more evident, social network analysis (SNA) is utilized. A key concept in this context is centrality, the extent to which a single journal is the focal point of the myriad of individual citations. One way of conceiving this is the number of total citations a journal is involved in, whether being export-citations or import-citations and including or excluding self-citations; the journal with the most total citations over a defined period might be considered the most central journal in the discipline. This view of centrality (degree centrality) is encompassed in the bibliographic counts in the preceding analysis. However, a concentration on "big hitters" often overlooks other important players who engage different parts of a community without being highly cited in raw terms themselves. So a journal may be significant because it is cited by two big hitters who may not directly cite each other. This idea that raw degree centrality should be offset by the extent to which citations engage journals that are more central to the discipline is termed eigenvector centrality (EC). Alternatively, a journal may be significant not because it engages with journals that are highly central, but because it spans parts of the discipline that are otherwise weakly connected, a brokering role termed betweenness centrality (BC). SNA also allows the identification of groups of more closely related journals, that is, different regions of a network (k-cores), and the discrimination of different roles in brokering situations between these groups, such as representing or gate-keeping in relation to a group (Bonacich 1972; Freeman 1979; Seidman 1983; Cronin 2008; Dolfsma and Leydesdorff 2008).

In terms of assessing the contribution to building both specialized and integrative scientific knowledge, within the citation relationships among heterodox journals, eigenvector centrality (EC) reveals concentrations of specialized knowledge within a discipline and betweenness (BC) demonstrates integration. Similarly, in Gould and Fernandez's (1989) demarcation of brokerage roles, some are oriented towards the group of origin, which reinforces specialization, the coordinator (C), itinerant broker (I), and gatekeeper (G) roles. Others are orientated externally, that is, integrative, the representative (R) and liaison (L) roles. Thus, in the same manner as the preceding analysis a single metric of disciplinary importance in network terms can be constructed by summing these indicators. Each indicator is normalized as proportions of the highest result, thus each has a maximum of one. Each is weighted equally with the exception of the three specialization and the two integrative brokerage roles, where a single specialization and integrative broker score is drawn from the mean:

$$\text{Journal Network Quality Score (JNQS)} = [EC] + [BC] + ([C] + [I] + [G])/3 + ([R] + [L])/2. \tag{2}$$

As in the preceding analysis, the closer each component score is to one, the more effective is the journal in building specialized knowledge and promoting research dependency, thus the greater its research quality. To allow comparison with the JBQSs, the JNQS is rescaled on a 1–7 range so that the highest score (JNQS*) possible on this indicator is seven, which would highlight a journal with a pattern of citations maximizing specialization and integration within the network.

Peer Evaluation and Research Quality

Bibliometric methods distinguish between journals that make a significant contribution to research discourse and those that do not, but they are not very good for making more refined distinctions. To do the latter with a significant degree of accuracy, peer evaluation is needed. In the numerous studies on the correlation between bibliometric and peer evaluation ranking of journals (and academic departments), the results are positive, but not perfect. This is to be expected since peer evaluation of journals has an impact on where to publish and what to cite, while citation patterns have an impact on peer evaluations. It is because of this interdependency that peer evaluation can be used to inform the ranking of journals. That is, it is through peer evaluation that qualitative, informed judgments of heterodox economists have an impact on the final ranking of journals (Moed 2005; van Raan 1996; Weingart 2005).

To obtain the peer evaluation of the research quality of a journal, a questionnaire was used. It consisted of two pages explaining its purpose, defining research quality, and asking for country affiliation and JEL classifications of research and research interests. For each of the 62 heterodox journals, three questions were asked. The first was familiarity with the journal. If the response was "not familiar," the respondent went to the next journal. However, if the response was "some" or "considerable," the respondent was asked in what way and given five possibilities to choose from, including subscribing to it, publishing in it, being its editor, being on its editorial board, and/or consulting it for research. Given positive responses for the first two questions, the respondent was then asked to evaluate the research quality of the journal as "distinguished," "strong," "good," "adequate," "minimal," or "no response." The questionnaire ended with an invitation to the respondent to add any comments—see Appendix I, Table 4A. The criteria for scoring the peer evaluation of the research quality of the journals first involved assigning a numerical value to each of the research quality categories: distinguished (5), strong (4), good (3), adequate (2), minimal (1), and no response (0). The next step was to weight the scores in terms of the respondent's familiarity with the journal: considerable (1) or some (0.5). The third step was to aggregate the scores of all the respondents for each journal and then apply an overall familiarity weight, which is the ratio of all the respondents who had some or considerable familiarity with the journal to the total number of respondents. Finally, to get the average peer evaluation research quality score for the journal, the weighted aggregate score was divided by the number of respondents. Thus we have the following:

Journal Peer Evaluation Quality Score $(JPEQS) =$

$$
(w_j)(1/n_j)\sum_{j=1}^{n}(z_j \times v_j) = (1/R)\sum_{j=1}^{n}(z_j \times v_j), \tag{3}
$$

where $w_j = n_j/R$ is the overall familiarity weight for the j-th journal;

n_j is the number of respondents who had some or considerable familiarity with the j-th journal;

R is the total number of respondents;

z_j is equal to 1 or 0.5 when the respondent has considerable or some familiarity with the j-th journal; and

v_j is equal to 1, . . . , 5 depending on the research quality score chosen by the respondents for the j-th journal.

The maximum JPEQS and hence benchmark for a journal is five, but this would require that all respondents answering the questionnaire are considerably familiar with the journal and evaluated its research quality as distinguished; on the other hand, the minimum score is zero when no respondent is familiar with the journal. Thus, a journal with a score of four has achieved an 80 percent success of reaching the benchmark and is twice as successful in attaining it relative to a journal with a score of two.

Data

Because economics is a discipline with nonhomogeneous knowledge that is divided into theoretically distinct subdisciplines of mainstream and heterodox economics, it is possible to develop a ranking
methodology specifically adapted for heterodox economics. The first
step is to identify or target the journals relevant to heterodox economics. The *Informational Directory for Heterodox Economists* (Lee
2008b) provides the most comprehensive selection of generalist,
specialist, and interdisciplinary heterodox economic journals. It
includes 122 journals, but some are not accessible for the study
while others, such as multidisciplinary and popular journals, are of
interest to heterodox economists yet are not considered relevant for
ranking since they are not directly relevant to the building of heterodox economics. That is, since the purpose of ranking heterodox
journals is to evaluate how they contribute to the building of heterodox economics, the relevant journals are those that engage in
scholarly communication through publishing scholarly works
between scholars. Thus heterodox journals whose aims are to communicate heterodox economics to a popular or practical-political
oriented audience are not included (Borgman and Furner 2002).
From the *Directory* 62 heterodox journals are selected for research
quality ranking: 27 generalist, 13 specialist, and 22 interdisciplinary
journals—see Appendix I, Table 1A, columns 1 and 2.[10] The second
step is to collect from the journals their citation data for the period
2002 to 2008 for the 62 heterodox journals (see Appendix II,
Table A1).[11] Since our concern is with journals that contribute to
heterodox economics, only citations to the 62 heterodox journals
were collected;[12] and they were not collected from a specific citation
source (such as is the case for the SSCI), but from a number of
different sources including Scopus, hardcopies, and electronic and
online copies—see Appendix I, Table 1A, column 4.[13] Citations were
obtained from articles and notes and reviews (if they were longer
than four pages). The citation counts were done by hand count of
physical journals, PDF files, or through Scopus, which aggregated
the per-year count electronically. The resulting 62 × 62 matrix of
citations plus 2008 RDIF citations were used to derive the JBQSs

and the JNQSs for the 62 heterodox journals—see Appendix I, Tables 2A and 3A and Appendix II, Tables A1 and A2.

Initially the questionnaire was sent to 20 heterodox economists to get feedback. After making minor revisions to the questionnaire, it was converted into a web-based questionnaire: http://cei.umkc.edu/Lee. Then on 18 August 2009 it was sent to approximately 3,550 to 4,000 economists that are on the *Heterodox Economics Newsletter* listserv: over 1,000 located in the United States and Canada, over 400 in Latin America, over 1,500 in Europe including the British Isles, and finally over 450 elsewhere around the world; a reminder e-mail was sent out on 9 September 2009. As of 15 November 2009, the total number of responses was 408 of which 405 were usable.[14]

The creditability of any peer evaluation depends on the qualifications of the peers doing the evaluation; and if the peer evaluation is to carry an "international" weight, the peers cannot be selected from just one or two countries, but must draw upon peers around the world. Of the 405 respondents, 200 are located in Europe, 102 in the United States, 34 in Latin America, and 69 elsewhere. Each respondent on average knew, at least to some degree, nearly 17 journals, but only between 14 well enough to evaluate their research quality. The basis of their knowledge includes journal subscriptions for 186 respondents (who subscribed to on average three heterodox journals); publishing in the journal for 242 respondents (who published on average in three to four different heterodox journals); being an editor of a journal for 23 respondents (who on average were editors of two different heterodox journals); being on the editorial board of a journal for 74 respondents (who on average were on the editorial board of almost two heterodox journals); and/or consulting the journal for research purposes for 356 respondents (who on average consulted over 12 heterodox journals when doing research). All together, the 384 respondents had on average 2.5 different relationships to each of the nearly 17 journals with which they were familiar. Moreover, the research interests of the respondents include all of the JEL classifications and the research interests of the individual respondent cover on average over five JEL classifications. The most popular classification is the "schools of economic thought, methodology, and heterodox approaches" (392 respondents), followed by "economic development, technological change and growth" (237 respondents) and "macroeconomics and monetary policy" (202 respondents). So overall, the respondents are geographically dispersed, have a working to quite intimate knowledge of 14 heterodox journals, and have a sufficient range of research interests to be able to evaluate distinctly different heterodox journals. Thus, as a whole the respondents are well qualified to evaluate the research quality of the heterodox journals; and their evaluations are as "objective" as citation-based evaluations. That is, the respondents use hands-on working (as opposed to impressionistic) knowledge to evaluate a journal's research quality. Hence, although different, peer evaluation of journals is equal to and hence objective as any citation-based evaluation of journals (Appendix I, Table 4A.1).

Results and Discussion

The bibliometric approach produces interesting but unexpected results. First, *Development and Change* has the top score of 5.23, which amounts to nearly 75 percent of the benchmark score (see Appendix I, Table 2A, column 9). This suggests that all heterodox journals have much to do to improve their research quality. Secondly, *Development and Change* bibliometric research quality is 131 percent more than that of the *Cambridge Journal of Economics (CJE)*, clearly an unexpected result. It arises because the bibliometric approach emphasizes research interdependency as the driving force for its research quality score and uses an algorithm that neutralizes the impact of a journal's citation size on its JBQS, hence its ranking; thus interdisciplinary, specialist, and smaller generalist journals have a better chance of scoring well relative to a larger citation generalist journal. Therefore, we find that the bibliometric rankings of heterodox journals include in the top 20 large and not-so-large interdisciplinary, specialist, and generalist journals—see Table 1, column 3. However, the absence in the top 20 journals of well-known heterodox journals, such as *CJE, Review of Social Economy (ROSE), Metroeconomica*, and *Review of Political Economy (ROPE)*, suggests that the bibliometric approach captures only part of the contributions a journal makes towards building specific heterodox economic

Table 1

Research Quality Ranking of the 62 Heterodox Journals

Journal Name	Type of Journal	Bibliometric Ranking	Social Network Ranking	Total Citation Ranking	Peer Evaluation Ranking	Final **Ranking** —HJQS (*Z Score*)
Cambridge Journal of Economics	General	24	2	5	1	**1** 0.5419 *(3.43)*
Journal of Economic Issues	General	5	19	6	3	**2** 0.4412 *(2.32)*
Journal of Post Keynesian Economics	General	18	30	23	2	**3** 0.3931 *(1.79)*
Review of Radical Political Economics	General	14	15	8	4	**4** 0.3802 *(1.65)*
Economy and Society	Interdisciplinary	9	7	4	13	**5** 0.3521 *(1.34)*
Development and Change	Specialist	1	12	2	28	**6** 0.3480 *(1.29)*
Review of Political Economy	General	46	5	17	5	**7** 0.3373 *(1.17)*
Review of International Political Economy	Specialist	11	1	1	34	**8** 0.3277 *(1.07)*
Journal of Economic Behavior and Organization	General	23	20	15	6	**9** 0.3211 *(0.99)*
International Labour Review	Interdisciplinary	6	4	3	38	**10** 0.3062 *(0.83)*
American Journal of Economics and Sociology	General	26	3	7	26	**11** 0.3022 *(0.79)*
Capital and Class	General	16	14	9	20	**12** 0.3009 *(0.77)*

Table 1   *Continued*

Journal Name	Type of Journal	Bibliometric Ranking	Social Network Ranking	Total Citation Ranking	Peer Evaluation Ranking	Final **Ranking** —HJQS (*Z Score*)
Metroeconomica: International Review of Economics	General	35	9	21	10	**13** 0.2991 *(0.75)*
European Journal of the History of Economic Thought	Specialist	41	13	26	8	**14** 0.2964 *(0.72)*
Review of Social Economy	General	25	10	14	18	**15** 0.2936 *(0.69)*
Journal of the History of Economic Thought	Specialist	21	26	24	12	**16** 0.2919 *(0.67)*
Science and Society	Interdisciplinary	3	32	10	24	**17** 0.2910 *(0.66)*
Feminist Economics	General	4	31	11	23	**18** 0.2905 *(0.66)*
Journal of Evolutionary Economics	General	36	17	25	11	**19** 0.2882 *(0.63)*
Rethinking Marxism	Interdisciplinary	12	21	12	27	**20** 0.2824 *(0.57)*
Journal of Development Studies	Interdisciplinary	7	38	19	21	**21** 0.2742 *(0.48)*
Journal of Economic Methodology	Specialist	22	45	30	14	**22** 0.2547 *(0.26)*
History of Political Economy	Specialist	39	40	40	9	**23** 0.2538 *(0.25)*
Structural Change and Economic Dynamics	Specialist	20	46	31	16	**24** 0.2502 *(0.21)*

Table 1   *Continued*

Journal Name	Type of Journal	Bibliometric Ranking	Social Network Ranking	Total Citation Ranking	Peer Evaluation Ranking	Final **Ranking** —HJQS (*Z Score*)
International Review of Applied Economics	General	34	27	29	17	**25** 0.2495 *(0.20)*
Economics and Philosophy	Specialist	31	36	34	15	**26** 0.2466 *(0.17)*
International Journal of Social Economics	Interdisciplinary	32	6	13	42	**27** 0.2447 *(0.15)*
Capitalism, Nature, Socialism	Interdisciplinary	2	53	16	40	**28** 0.2347 *(0.04)*
International Journal of Political Economy	General	55	8	32	22	**29** 0.2342 *(0.04)*
New Left Review	Interdisciplinary	62	24	55	7	**30** 0.2292 *(−0.02)*
Contributions to Political Economy	General	53	22	37	25	**31** 0.2225 *(−0.09)*
New Political Economy	Interdisciplinary	15	39	27	36	**32** 0.2203 *(−0.12)*
Journal of Socio-Economics	Interdisciplinary	19	51	36	29	**33** 0.2192 *(−0.13)*
Journal of Institutional Economics	General	43	42	46	19	**34** 0.2174 *(−0.15)*
Constitutional Political Economy	General	8	37	18	53	**35** 0.2147 *(−0.18)*
Antipode	Interdisciplinary	30	16	22	47	**36** 0.2120 *(−0.21)*

Table 1   *Continued*

Journal Name	Type of Journal	Bibliometric Ranking	Social Network Ranking	Total Citation Ranking	Peer Evaluation Ranking	Final **Ranking** —HJQS (*Z Score*)
Review of Austrian Economics	General	17	29	20	54	**37** 0.2101 (*−0.23*)
Historical Materialism	Interdisciplinary	45	23	35	31	**38** 0.2052 (*−0.28*)
History of Economics Review	Specialist	37	28	33	33	**39** 0.1994 (*−0.35*)
Journal of Income Distribution	Specialist	10	46	28	49	**40** 0.1881 (*−0.47*)
Oxford Development Studies	Interdisciplinary	57	18	39	35	**41** 0.1848 (*−0.51*)
Ecological Economics	Interdisciplinary	47	43	51	30	**42** 0.1838 (*−0.52*)
Cepal Review	Specialist	58	25	50	32	**43** 0.1765 (*−0.60*)
Studies in Political Economy	Interdisciplinary	13	61	38	48	**44** 0.1704 (*−0.67*)
Review of African Political Economy	Specialist	27	50	41	44	**45** 0.1677 (*−0.70*)
Revista de Economia Politica/Brazilian Journal of Political Economy	General	61	11	42	43	**46** 0.1674 (*−0.70*)
Forum for Social Economics	General	49	41	51	37	**47** 0.1629 (*−0.75*)
Econ Journal Watch	General	28	54	43	45	**48** 0.1602 (*−0.78*)

Table 1   *Continued*

Journal Name	Type of Journal	Bibliometric Ranking	Social Network Ranking	Total Citation Ranking	Peer Evaluation Ranking	Final **Ranking** —HJQS (*Z Score*)
Economic Systems Research	General	29	52	44	46	**49** 0.1582 (*−0.80*)
Journal of Australian Political Economy	General	50	33	47	51	**50** 0.1504 (*−0.89*)
Quarterly Journal of Austrian Economics	General	33	49	45	57	**51** 0.1460 (*−0.94*)
Critical Sociology	Interdisciplinary	40	48	49	55	**52** 0.1443 (*−0.96*)
Research in the History of Economic Thought and Methodology	Specialist	60	34	58	41	**53** 0.1363 (*−1.04*)
Organization and Environment	Interdisciplinary	54	35	48	60	**54** 0.1355 (*−1.05*)
Work, Employment and Society	Interdisciplinary	42	57	56	50	**55** 0.1320 (*−1.09*)
Advances in Austrian Economics	General	48	47	54	56	**56** 0.1317 (*−1.10*)
Journal of Interdisciplinary Economics	Interdisciplinary	51	44	53	58	**57** 0.1287 (*−1.13*)
International Journal of Green Economics	Interdisciplinary	38	59	57	59	**58** 0.1229 (*−1.19*)
Intervention: European Journal of Economics and Economic Policy	General	59	55	62	39	**59** 0.1171 (*−1.26*)

Table 1   *Continued*

Journal Name	Type of Journal	Bibliometric Ranking	Social Network Ranking	Total Citation Ranking	Peer Evaluation Ranking	Final **Ranking** —HJQS *(Z Score)*
Review of Black Political Economy	General	52	60	59	52	**60** 0.1091 *(−1.35)*
Critical Perspectives on International Business	Interdisciplinary	56	58	61	61	**61** 0.0928 *(−1.52)*
Debatte	Interdisciplinary	44	62	60	62	**62** 0.0873 *(−1.59)*

Derived from Appendix I: Table 5A.

knowledge and integrated heterodox theory through research dependency.

SNA directly addresses this weakness in part because a journal's citation size is not neutralized. Using the same data set, it shows that the *CJE* has the second-rank JNQS* of 3.96, which amounts to 56 percent of the benchmark score, and that its social network research quality is 44 percent more than that of *Development and Change* (see Appendix I, Table 3A). More generally, the above four journals are in the SNA's top 10 ranking, while 13 of the top 20 bibliometric-ranked journals are not included in the top 20 SNA-ranked journals—see Table 1, column 4. More specifically, the Spearman rank correlation between the bibliometric and SNA rankings is a quite small ($R_s = 0.129$). Journals such as the *Review of International Political Economy (RIPE), CJE, ROPE, Metroeconomica,* and *American Journal of Economics and Sociology (AJES)* have much higher network rankings than in the bibliometric rankings. The disparity between the two rankings is least with interdisciplinary journals ($R_s = 0.178$) and generalist journals ($R_s = 0.142$) and the greatest with specialist journals ($R_s = −0.071$). Thus SNA makes a substantive contribution towards capturing the specialization and integrative impact of heterodox journals.

The bibliometric and social network approaches utilize the same citation data but in different ways to measure research quality; thus they stand on equal footing with each other. Consequently, to combine their contributions, the social network scores are rescaled to make them equivalent to the bibliometric scores and then added together, which means that the total citation benchmark score is now 14:

$$\text{Total Citation Score (TCS)} = \text{JBQS} + \text{JNQS*}. \qquad (4)$$

The journal with the top TCS is the *RIPE* (8.10), which is 58 percent of the benchmark score, suggesting, as above, that all heterodox journals have much to do to improve their research quality. Moreover and unexpectedly, none of the top four journals are noted heterodox journals. In addition, despite the fact that the total citation ranking includes some (but not all) noted heterodox journals in the top 20, it would be difficult to convince a majority of heterodox economists that the *RIPE* contribution to research quality and hence to the development of heterodox economics is 53 percent more than that of the *Journal of Post Keynesian Economics (JPKE)* (see Table 1, column 5 and Appendix I, Table 5A). In short, although the total citation rankings are based on a comprehensive evaluation of the journal citations,[15] they lack "believability" because they lack "peer accuracy."

To increase the accuracy of the journal rankings it is necessary to turn to peer evaluation. Over 75 percent of the journal evaluations are good, strong, or distinguished, while half of the journals have an average score of two or better. On the other hand, the familiarity weightings range from nearly 90 percent down to nearly 2 percent. However, because the average scores are positively correlated with the familiarity weight ($R = 0.74$), they reinforce each other. Thus the JPEQSs range from 2.9 for the *CJE* down to 0.02 for *Debatte* (see Appendix I, Tables 4A.2 and 4A.3). The rankings derived from the JPEQSs are different from the total citation ranking ($R_s = 0.536$).[16] In particular, the top 10 journals are dominated by generalist heterodox journals, while none of the top four total citation ranked journals are included (see Table 1, columns 5 and 6). Hence, from a bibliometric qua citation-base perspective, peer evaluation contributes to the accuracy of ranking journals. But since peer evaluations are as "objective" as citation-based evaluations, it can also be said that the latter contributes to the accuracy of the former. Because the different approaches contribute different but compatible evaluations of journals, they can be combined on an equal footing to each other. So to construct the best possible ranking of heterodox journals, the contributions of both approaches are combined into a single overall score qua ranking that indicates the extent a journal has achieved research quality relative to the benchmarks noted above (normalized to equal one):

Heterodox Journal Quality Score $(HJQS) = [0.5][TCS/14 + JPEQS/5]$.

$$(5)$$

Thus, each HJQS represents a journal's overall percentage attainment of achieving 100 percent benchmark research quality.

The HJQS scoring and final ranking of heterodox journals reveal a number of interesting results and outcomes. The first is that the research quality of heterodox journals is less than 50 percent of the benchmark maximum. That is, the *CJE* has the top HJQS score of 0.54 or that it has obtained only 54 percent of attainable research quality; but the next HJQS is 0.44 (or 44 percent of the attainable research quality) for the *Journal of Economic Issues (JEI)* and it declines down to 0.09 for *Debatte*. Since research quality is defined as building specific economic knowledge and integrating heterodox theory through research dependency, the *CJE* as well as all other heterodox journals have significant room to improve their contributions to heterodox economics. Because of the positive rank correlation between total citations and peer evaluation ($R_s = 0.536$), improving TCSs would also improve JPEQs and vice versa; thus citation improvements coincides with peer evaluation improvements. This interlocking virtuous reinforcing outcome implies that improving a journal's research quality can be done by improving its familiarity with heterodox economists and by promoting dependency (and specialized) citation practices.[17] A second result is that the rankings of the HJQSs have generalist journals making more of a contribution to research quality than interdisciplinary journals: of the top 20 journals, 12 are generalist journals while four are interdisciplinary journals, but of the bottom 42 journals, 18 are interdisciplinary while 15 are generalist journals—see Table 1. This outcome suggests that there is a limit to the extent that interdisciplinary journals can contribute to the development of heterodox economics. In particular, because not all their articles qua citations are necessarily relevant to heterodox economics, the JNQSs of interdisciplinary journals are depressed; and similarly because heterodox economists are not as familiar with interdisciplinary journals as a whole, their JPEQSs are also depressed. Together, the two factors "explain" why the contributions of interdisciplinary journals to heterodox economics are not on par with generalist heterodox journals (Appendix I, Tables 2A and 4A.3).[18]

Regarding the final ranking, the top 10 journals include the top six journals of both the total citation and peer evaluation ranking; and the top 20 journals include 15 of the top 20 journals in the total citation rankings and 13 of the top 20 journals in the peer evaluation ranking. This suggests that the HJQSs qua final rankings are more believable than either the TCSs or the JPEQSs and their rankings are individually. Thus by combining the two scores, a more accurate research quality score is produced and a more believable journal ranking is achieved.[19] In particular, the top four journals—*CJE, JEI, JPKE,* and *Review of Radical Political Economics (RRPE)*—represent the heterodox approaches of post-Keynesian-Sraffian, institutional, and Marxian-radical economics; and within the top 20 journals, there is *Feminist Economics, ROSE,* and the *Journal of Evolutionary Economics,* each representing the heterodox approaches of feminist, social, and evolutionary economics. So, most of the various heterodox approaches are represented in the top 20 journals. The final rankings also reveal interesting clustering of heterodox journals. First, of the seven Marxist-radical journals (ranked 4, 12, 17, 20, 30, 38, 44), four are in the top 20; and of the eight post-Keynesian-Sraffian-institutional journals (ranked 1, 2, 3, 7, 13, 29, 46, 59), five are also in the top 20. This suggests that these two broad heterodox approaches collectively play a significant role in developing heterodox economics. Secondly, of the eight history of thought, methodology, and philosophy journals (ranked 14, 16, 22, 23, 26, 31, 39, 53), two appear in the top 20 and five appear in the top 30 journals. This clearly points to the centrality of these research areas for the development of heterodox economics. Just below these three clusters of journals in terms of contributing are the five development journals (ranked 6, 21, 41, 43, 45) and the four social economic journals (15, 27, 33, 47). Finally, the three environment-ecological journals (ranked 28, 42, 58) and the five Austrian journals (ranked 35, 37, 48, 50, 56) are all but one in the lower half of the journal rankings. This suggests that these research areas are currently not central to the development of heterodox economics.[20]

The final journal ranking reveals which journals individually and in clusters are better at contributing to the development of heterodox economics. However, this ranking should not be deified since none of the heterodox journals are outstanding in this regard—there is much room for improvement. Moreover, except for the *CJE* and *JEI*, the distribution of the HJQSs is so compact (as indicated by their Z scores) that their differences are not very significant. Therefore, it is perhaps more appropriate to view the rankings as simply showing that all heterodox journals contribute to the development of heterodox economics (which is after all what is important) although in different amounts.

Research Quality-Equality Ranking of Heterodox and Mainstream Journals

Methodology and Data

Economics is about explaining the provisioning process. Even though heterodox and mainstream economics contest each other's explanation of it, they both adhere to the discipline's goal of producing more scientific knowledge about it. Thus, the research quality of a journal is broadly the same for both—the usefulness of its articles to researchers in their analysis of the provisioning process. What constitutes advancement in scientific knowledge for heterodox and mainstream economists, however, is quite different. Therefore, a research quality metric utilized for mainstream economics is not appropriate for identifying quality research in heterodox economics; or putting it another way, heterodox journals perform poorly when evaluating the usefulness of their research for mainstream economists and vice-versa. In the previous section, the HJQS was developed to measure the research quality of heterodox journals and hence rank them accordingly. As noted below, the SSCI impact factor is widely used by mainstream economists to measure the research quality of mainstream journals and also rank them accordingly. While these two measures for research quality are different in that they represent two distinct subdisciplines of different economic knowledge, they can be synthesized into a quality-equality economic journal ranking where heterodox and mainstream journals can be compared in terms of their research quality relative to their paradigm-based benchmark (Lee, Grijalva, and Nowell 2010).

The SSCI impact factor measures the importance of a journal to a predetermined collection of journals in terms of usefulness or relevance. That is, the impact factor for a journal in 2008 is calculated based on a two-year or a five-year period prior to 2008. The number of times the journal's articles in the previous two- or five-year period are cited in the collection of journals during 2008 is divided by the number of "citable items" in the preceding time periods produces a two- or a five-year impact factor. Thus, the impact factor is one way to measure the usefulness of a journal's articles to the research community that is represented by the collection of journals; that is, the impact factor is one way to measure research quality. Ideally, a journal's impact factor is derived only from a collection of journals like itself in that they all are engaged in similar research issues and building a common body of scientific knowledge and, as a result, have similar referencing and citation practices. However, this is not the case for SSCI impact factor scores. In particular, the impact factor scores for economic journals are not constrained to the subdiscipline of economics but include all the Web of Science social science journals, which means they are greater than if restricted to the 209 journals the SSCI identifies as economic journals. Yet, despite the misspecification of the impact factor scores for economic journals and other criticisms (see note 6 and its references), mainstream economists generally accept them as a legitimate measure of a journal's research quality relative to the research agenda and the building of scientific knowledge of mainstream economics.

For 2008, the SSCI identifies 209 economic journals that also include 17 heterodox journals; excluding the latter journals reduces the number of mainstream journals to 192. For 165 journals, the SSCI five-year impact factor scores are used; and for the remaining recently added 27 journals, the SSCI two-year impact factor scores are used—see Appendix I, Table 6A.[21] The HJQS represents a heterodox journal's overall percentage attainment of achieving the research quality benchmark, while the SSCI impact factor does not do this directly. Following Lee, Grijalva, and Nowell (2010), it is possible to revise the impact factor to do this by using the scores of the top five journals as the benchmark to which all mainstream journals can aspire. That is, for 2008 the five journals with the highest impact factor scores are *Quarterly Journal of Economics* (8.716), *Journal of Economic Literature* (8.380), *Journal of Economic Growth* (6.032), *Journal of Political Economy* (5.742), and *Journal of Financial Economics* (5.203); and the average of their scores is 6.814. Taking this as the impact factor benchmark for mainstream journals, a journal's score that indicates its achieved degree of research quality relative to the benchmark is:

$$\text{Mainstream Journal Quality Score (MJQS)} = \text{MIF}/6.814, \quad (6)$$

where MIF is the impact factor score for the mainstream journal.

Thus, each MJQS represents a mainstream journal's percentage attainment of achieving benchmark research quality. Because HJQS and MJQS are a percentage of a heterodox or mainstream benchmark research quality, they can be synthesized into a composite *quality-equality* ranking of economics journals in which heterodox and mainstream journals can be compared in terms of research quality achievement:

$$\text{Journal Quality-Equality Score (JQES)} = (\text{HJQS, MJQS}), \quad (7)$$

where for any heterodox (mainstream) journal JQES = HJQS (MJQS).

Results and Discussion

Before examining the quality-equality rankings, it is noticeable that in comparison to the MJQSs for the 17 SSCI heterodox economics journals, the HJQSs are, except for two journals, 1.2 to over 10 times higher and the scores of the *CJE, JEI,* and the *JPKE* (the top three

Table 2

Comparative Research Quality Scores for Heterodox Journals

JOURNAL	MJQS	HJQS	HJQS/MJQS
American Journal of Economics and Sociology	0.053	0.302	5.70
Cambridge Journal of Economics	0.139	0.542	3.90
Ecological Economics	0.348	0.184	0.53
Economics and Philosophy	0.104	0.247	2.38
Economy and Society	0.288	0.352	1.22
European Journal of the History of Economic thought	0.030	0.296	9.87
Feminist Economics	0.170	0.290	1.71
History of Political Economy	0.025	0.254	10.16
Journal of Development Studies	0.174	0.274	1.57
Journal of Economic Behavior and Organization	0.242	0.321	1.33
Journal of Economic Issues	0.069	0.441	6.39
Journal of Evolutionary Economics	0.210	0.288	1.37
Journal of Post Keynesian Economics	0.057	0.393	6.89
New Political Economy	0.108	0.229	2.12
Review of International Political Economy	0.197	0.328	1.66
Revista de Economia Politica	0.017	0.167	9.82
Work Employment and Society	0.293	0.132	0.45

heterodox journals) are four to seven times higher—see Table 2. This suggests that heterodox journals contribute much less to mainstream economics than they do to heterodox economics, an expected outcome since, as argued above, mainstream and heterodox economics are distinct subdisciplines in economics and the SSCI does not include many heterodox journals.[22] Therefore, the SSCI impact factor is simply the wrong measure to access the research quality of heterodox journals.

The JQES ranking of 254 mainstream and heterodox journals shows the degree to which each has attained its research quality benchmark and hence provides a basis for comparing research quality—see Table 3. Consider the first 25 journals, of which three are heterodox journals. The JQES for the *CJE* is slightly below that of the *American Economic Review* and slightly above the *Review of Economics and Statistics*. Thus in terms of their quality relative to their respective but different benchmarks, they are roughly the same—different but equal.

Table 3

Research Quality Ranking of 254 Heterodox and Mainstream Journals

JOURNAL	JQES	ARE	BRE
Quarterly Journal of Economics	1.279	A1	A1
Journal of Economic Literature	1.230	A1	A1
Journal of Economic Growth	0.885	A1	A2
Journal of Political Economy	0.843	A1	A1
Journal of Financial Economics	0.764	A1*	A1
Journal of Economic Perspectives	0.742	A1	A1
Econometrica	0.725	A1	A1
Journal of Economic Geography	0.669	A2	
Journal of Accounting and Economics	0.646	A1	
Review of Economic Studies	0.592	A1	A1
American Economics Review	0.554	A1	A1
Cambridge Journal of Economics	**0.542**	**A2**	**A1**
Review of Economics and Statistics	0.533	A1	A1
Journal of Health Economics	0.526	A1	A2
Economic Geography	0.525	A2	
Brookings Papers of Economic Activity	0.518	A2	A2
Journal of Economic Issues	**0.441**	**C**	**A2**
Economic Policy	0.422	A2	
Economic Journal	0.406	A1	
Journal of International Economics	0.403	A1	A1
Journal of Monetary Economics	0.402	A1	
Journal of Labor Economics	0.400	A1	A2
Energy Economics	0.400	A2	B3
Journal of Post Keynesian Economics	**0.393**	**A2**	**A1**
Health Economics	0.385	A2	B1
Journal of Econometrics	0.385	A1	A1
Review of Radical Political Economics	**0.380**	**B**	**A2**
Journal of Environmental Economics and Management	0.378	A2	A2
Economy and Society	**0.352**	**A2***	**B1**
Development and Change	**0.348**	**B**	**B3**
World Development	0.342	A2	B1
Review of Political Economy	**0.337**	**B**	**A2**
Rand Journal of Economics	0.336	A1	A1
Review of International Political Economy	**0.328**	**A2**	**B4**
Journal of Human Resources	0.328	A1	A2
World Bank Research Observer	0.325	B*	B3
Journal of Financial and Quantitative Analysis	0.325	A2	

Table 3   *Continued*

JOURNAL	JQES	ARE	BRE
World Bank Economic Review	0.322	A2	B1
Journal of Economic Behavior and Organization	**0.321**	**A2**	**A2**
Journal of Risk and Uncertainty	0.316	A1*	B1
Journal of Public Economics	0.312	A1	A1
Industrial and Corporate Change	0.307	A2*	A2
International Labour Review	**0.306**	**B***	
American Journal of Economics and Sociology	**0.302**	**B**	
Capital and Class	**0.301**	**B***	**B3**
Journal of Law and Economics	0.301	A1	A2
Metroeconomica	**0.299**	**B**	**B1**
Journal of Business and Economic Statistics	0.298	A1	A1
Resource and Energy Economics	0.298	A2	B2
Journal of Money, Credit, and Banking	0.296	A1	A1
European Journal of the History of Economic Thought	**0.296**	**A2**	
Review of Social Economy	**0.294**	**B**	**B3**
Journal of the History of Economic Thought	**0.292**	**A2**	
Science and Society	**0.291**	**B***	**B3**
Feminist Economics	**0.290**	**B**	
Journal of Applied Econometrics	0.289	A1	A2
Journal of Evolutionary Economics	**0.288**	**A2**	
Food Policy	0.282	B*	
Rethinking Marxism	**0.282**	**C**	
Journal of Law Economics and Organization	0.279	A1	A2
Experimental Economics	0.275	A2	
Energy Journal	0.274	A2*	B1
Journal of Development Studies	**0.274**	**A2**	**B1**
Journal of Development Economics	0.273	A1	A2
China Economic Review	0.270	B	
Journal of Urban Economics	0.270	A1	B1
Journal of Industrial Economics	0.266	A1	A2
Journal of Economic Surveys	0.263	A2	
European Economic Review	0.258	A1	A1
Journal of Economic Methodology	**0.255**	**B**	**A1**
History of Political Economy	**0.254**	**A1**	**A1**
Economics and Human Biology	0.253	B	B4
Transform Business Economics	0.251	—	
Small Business Economics	0.251	A2*	B3
Structural Change and Economic Dynamics	**0.250**	**B**	**B1**
International Review of Applied Economics	**0.249**	**B**	

Table 3 *Continued*

JOURNAL	JQES	ARE	BRE
Land Economics	0.249	A2	B1
Journal of Common Market Studies	0.248	A2*	B3
Economics and Philosophy	**0.247**	**A2**	**B1**
European Review of Agricultural Economics	0.246	A2	B3
International Journal of Social Economics	**0.245**	**B**	**B1**
Mathematical Finance	0.244	A1*	
Journal of Policy Reform	0.238	—	B2
Game and Economic Behavior	0.238	A1	A1
Capitalism, Nature, Socialism	**0.235**	**C**	
International Journal of Political Economy	**0.234**	**C**	**B3**
International Journal of Forecasting	0.234	A2	
International Journal of Industrial Organization	0.234	A2	
Journal of Comparative Economics	0.234	A2	B2
Journal of Economics and Management Strategy	0.233	A2	B1
Insurance: Mathematics and Economics	0.231	A2	
Regional Science and Urban Economics	0.230	A2	B1
New Left Review	**0.229**	**A2***	
Journal of Economic Theory	0.228	A1	A1
International Economic Review	0.228	A1	A1
American Journal of Agricultural Economics	0.225	A1	B1
Journal of Policy Analysis and Management	0.224	A2*	B1
Oxford Economic Papers	0.223	A2	B1
Contributions to Political Economy	**0.223**	**B**	**B5**
New Political Economy	**0.220**	**A2**	**B2**
Environmental and Resource Economics	0.220	A2	B1
Journal of Socio-Economics	**0.219**	**B**	**B5**
Journal of Institutional Economics	**0.217**	**B**	**B4**
Oxford Review of Economic Policy	0.216	A2	B1
Constitutional Political Economy	**0.215**	**B**	
Oxford Bulletin of Economics and Statistics	0.215	A2	B1
Antipode	**0.212**	**A2***	
Scandinavian Journal of Economics	0.211	A2	B1
Review of Austrian Economics	**0.210**	**C**	
Australian Journal of Agricultural and Resource Economics	0.206	A2	B3
Historical Materialism	**0.205**	**C**	
Journal of Agrarian Change	0.202	B	
History of Economics Review	**0.199**	**B**	
Journal of European Economics Association	0.199	A2	
Econometric Theory	0.198	A1	

Table 3   *Continued*

JOURNAL	JQES	ARE	BRE
Journal of Economic Psychology	0.195	A2	B2
Journal of Banking and Finance	0.190	A1*	A2
World Economics	0.188	B	B2
Journal of Income Distribution	**0.188**	**B**	**B4**
Journal of Agricultural Economics	0.186	A2	B2
Oxford Development Studies	**0.185**	**B**	**B2**
Ecological Economics	**0.184**	**A2**	**B1**
Labour Economics	0.183	A2	B1
Review of Economic Dynamics	0.181	A2	A2
Econometric Reviews	0.179	A2	B2
Cepal Review	**0.177**	—	**B2**
Journal of Economic Dynamics and Control	0.174	A1	A2
Economics of Transition	0.172	A2	
Economic Development and Cultural Change	0.172	A2	B2
Studies in Political Economy	**0.170**	**C**	**B4**
Journal of Risk and Insurance	0.170	A2*	
Real Estate Economics	0.169	A2	B2
Review of African Political Economy	**0.168**	**C**	
Revista de Economia Politca/Brazilian Journal of Political Economy	**0.167**	**C**	**B2**
Quantitative Marketing and Economics	0.166	B	
IMF Staff Papers	0.165	C	B1
Journal of Regional Science	0.165	A2	B3
Bulletin of Indonesian Economic Studies	0.164	A2	B4
Journal of Housing Economics	0.163	B	B2
Forum for Social Economics	**0.163**	**C**	
Economica	0.162	A2	B1
Econ Journal Watch	**0.160**	**C**	
Journal of Transport Economics and Policy	0.160	A2	B2
Futures	0.158	B*	
Economic Systems Research	**0.158**	**C**	
Journal of Population Economics	0.155	A2	B1
Quantitative Finance	0.154	B*	B1
Post-Soviet Affairs	0.153	B*	
Economics of Education Review	0.151	A2	B1
Journal of Australian Political Economy	**0.150**	**B**	
Journal of Productivity Analysis	0.149	A2	B2
Economic Inquiry	0.148	A2	A2
Quarterly Journal of Austrian Economics	**0.146**	**C**	
Kyklos	0.146	A2	

Table 3 *Continued*

JOURNAL	JQES	ARE	BRE
Critical Sociology	**0.144**	**B***	
Journal of Regulatory Economics	0.144	A2	B1
Studies in Nonlinear Dynamics and Econometrics	0.143	A2	
Canadian Journal of Economics	0.141	A2	A2
Review of Agricultural Economics	0.138	B	B1
Research in the History of Economic Thought and Methodology	**0.136**	**B**	
Information Economics and Policy	0.136	B*	B4
Organization and Environment	**0.135**	**C***	
International Tax and Public Finance	0.134	B	
Agricultural Economics	0.134	A2	B2
ASTIN Bulletin	0.132	B*	
Work, Employment and Society	**0.132**	**A2***	
Advances in Austrian Economics	**0.132**	**—**	
Economic History Review	0.130	A1	B2
Economic Record	0.130	A2	B3
Public Choice	0.129	A2	B1
Journal of Interdisciplinary Economics	**0.129**	**C**	**B5**
Journal of Economic History	0.126	A2	B1
Tijdschrift voor Economisch en Sociale Geografre	0.123	B	
International Journal of Green Economics	**0.123**	**C**	
Economic Theory	0.123	A1	A1
Journal of Real Estate Finance and Economics	0.120	B	
Review of World Economics	0.120	B	B1
Journal of Policy Modeling	0.120	B*	B3
Review of Industrial Organization	0.118	A2	
Intervention: European Journal of Economics and Economic Policy	**0.117**	**C**	
Applied Economics	0.114	A2	B1
Journal of Forest Economics	0.114	C	
Review of Income and Wealth	0.113	A2	B1
Econometrics Journal	0.110	A2	
Review of Black Political Economy	**0.109**	**A2**	**B3**
Explorations in Economic History	0.108	A2	B1
Fiscal Studies	0.108	A2	
Contemporary Economic Policy	0.107	B*	B2
Economic Development Quarterly	0.107	B	B4
Journal of Economics	0.106	B	
Macroeconomic Dynamics	0.106	A2	A2
Southern Economic Journal	0.105	A2	B1

Table 3   *Continued*

JOURNAL	JQES	ARE	BRE
Journal of Macroeconomics	0.103	A2	B3
Emerging Markets Financial and Trade	0.103	C	
Journal of Japanese and International Economics	0.103	A2	B2
CESifo Economic Studies	0.098	C	
Economics Letters	0.095	A2	A2
Canadian Journal of Agricultural Economics	0.095	A2	
Federal Reserve Bank St. Louis	0.095	—	
Europe-Asian Studies	0.094	B*	
Review of Development Economics	0.093	B	
Scottish Journal of Political Economy	0.093	A2	B3
Theory and Decision	0.093	A2*	
Critical Perspectives on International Business	**0.093**	**C***	
Journal of Agricultural and Resource Economics	0.092	B	
Social Choice and Welfare	0.091	A2	A2
Economic Modelling	0.088	A2	B3
Debatte	**0.087**	**B***	
Defence and Peace Economics	0.085	B	
Journal of Mathematical Economics	0.084	C	A2
Journal of Media Economics	0.084	B	B4
National Tax Journal	0.082	A1*	A2
Journal of Institutional and Theoretical Economics	0.080	A2	B3
Journal of African Economics	0.079	B	
International Journal of Game Theory	0.078	B	
Manchester School	0.076	B	B2
International Review of Law and Economics	0.072	A2	B3
Geneva Risk Insurance Review	0.068	B*	
Japan Economic Review	0.066	B	
South African Journal of Economics	0.065	B	
Journal of Real Estate Research	0.064	B*	
Open Economies Review	0.064	B	B4
Australian Economic History Review	0.062	A2	
Empirical Economics	0.062	B	B3
China and World Economy	0.061	C	
Journal of Economic Policy Reform	0.060	B	
Applied Economics Letters	0.058	B	B2
Eastern European Economics	0.057	B	B4
Post-Communist Economies	0.056	B	
De Economist	0.055	C	B4
Finanzarchiv	0.053	C*	

Table 3   *Continued*

JOURNAL	JQES	ARE	BRE
Japan and the World Economy	0.052	B	B2
Portuguese Economic Journal	0.049	C	
Australian Economic Review	0.048	B	
Politicka Ekonomie	0.048	B	
Developing Economies	0.047	B	B3
Independent Review	0.045	C	
Journal of Economic Education	0.043	B*	B2
Spanish Economic Review	0.037	B	
Pacific Economic Review	0.036	B	
International Journal of Transport Economics	0.034	C*	
Journal of Applied Economics	0.031	B	
Revue d'Etudes Comparative Est-Quest	0.028	B	
Ekon CAS	0.027	—	
Desarrollo Economico	0.026	B	
Invest Econ-Spain	0.025	—	
Hitotsubashi Journal of Economics	0.025	B	B4
Trimestre Economico	0.024	B	B3
Jahrbuecher fuer Nationaloekonomie und Statistik	0.021	B	
South African Journal of Economics and Management Science	0.017	C	
Hacienda Publica Esp	0.015	—	
Invest Econ-Mex	0.007	—	
Ekonomiska Samfundets Tidskrift	0.004	C	
Revista de Economia Aplicada	0.000	C	B2

JQES—journal quality-equality score—heterodox journals and their scores are in **bold**.
ARE—Australian Ranking Exercise—if denoted by an * the journal does not have an economics classification.
BRE—Brazil Ranking Exercise.

Similarly, the research quality of the *JEI* is slightly above the *Economic Journal*, while the research quality of the *JPKE* is slightly below the *Journal of International Economics* and the *Journal of Monetary Economics* but above the *Journal of Econometrics*. Moreover, if the research quality of the top 25 mainstream journals is judged as excellent, then the research quality of the top four heterodox journals must prima facie also be judged as excellent. Finally, if the research quality of an individual mainstream journal is judged as excellent, then the research quality of a heterodox journal whose JQES is within, say,

5 percent of the mainstream journal's score can also be judged as excellent or nearly so, such as the *Journal of Law and Economics* and *AJES, Capital and Class,* and *Metroeconomica.* So it is not that the research quality of mainstream journals is intrinsically better than heterodox journals (or vice versa), but they are different. Some mainstream journals contribute more to mainstream economics than some heterodox journals contribute to heterodox economics and some do not. Thus, the JQES ranking is a *quality-equality* ranking of both mainstream and heterodox journals.

The implications of the JQES ranking on the perceptions of which are the high impact, top tier, excellent research quality journals are dramatic. For example, in 2007 the Australian Department of Education, Science and Training invited the Academy of Social Sciences of Australia to participate in the ranking of academic journals for the ongoing research assessment exercise. In turn, the Economic Society of Australia was asked to rank 602 journals, which it did by using peer evaluation obtained via a questionnaire. As a result of the survey, an additional 288 journals were subject to peer evaluation. The end result, after due deliberation, is the publication of a four-tier ranking of 20,712 journals, of which 628 are classified as economics, on 9 February 2010. In economics, the top tier contains 46 journals (but only 37 are in the economics SSCI), and only one is a heterodox journal, *History of Political Economy*—see Table 3. The dispersion of first-tier journals goes from the *Quarterly Journal of Economics* (ranked 1) to *Economic Theory* (ranked 175) and includes 58 of the 62 heterodox journals. If the bottom 25 percent of the first tier is eliminated, which reduces the dispersion to *European Economic Review* (ranked 69), 21 heterodox journals are included; and repeating the exercise but eliminating the bottom 50 percent, nine heterodox journals still remain. Thus, utilizing the JQES ranking, anywhere from the top nine to the top 21 heterodox journals should be included in the first tier; and if the first and second tiers are combined, then between 40 and 56 heterodox journals should be included. The analysis reveals quite clearly that however the high impact, top tier, excellent research quality mainstream journals are identified, there are a nonnegligible number of heterodox journals that are their equivalents. Moreover, the JQES quality-equality rankings reveal that the

Australian rankings systematically undervalue the heterodox journals that are included in that the first tier equivalent heterodox journals are ranked in the second tier or lower, while the second tier equivalent heterodox journals are generally ranked in the third tier or lower (Abelson 2009; Bloch 2010; http://www.arc.gov.au/era/era_journal_list.htm).

Conclusion

Evaluating the research quality of heterodox journals and comparing it to the research quality of mainstream journals is an unexplored area in the economics ranking literature. By separating economics into two subdisciplines of mainstream and heterodox economics and then identifying a set of heterodox journals, it is possible to develop a bibliometric and peer evaluation measure of research quality specific to them. The measure produces a ranking of heterodox journals in their own terms; but it can also be used to compare the research quality of heterodox journals to mainstream journals, as delineated in the JQES quality-equality rankings. That is, following conventional bibliometric methods combined with peer evaluation, it is possible to construct a research quality-equality measure relative to a benchmark that shows the contribution a journal makes to a subdiscipline and that can be used in an unbiased manner to compare journals" research quality across subdisciplines relative to the quality benchmarks of the subdiscipline. What the quality-equality rankings illuminate is the systematic discrimination against heterodox journals by mainstream economists.

In 2009 the Brazilian Ministry of Education undertook a ranking of academic journals, including economic journals, which are to be used to rate graduate programs and assess Brazilian research output. The committee appointed to rank the journals was made up of mainstream and heterodox economists and its journal ranking reflected this—see Table 3. In particular, 15 heterodox journals are included in the tier rankings of A1, A2, and B1 (which are the equivalent of the first and second tier in the Australian rankings) and another 15 to 25 could have been included. Despite of the effort to arrive at a more quality-equality tier ranking of heterodox and mainstream journals, some

Brazilian mainstream economists find it unacceptable. In his evaluation of the rankings, Da Silva (2009) stated that the inclusion of *History of Political Economy, JPKE,* and *RRPE* in the first two tiers reveals a left-wing bias in the rankings; moreover, he argued that the *CJE* and virtually all other heterodox journals should be downgraded and their places taken by better mainstream journals. To buttress his position, Da Silva refers to the RePEc impact factors, which are just as biased and invalid for evaluating the research quality of heterodox journals as are the SSCI impact factors. But, if the above method applied to the SSCI impact factors for measuring the research quality of mainstream journals is applied to the RePEc impact factors, the resulting quality-equality ranking would be somewhat the same, except that all the heterodox journals would be included in the first two tiers. Thus, Da Silva's recommendations for changes in the Brazilian journal rankings is to substitute lower quality mainstream journals for higher quality heterodox journals so to eliminate the supposed left-wing bias and impose a neoliberal right-wing bias.

The quality-equality measure shows which mainstream and heterodox journals have the same research quality. As a result, many heterodox journals appear on par with highly rated mainstream journals. Mainstream economists, such as Da Silva, may find this unacceptable and hence refuse to accept the rankings. However, because the measure is an unbiased one, it is not possible to argue that, for example, the *CJE* is not quality comparable to the *American Economic Review* or the *JPKE* is not comparable to the *Journal of Monetary Economics.* Thus, the mainstream response must be to condemn heterodox economics as noneconomics and reject it entirely. But this is not one based on ranking journals according to their research quality; rather it is quite different. In this case, it is an issue of cross-paradigm engagement and political/social tolerance or intolerance of different ideas and arguments. And this is quite a far distance from the issue of research quality ranking of heterodox journals.

Appendices

Appendix I and Appendix II are available online at http://cas.umkc.edu/economics/people/facultyPages/lee/.

Notes

1. Bibliometric refers to the use of citation and other bibliographic data to carry out quantitative and statistical analysis of scholarly research.

2. In this article, citations are interpreted as quantitative proxies of intellectual influence (Moed 2005).

3. In economics, there are subdiscipline rankings of journals in the areas of applied economics and socioeconomics (Barrett, Olia, and von Bailey 2000; Azar 2007).

4. Similar arguments have been advanced with regard to the subdisciplines of econometrics, applied econometrics, and applied economics (Baltagi 1998, 1999; Barrett, Olia, and von Bailey 2000).

5. Combining bibliometric measures with peer-based evaluation of the research quality of journals is considered good research practice in part because it provides a "check and balance" on the two approaches that if left to themselves may generate clearly "wrong" outcomes (van Raan 1996; Moed 2005). For an example of journal ranking that combines bibliometric measures with peer-based evaluation, see DuBois and Reeb (2000).

6. The research dependency impact factor for a journal is defined as the number of 2008 citations to its articles, reviews, and notes published in 2003–2007 divided by the total number of 2008 citations received by the journal—see Appendix II, Table A2. It represents the degree to which the building of heterodox knowledge draws upon recent as well as older contributions. That is, the RDIF encapsulates one of the research values of heterodox economists that both current and past research make valuable contributions to the building of heterodox economics. RDIF is used in place of the traditional impact factor, in part, because the latter is lagged only two years whereas for economics the lag should be five years, but largely because the impact factor does not capture the issue of research dependency on current publications. The other usual criticisms directed at the impact factor, such as possible wide yearly swings in its value and that it measures the "average impact" of all the journal's articles ignoring the skewed distribution of citations per article, do not apply to RDIF because its value is constrained and is embedded in an algorithm that takes other factors into account when scoring the research qualities of a journal (Adler, Ewing, and Taylor 2008; Nederhof 2008; Carmona, Garcia-Ferrer, and Poncela 2005; Seglen 1998; Glanzel and Moed 2002; Nisonger 2004; Moed 2005).

7. The value of the constraint can range from zero to one. However, 0.50 is selected to emphasis the relative importance of promoting research dependency of recently produced scientific knowledge while at the same time maintaining the research importance of older publications.

8. For example, for the period 2002–2008, the *Cambridge Journal of Economics* (*CJE*) imported 927 citations and exported 1541 citations, and its domestic production of citations was 437, resulting in a total of 2,905 citations.

In addition, it imported citations from 29 heterodox journals and exported citations to 43 heterodox journals. Finally, of its 211 citations for 2008, 86 were to heterodox publications in the previous five years. Therefore, the JBQS for the *CJE* is:

$$JBQS = 3[437/2905] + [1541/437] + [927/437] + [927/1541] + \qquad (1.1)$$
$$[43/61] + 29/61] + 2[86/211]$$

$$JBQS = 0.4512 + 3.526 + 2.121 + 0.6015 + 0.7049 + 0.4754 + 0.8151. \quad (1.2)$$

Because (E/DP) and (I/DP) cannot be greater than two, their scores are reduced to zero. Therefore, the final JBQS for the *CJE* is 3.4540 (see Appendix I, Table 2A).

9. Because this approach to scoring research quality utilizes a benchmark that includes a balance of trade citations and implies a given citation-interdependent collection of heterodox journals, the issue of size and field-dependent normalization is not relevant (Moed 2005).

10. The criteria for the selection were that the journal had to be in existence for at least three years and accessible in a manner that counting citations was possible. This latter criterion meant that nearly all non-English language heterodox journals were excluded.

11. Citation data for the entire period were collected for 46 journals. Of the remaining 16 journals, five were started after 2002 and for the remaining 11 journals, it was not possible to obtain copies of the journals to fill in the gaps—see Appendix I, Table 1A, column 3.

12. Thus citations to mainstream and other journals were not collected. For all the journals, citations to heterodox journals constituted a minority of all journal citations.

13. Of the 62 journals, the SSCI only covers 22 of them (and not all of them completely). Of the 22 journals, 17 are in the subject category of economics while the remaining five are found in the industrial relations and labor, planning and development, interdisciplinary social sciences, and geography categories. The remaining 40 journals are covered by Scopus or no index whatsoever—see Appendix I, Table 1A, column 4.

14. A response rate is difficult to calculate. However, each *Newsletter* sent out over the listserv gets around 1,000 hits. If this is used as a benchmark, then the response rate is 40 percent.

15. The rank correlation between total citation and bibliometric rankings is $R_s = 0.786$; and the correlation between total citation and social network ranking is $R_s = 0.772$. Thus, together the bibliometric and social network scores produce a more accurate total citation score qua ranking than when separate.

16. In addition, the rank correlation between peer evaluation and bibliometric rankings is $R_s = 0.244$ and between peer evaluation and social network

ranking is $R_s = 0.563$. Thus, as in other studies, the Spearman rank correlation of peer evaluation and citation-based rankings are positive but not perfect.

17. Such practices include emphasizing to potential authors that submissions should include citations to articles previously published in the journal and citing relevant articles in other heterodox journals.

18. If either or both limiting factors are reduced, the interdisciplinary journals would lose their distinctiveness and become more like generalist or specialist heterodox journals.

19. The rank correlation between total citation and final rankings is $R_s = 0.893$; and the correlation between peer evaluation and final rankings is $R_s = 0.837$. In contrast, the rank correlation between total citation and peer evaluation rankings is $R_s = 0.536$. Thus, together the total citation and peer evaluation scores produce a better, more accurate final score and ranking than when separate.

20. The social network and peer-review ranking of these eight journals are mostly in the bottom third, suggesting that they are neither well integrated into heterodox economics nor very familiar to heterodox economists—see Table 1.

21. Traditionally, economists have used the two-year impact factor scores to measure the research quality of a journal. But the evidence shows that impact factor scores in economics (and in the other social sciences) generally reach their highest value after five years; thus it is a better metric for research quality (Moed 2005; Adler, Ewing, and Taylor 2008; Nederhof 2008; Engemann and Wall 2009).

22. In fact, given the near absence of mainstream citations of heterodox journals (see Lee 2010), it appears that heterodox journals contribute nothing at all to mainstream economics and that their positive MJQSs are largely due to citations made by noneconomic journals in the SSCI.

References

Abelson, P. (2009). "The Ranking of Economics Journals by the Economic Society of Australia." *Economic Papers* 28(2): 176–180.

Adler, R., J. Ewing, and P. Taylor. (2008). "Citation Statistics." A Report from the International Mathematical Union in Cooperation with the International Council of Industrial and Applied Mathematics and the Institute of Mathematical Statistics, available at: http://www.mathunion.org/fileadmin/IMU/Report/CitationStatistics.pdf.

Aliseda, A., and D. Gillies. (2007). "Logical, Historical and Computational Approaches." In *General Philosophy of Science: Focal Issues*. Ed. T. A. F. Kuipers, pp. 431–513. Elsevier: Amsterdam.

Azar, O. H. (2007). "Behavioral Economics and Socio-Economics Journals: A Citation-Based Ranking." *Journal of Socio-Economics* 36: 451–462.

Baltagi, B. H. (1998). "Worldwide Institutional Rankings in Econometrics: 1989–1995." *Econometric Theory* 14(1): 1–43.

———. (1999). "Applied Econometrics Rankings: 1989–1995." *Journal of Applied Econometrics* 14(4): 423–441.

Barrett, C. B., A. Olia, and D. von Bailey. (2000). "Subdiscipline-Specific Journal Rankings: Wither Applied Economics?" *Applied Economics* 32: 239–252.

Bloch, H. (2010). "Research Evaluation Down Under: An Outsider's View from the Inside of the Australian Approach." *American Journal of Economics and Sociology* 69(5): 1530–1552.

Bonacich, P. (1972). "Factoring and Weighting Approaches to Status Scores and Clique Identification." *Journal of Mathematical Sociology* 2: 113–120.

Borgman, C. L., and J. Furner. (2002). "Scholarly Communication and Bibliometrics." *Annual Review of Information Science and Technology* 36: 3–72.

Carmona, S., A. Garcia-Ferrer, and P. Poncela. (2005). "From Zero to Infinity: The Use of Impact Factors in the Evaluation of Economic Research in Spain." Instituto de Empresa Working Paper WP05-22. Available at: http://latienda.ie.edu/working_paper_economia/WP05-22.pdf.

Cronin, B. (2008). "Journal Citation Among Heterodox Economists, 1995–2007: Dynamics of Community Emergence." *On the Horizon* 16(24): 226–240.

Da Silva, S. (2009). "Going Parochial in the Assessment of the Brazilian Economics Research Output." *Economics Bulletin* 29(4): 2826–2846. Available at: http://works.bepress.com/sergiodasilva/88/.

Dolfsma, W., and L. Leydesdorff. (2008). "Journals as Constituents of Scientific Discourse: Economic Heterodoxy." *On the Horizon* 16(4): 214–225.

DuBois, F. L., and D. Reeb. (2000). "Ranking the International Business Journals." *Journal of International Business Studies* 31(4): 689–704.

Engemann, K. M., and H. J. Wall. (2009). "A Journal Ranking for the Ambitious Economist." *Federal Reserve Bank of St. Louis* 91(3): 127–139.

Freeman, L. (1979). "Centrality in Social Networks: Conceptual Clarification." *Social Networks* 1: 215–239.

Glanzel, W., and H. F. Moed. (2002). "Journal Impact Measures in Bibliometric Research." *Scientometrics* 53(2): 171–193.

Gould, J., and J. Fernandez. (1989). "Structures of Mediation: A Formal Approach to Brokerage in Transaction Networks." *Sociological Methodology* 19: 89–126.

Hirst, G. (1978). "Discipline Impact Factors: A Method for Determining Core Journal Lists." *Journal of the American Society for Information Science* 29(4): 71–72.

Kodrzycki, Y. K., and P. Yu. (2006). "New Approaches to Ranking Economics Journals." *Contributions to Economic Analysis and Policy* 5(1): article 24. Available at: http://www.bepress.com/bejeap/contributions/vol5/iss1/art24.

Lee, F. S. (2006). "The Ranking Game, Class, and Scholarship in American Economics." *Australasian Journal of Economics Education* 3(1–2): 1–41.

———. (2008a). "A Case for Ranking Heterodox Journals and Departments." *On the Horizon* 16(4): 241–251.

———. (2008b). *Informational Directory for Heterodox Economists: Graduate and Undergraduate Programs, Journals, Publishers and Book Series, Associations, Blogs, and Institutes and other Websites*, 3rd ed. Available at: http://www.heterodoxnews.com/directory/heterodoxdirectory.pdf.

———. (2009). *Challenging the Mainstream: Essays on the History of Heterodox Economics in the Twentieth Century.* Routledge: London.

———. (2010). "Who Talks to Whom: Pluralism and Identity of Heterodox Economics Journals." Unpublished.

———. (Forthcoming). "The Pluralism Debate in Heterodox Economics." *Review of Radical Political Economics.*

Lee, F. S., T. C. Grijalva, and C. Nowell. (2010). "Ranking Economics Departments in a Contested Discipline." *American Journal of Economics and Sociology* 69(5): 1345–1375.

Liner, G. H., and M. Amin. (2004). "Methods of Ranking Economic Journals." *Atlantic Economic Journal* 32(2): 140–149.

Lockett, A., and A. McWilliams. (2005). "The Balance of Trade Between Disciplines: Do We Effectively Manage Knowledge?" *Journal of Management Inquiry* 14(2): 139–150.

Moed, H. F. (2005). *Citation Analysis in Research Evaluation.* Dordrecht: Springer.

Nederhof, A. J. (2008). "Policy Impact of Bibliometric Rankings of Research Performance of Departments and Individual in Economics." *Scientometrics* 74(1): 163–174.

Nisonger, T. E. (2004). "The Benefits and Drawbacks of Impact Factor for Journal Collection Management in Libraries." *Serial Librarian* 47(1/2): 57–75.

Pieters, R., and H. Baumgartner. (2002). "Who Talks to Whom? Intra- and Interdisciplinary Communication of Economic Journals." *Journal of Economic Literature* 40(2): 483–509.

Schubert, A., and T. Braun. (1993). "Reference Standards for Citation Based Assessments." *Scientometrics* 26(1): 21–35.

Seglen, P. O. (1998). "Citation Rates and Journal Impact Factors Are Not Suitable for Evaluation of Research." *Acta Orthop Scand* 69(3): 224–229.

Seidman, S. (1983). "Network Structure and Minimum Degree." *Social Networks* 5: 269–287.

Stigler, G. J., S. M. Stigler, and C. Friedland. (1995). "The Journals of Economics." *Journal of Political Economy* 103(2): 331–359.

Stigler, S. M. (1994). "Citation Patterns in the Journals of Statistics and Probability." *Statistical Science* 9(1): 94–108.

Thomas, P. R., and D. S. Watkins. (1998). "Institutional Research Rankings via Bibliometric Analysis and Direct Peer Review: A Comparative Case Study with Policy Implications." *Scientometrics* 41(3): 335–355.

Van Raan, A. F. J. (1996). "Advanced Bibliometric Methods as Quantitative Core of Peer Review Based Evaluation and Foresight Exercises." *Scientometrics* 36(3): 397–420.

Vinkler, P. (2002). "Subfield Problems in Applying the Garfield (Impact) Factors in Practice," *Scientometrics* 53(2): 267–279.

Weingart, P. (2005). "Impact of Bibliometrics Upon the Science System: Inadvertent Consequences?" *Scientometrics* 62(1): 117–131.

Increasing the Impact of Heterodox Work: Insights from *RoSE*

By MARTHA A. STARR*

ABSTRACT. To help understand what enhances the prospects for heterodox work to have strong research impact, this article analyzes the pool of articles published in the *Review of Social Economy* in the past 15 years, aiming to identify what differentiates well-cited articles from others. Well-cited papers tend to be in areas of core concern in social economics (labor, health, social theory) and attract attention in related social sciences and policy fields. Yet about half the articles published in *RoSE* are not cited in another scholarly journal within three years of publication, suggesting that, as well done and interesting as these papers may be, problems like narrow focus seem to limit their influence on other people's work. The article's results suggest that increasing the impact of heterodox work requires articles to be interesting and accessible to intentionally broad audiences, and to prompt people to change their thinking. Better still if they open up channels of communication between diverse communities of scholars that are likely to be sustained.

Introduction

Recent work by Fred Lee and others shows that research "impact" is hard to measure, and that widely used methods of quantifying impact

*Please address correspondence to: Prof. Martha A. Starr, Department of Economics, American University, 4400 Massachusetts Ave. NW, Washington, DC 20016. Phone: 202-885-3747. E-mail: mstarr@american.edu. The author's research interests include consumption, saving, wealth, inequality, macroeconomics, monetary policy, business cycles, and social economics. She is grateful to Paul Davidson, John Davis, Wilfred Dolfsma, Jakob Kapeller, Fred Lee, Robert McMaster, Jack Reardon, participants in the URPE sessions on heterodox journals organized by Fred Lee at the 2010 ASSA meetings, and two anonymous referees for valuable comments on an earlier version of this article. Views expressed in this article are hers and do not necessarily reflect any editorial position of the *Review of Social Economy*.

American Journal of Economics and Sociology, Vol. 69, No. 5 (November, 2010).

tend to give heterodox journals the short end of the stick.[1] Yet it is also true that, qualitatively, heterodox research tends to fall short of its desired impact, in terms of creating and sustaining a lively, productive, and socially relevant discourse different from that of the mainstream, and/or changing the knowledge practices and priorities in the profession's work. Thus, for example, awareness of heterodox discourse outside of heterodox discourse is very low, as shown by mainstream tendencies to start from scratch when revisiting issues well-researched in the heterodox literature (e.g., relational preferences, conspicuous consumption). Moreover, the typical article published in a heterodox journal has a low probability of being cited in any scholarly journal (in the ISI or not), in a timely way. This suggests that, even if the ratings game is stacked against heterodox outlets, other problems probably also contribute to low impact.

To help understand what gives heterodox work good prospects of having good impact, this article analyzes the pool of articles published in the *Review of Social Economy* in the past 15 years, aiming to identify what differentiates articles that get cited from those that do not. As a matter of background, *RoSE* is a 68-year-old journal, presently published by Routledge, that aims to promote scholarship on the many intersections between social values and economic life. Work published in *RoSE* covers a relatively eclectic mix of subjects that fall broadly under the heading of "social economics," including empirical and conceptual studies of qualitative dimensions of social welfare (health, human dignity, economic security, basic needs, social justice); theories relating social, cultural, religious, and ethical values to economic behavior and institutions; and characterizations of economic activity organized by rationales other than the profit motive (the "social economy" or third or nonprofit sector).[2] In the spirit of open-minded inquiry, it also publishes work in related areas of interest, such as economic thought; social ontology; institutional, radical, and post-Keynesian economics; and applied fields sharing *RoSE*'s concern with inclusion and social welfare, such as gender/feminist economics, development, and ecological economics. *RoSE* is not presently included in the ISI, although it does appear in widely circulated rankings such as that of Kalaitzidakis, Mamuneas, and Stengos (2003), usually in a respectable but lower-tier rank.

A key assumption made in this article is that, at a journal like *RoSE,* which publishes only 10–20 percent of submitted papers, those that make it through the process of double-blind peer review by expert referees should be viewed as high in quality: to the extent that they fail to have much subsequent impact on economic knowledge, prob-lem(s) are of other kinds—such as overly narrow topics, overly narrow pools of interested scholars, topics of limited current interest, etc. Thus, we go through and code up the various articles and examine what correlates with being cited or highly cited. An interest-ing finding is that the distribution of citations is highly skewed: About half of all articles are not cited at all within three years, while a large share of total citations comes from a small number of "big hit" articles. The article analyzes the characteristics of these articles, aiming to identify what made them interesting to broad audiences. The article concludes with some implications of the evidence from *RoSE* for efforts to increase the impact of heterodox work.

Methodology and Descriptive Statistics

To examine the impact of articles published in *RoSE* on other pub-lished work, I collected citation information for all original articles published in the journal between 1993 and 2006. The start date was chosen as a matter of analyzing patterns relevant to the present, and also because electronic means of identifying citations become more reliable for work published after the early 1990s. The end date was chosen because some of the analysis focuses on citations in the three years after publication, for which the "observation period" is truncated for articles published in 2007–2009. As the emphasis is on original work, book reviews are excluded from the analysis, although a small number of book-oriented symposia are not. Also omitted are articles reprinted in a "Best of *RoSE,* 1944–1999" issue in 2005.[3]

Google Scholar was used as the main means of identifying citations. Because Google Scholar aims to include all possible scholarly citation venues, it enables us to include citations in journals not included in the ISI Social Science Citation Index, along with citations in books.[4] Not infrequently, citations appear in Google Scholar multiple times; to guard against double-counting, citations were examined one by one and duplicates discarded. To guard against omissions, we also ran *RoSE* articles through the "publish or perish" software developed by Harzing.com and searched electronically for references to the "Review of Social Economy" in the other main heterodox journals; this resulted in some additional citations, though not many. Citations in unpublished working papers are not included in the analysis due to difficulties in eliminating double-counting (e.g., papers may appear in multiple working paper series, revised versions may appear under a different title, etc.). A small number of citations in non-English-language journals and books were also omitted due to difficulties establishing what they were. These procedures yielded a total of 1,248 citations to 349 original *RoSE* articles published over the 1993–2006 period.

As shown in Table 1, 83.9 percent of citations to *RosE* articles appeared in journals while 16.1 percent were in books. While the focus in this article is on citations in journals, it is worth noting the importance of five book publishers—Edward Elgar, Routledge, Springer, Ashgate, and M. E. Sharpe—which together accounted for about 70 percent of citations to *RoSE* articles in books. This underlines

Table 1

Distribution of Citations Across Journals and Books

	# cites	% of total
Total	1248	100.0
Journals	1047	83.9
Books	201	16.1
Distribution of citations in books across publishers	201	100.0
Edward Elgar	51	25.4
Routledge	47	23.4
Springer	20	10.0
Ashgate	11	5.5
M. E. Sharpe	11	5.5
Cambridge University Press	5	2.5
Oxford Univ. Press	5	2.5
Others ($n = 32$)	51	25.4

the valuable contribution these publishers make in securing broader audiences for heterodox discourse.

Table 2 provides information on the types of journals in which *RoSE* articles appear.[5] Of the 1,047 journal citations, only about half were in what might be thought of as the core set of journals with which *RoSE* is connected. The single largest source of citations to *RoSE* articles is other *RoSE* articles, accounting for 16 percent of the total. Another 21 percent appear in other heterodox journals, especially the *Journal of Economic Issues, Cambridge Journal of Economics, Review of Political Economy, Review of Radical Political Economics,* and *Journal of Post Keynesian Economics*. An additional 13 percent came from journals that share *RoSE*'s orientation to intersections between social phenomena and economic life, including the *International Journal of Social Economics, Journal of Socio-Economics, Forum for Social Economics,* and *American Journal of Economics and Sociology*. There are 56 journals in this "core" journal category, accounting for a total of 527 citations, for an average of 9.4 each.

However, an almost equally large number of citations to *RoSE* articles (520) can be found scattered across a vast array of other journals—in categories as varied as business ethics, mainstream economics, fields of applied economics (labor, gender/family, development, environmental/ecological), health-care research, public policy and administration, geography/urban studies, and other social sciences (psychology, sociology, anthropology). Here a surprising 325 journals provide 520 citations to *RoSE* articles, for an average of 1.6 citations each. This is consistent with a result found in quantitative analyses of citation flows between heterodox journals: that *RoSE* does not show the same centrality in heterodox discourse as some other of its other well-regarded journals, such as the *Cambridge Journal of Economics, Journal of Economic Issues,* or *Journal of Post-Keynesian Economics* (Lee 2008; Dolfsma and Leydesdorff 2008); rather, like *Feminist Economics*, it has highly diversified set of ties to other journals sharing its topical interests (Woolley 2005).

This raises two important questions about the issue of the "impact" of heterodox journals. The first has to do with the method of ranking heterodox journals proposed by Lee (e.g., 2008, 2010), which emphasizes citation flows among heterodox journals. In Lee's method, a

Table 2

Distribution of Citations Across Journal Categories

	# of citations	% of all cites	# of journals	Journals in category having 5 citations or more
All journals	1047	100	381	
Core journals	**527**	**50.3**	**56**	
RoSE	166	15.9	1	
Hcterodox, political economy, history of thought, methodology	222	21.2	26	*Journal of Economic Issues* (52), *Cambridge Journal of Economics* (51), *Review of Political Economy* (26), *Review of Radical Political Economics* (21), *Journal of Post Keynesian Economics* (11)
Other social	139	13.3	29	*International Journal of Social Economics* (34), *Journal of Socio-Economics* (27), *Forum for Social Economics* (17), *American Journal of Economics and Sociology* (6), *Journal of Human Behavior in the Social Environment* (6), *Social Forces* (6), *Journal of Economic and Social Measurement* (5)
Other journals	**520**	**49.7**	**325**	
Business, law, IT	85	8.1	63	*Journal of Business Ethics* (9)

Table 2   *Continued*

	# of citations	% of all cites	# of journals	Journals in category having 5 citations or more
Economics	58	5.5	35	*Economic Journal* (6), *Applied Economics* (5), *Kyklos* (5), *Oxford Economic Papers* (5)
Geography, urban studies	43	4.1	24	*Urban Studies* (7), *Environment and Planning A* (5)
Sociology & anthropology	42	4.0	27	
Labor	40	3.8	26	
Development, ag.	39	3.7	19	*Journal of Development Studies* (5)
Environment	39	3.7	21	*Ecological Economics* (10)
Public services, public policy	39	3.7	28	
Household, family, feminist	35	3.3	13	*Journal of Marriage and Family* (17), *Feminist Economics* (12), *Community, Work & Family* (6), *Journal of Family and Economic Issues* (6), *Journal of Family Issues* (6)
Health	30	2.9	24	
Psychology	30	2.9	13	*American Behavioral Scientist* (16)
Consumer	16	1.5	10	
Philosophy & religion	14	1.3	12	
Education	6	0.6	6	
Misc	4	0.4	4	

heterodox journal that is both citing other heterodox journals heavily and being heavily cited in them comes out most highly ranked—on the grounds that it is contributing most actively to the construction of a lively and integrated heterodox discourse. This could be advantageous insofar as it promotes the development of a more integrated, cohesive, and advanced body of heterodox theory, methodology, and knowledge; this could potentially increase the ability of heterodox economists to challenge mainstream approaches and produce compelling alternatives to them in research, teaching, and policy analysis. But intensifying flows of ideas *among* heterodox economists is only one way in which heterodox discourses could become livelier, more creative, and more influential. As the experiences of *RoSE* and *Feminist Economics* suggest, another way is via creating and sustaining strong productive flows of ideas with scholars outside of the heterodox community who work on topics of shared interest—whether they are open-minded mainstream economists, scholars with other disciplinary or interdisciplinary identifications, and/or people working in the public-policy community. This is consistent with Cronin's (2010) discussion of the potential strategic value of aligning heterodox work with "adjacent" discourses, by highlighting the salience of their shared values. It is also consistent with Colander's (2009) recommendation that, to secure a healthy future of heterodox discourse, heterodox economists could increase their connections with innovative mainstream economists and work to secure broader audiences for their ideas.[6]

But the second issue here concerns the great diversity of *RoSE's* citations outside of the core social and heterodox journals. The fact that so many journals cite *RoSE* articles only once suggests that scholars in other fields may find a specific *RoSE* piece valuable for their work—but that their interests only partly overlap with the range of topics on which *RoSE* focuses, and/or their theoretical frameworks and/or methodological approaches do not articulate well with those in use in social- or heterodox-economics circles, so that a regular exchange of ideas does not materialize. Thus, for example, a special issue on consumption in 2004 generated citations in a number of journals in other fields—in consumer studies, marketing, sociology, environmental/ecological studies, and in studies of rural/agricultural/

local economies—but without creating sustained connections between social economists and people working in these fields.

The finding of high diversification also shows up in the range of topics covered in *RoSE* articles. To classify articles, I went through each article (mostly the abstract but sometimes also the introduction) and categorized them according to their main emphasis, using the coding scheme shown in Table 3.[7] As the table shows, about half of all articles can be categorized as dealing with core social economics topics, including discussions of social economics as a field; contemporary social theory (social capital, capabilities); theories of the individual transcending *homo economicus*; labor-economics work having a distinct concern with social welfare; analyses of poverty, inequality, and income support programs; and "other" social-economics topics (consumerism, business ethics, housing policy). Another 26 percent of articles were in fields closely related to social and/or heterodox economics, including institutions, development, gender/family, environment/ecological economics, and alternative macroeconomic approaches. One-fifth can be classified as "economic thought" (classical or contemporary), with the remaining 5 percent on miscellaneous subjects. This wide range of topics is both a strength and a weakness of *RoSE's* deliberately open-minded approach: it leads to a lot of variety, but the relatively eclectic mix of topics covered in the journal's pages may make its "identity" seem less than clear. We return to this issue below.

Citation Analysis

To analyze citations to a given article, one can look either at the *total* number of citations it acquires, or the number acquired within a certain number of years of publication. While the first is to some extent most interesting, it suffers from the problem of "right truncation"—that older articles have had longer periods of time over which to acquire citations than newer articles, so that newer ones inevitably have lower measured impact than older ones. To get around this problem, much of our analysis focuses on citations within three years of publication, or more precisely, citations to an article published in year t occurring in years t through t + 3. Using a fixed and

Table 3

Distribution of Articles Across Topics

		# of articles	% of total
Core social economics		166	52.4
Social economics as a field	Includes Catholic social thought, economic justice, needs, human dignity, Severyn Bruyn, Ed O'Boyle, Mark Lutz	34	9.7
Labor	Earnings, discrimination, human capital, work hours, job satisfaction, living wage, minimum wage, unemployment insurance, pensions/ social security, training, immigration, labor force participation	39	11.2
Poverty, welfare, & inequality	Poverty, welfare, inequality	24	6.9
Theory of the individual	Preferences, self-interested vs. altruistic behavior, rationality, cooperation, choice, utility	17	4.9
Contemporary social theory & its applications	Capabilities, social capital, subjective well-being, happiness, Bourdieu	14	4.0
Other SE topics	Health, housing/urban, religion & economics, consumption & social values, consumerism, economic security, business ethics	38	10.9

Table 3   *Continued*

		# of articles	% of total
Related applied fields		93	26.8
Institutions	Institutions, institutional economics, industrial organization, innovation, the corporation, Fordism	25	7.2
Gender/family	Household economics, gender-related wage & employment issues, children, feminist economics	25	7.2
Development/ international	Development, developing & emerging market countries, transition/ postsocialism, international, trade, globalization/neoliberalism, European Union	21	6.0
Environment/ ecology	Sustainability, ecological economics	11	3.2
Macro	Macro, Keynes, post-Keynesian, monetary, fiscal, radical political economy	11	3.2
Economic thought		70	20.1
History of economic thought	Smith, Mill, Hume, Mises, Kant, Carlyle, Locke, Knight, Austrian economics, Malthus, Schumpeter, Robinson, Tillich, Marx, Veblen, Sombart, Irving Fisher, Polanyi	37	10.6

Table 3   *Continued*

		# of articles	% of total
Contemporary economic thought	Boulding, Dugger, Sherman, Hodgson, Fred Hirsch, Ellerman, Roemer	20	5.7
Critical realism	Social ontology, closed vs. open systems	13	3.7
Misc.		20	5.7

relatively short window for measuring citations is advantageous, not only because it controls for differences across articles related to age; it also gauges the extent to which given articles are having a relatively timely impact on the ideas and strategies of others who are actively publishing. For purposes of comparison, we also show citations over a two-year time horizon, which corresponds to the interval over which the ISI Web of Knowledge computes "impact factors" for journals;[8] those accumulated over a five-year horizon, reflecting evidence that articles in the social sciences take four to five years to reach their "long-run" citation level (see, e.g., Hicks 2004); and all citations through the end of the observation period (2009).[9]

Table 4 shows the distribution of articles by the number of citations received over various time horizons. One of the most important findings of this article can be seen here: Over one-half of all articles published in *RoSE* in the 1993–2006 period were not cited within three years of publication, and another quarter received only one citation in the three-year window. Looking over a longer time horizon yields a better-looking picture: For example, two-thirds of all articles published between 1993 and 2003 had been cited at least once within five years of publication. Similarly, of all papers published before 2000, three-quarters had been cited at least once by mid-2009, even though only 45 percent had been cited within three years of publication. Still, it is not a good situation to have so many articles of good quality

Table 4

Distribution of Articles by Number of Citations

| | In years since publication | | | | | | | |
| | t to t+2 | | t to t+3 | | t to t+5 | | All citations | |
	# of articles	%	# of articles	%	# of articles	%	# of articles	%
Articles published 1993–2006, by # of citations:								
0	219	62.8	179	51.3	111	35.9	97	27.8
1	79	22.6	85	24.4	82	26.5	76	21.8
2–3	40	11.5	59	16.9	73	23.6	81	23.2
4+	11	3.2	27	7.4	43	13.9	95	27.2
All	349	100	349	100	309	100	349	100
Articles published 1993–2000, by # of citations:								
0	129	65.2	104	52.5	76	38.4	48	24.2
1	42	21.2	50	25.3	53	26.8	42	21.2
2–3	25	12.6	34	17.2	40	20.2	41	20.7
4+	2	1.0	10	5.1	29	14.6	67	33.8
All	198	100	198	100	198	100	198	100

showing so little evidence of having affected the thinking of other actively publishing scholars.

To gain insight into what factors are associated with getting cited in a timely way, Table 5 shows three-year citation rates by article topic and by type of article. There are some notable variations in citation rates across article topics. Several of the "topical" areas of social economics and closely related applied fields have relatively high citation rates. These include labor (59 percent), "other" social economics topics (60 percent), gender (60 percent), and the environment (81.8 percent), although only some of these citation rates are significantly higher than those of other articles. A relatively hot area was contemporary social theory and its applications (i.e., social capital, capabilities, subjective well-being): 78 percent of articles in this area were cited within three years, a significantly higher rate than for other articles. In contrast, papers on both classic and contemporary economic thought had citation rates significantly below those of other articles, with only about one-quarter getting cited within three years; similarly, only about one-third of articles on social economics as a field were cited in this time frame. This is especially worrisome because articles in these three areas made up more than a quarter of all articles published over the period; even though discriminating referees found them to be quality pieces making valuable contributions to the literature, evidently the discourses to which they contributed tended to be relatively slowly-evolving and/or thin. For the history-of-thought pieces it is also possible that they did not attract notice in a journal not specialized in this field.

There are also notable variations across types of articles in three-year citation rates. Compared to articles overall, those appearing in special issues are somewhat more likely to be cited in three years—reflecting both the fact that topics for special issues are selected for their likelihood of attracting broad interest, and the fact that thematically-related articles packaged together are more likely to attract attention than if they appeared separately. One might expect symposium articles—usually a collection of three or four thematically-related articles taking up less than a full issue—to have similarly higher citation rates, but in fact only one-third of them are cited within three years. Book-oriented symposia and presidential addresses are

Table 5

Shares of Articles Cited Within Three Years of Publication, by
Article Topic and Article Type

	Share cited within 3 years of publication	Statistically significant difference in citation probability?*	Share of all articles
All articles	49.0	—	100.0
By article topic:			
Environment	81.8	Higher @ 5%	3.2
Contemporary social theory	78.6	Higher @ 5%	4.0
Critical realism	61.5		3.7
"Other" SE topics	60.5	Higher @ 5%	10.9
Gender, households	60.0		7.2
Labor, discrimination, workplace	59.0		11.2
Misc.	55.0		5.7
Macro, monetary, fiscal, PE	54.5		3.2
Theory of the individual	52.9		4.9
Institutions	52.0		7.2
Poverty & inequality	45.8		6.9
Development, international	33.3	Lower @ 10%	6
Social economics as a field	32.4	Lower @ 5%	9.7
Contemporary economic thought	25.0	Lower @ 5%	5.7
History of economic thought	24.3	Lower @ 5%	10.6
By article type:			
Special issue	56.2	Higher @ 10%	20.9
Regular article	50.9		62.5
Symposia	37.5		5.7
Book-related symposia	29.0	Lower @ 5%	8.9
Presidential address	28.6		2.0
Potter award	64.3		4.0

*Based on *p*-values computed from the relevant one-tailed test (i.e., if the citation rate for articles on topic *i* exceeds the citation rate for other articles, the test is for whether the difference is significantly positive; but if the citation rate is lower, the test is for whether the difference is significantly negative).

Table 6

Distribution of Articles, by Number of Journal Citations
Within Three Years After Publication

# of cites in journals in 3 yrs	# of articles	% of articles	# of cites	% of cites
0	179	51.3	0	0
1	85	24.4	85	22.9
2	40	11.5	80	21.6
3–4	33	9.5	113	30.5
5+	12	3.4	93	25.1
Total	349	100.0	371	100.0

also not well-cited; possibly such pieces are interesting to members of the social-economics community, but they may tend to restate ideas given in other research. In contrast, papers that received the Helen Potter Award, given annually to the best paper published in *RoSE* in the previous year by a promising new scholar, had a relatively high citation rate. Almost two-thirds of Potter papers were cited within three years, versus about 50 percent of papers overall.[10]

A final, important point to note concerns the highly skewed distribution of citations. As has been found in other research on economics journals (e.g., Wall 2009), a small number of *RoSE* articles generated a large share of citations to the journal made in the three-year time frame. As shown in Table 6, of the 349 articles in our data set, about 45 articles (13 percent) accounted for 206 of the 371 citations made within three years—over 50 percent of all such citations. In fact, the 12 articles cited five or more times within three years (3.4 percent of the total) were responsible for one-quarter of all citations made in the three-year frame (93 of 371). In order to understand what enables papers to become "big hits," Table 7 lists the authors, titles, and years of the articles with 5+ citations in the three-year time frame. Although these are a fairly diversified bunch, they share some common attributes. Several were situated in "breaking areas" of social theory and aimed to expose a broad audience to new and influential ideas, and/or challenge or apply

Table 7

Articles Cited Five or More Times Within Three Years
of Publication

Year	Author	Article title	# of cites in 1st 3 yrs.
1995	Phillip Anthony O'Hara	Household Labor, the Family, and Macroeconomic Instability in the United States: 1940s–1990s	5
1997	Deborah M. Figart	Gender as More Than a Dummy Variable: Feminist Approaches to Discrimination	5
1998	Jerry Jacobs and Kathleen Gerson	Who Are the Overworked Americans?	14
1998	Barry Bluestone and Stephen Rose	The Macroeconomics of Work Time	5
1999	Brent McClintock	The Multinational Corporation and Social Justice: Experiments in Supranational Governance	5
2002	Lindon Robison, A. Allan Schmid, and Marcelo Siles	Is Social Capital Really Capital?	15
2003	Elizabeth Oughton and Jane Wheelock	A Capabilities Approach to Sustainable Household Livelihoods	7
2004	Philip Arestis and Malcolm Sawyer	On the Effectiveness of Monetary Policy and of Fiscal Policy	9
2004	Gill Seyfang	Consuming Values and Contested Cultures: A Critical Analysis of the UK Strategy for Sustainable Consumption and Production	5
2004	Frederic Lee and Steve Keen	The Incoherent Emperor: A Heterodox Critique of Neoclassical Microeconomic Theory	5
2005	Bruno Frey and Alois Stutzer	Happiness Research: State and Prospects	13
2006	M. G. Hayes	On the Efficiency of Fair Trade	5

such ideas; these include a paper on social capital by Robison, Schmid, and Siles (2002); one on the capabilities approach by Oughton and Wheelock (2003); and that on happiness research by Frey and Stutzer (2005). Another set addresses topics of strong public-policy interest that are little addressed in mainstream economics—work time (Bluestone and Rose 1998; Jacobs and Gerson 1998) and sustainable consumption (Seyfang 2004)—reflecting its difficulties in analyzing multifaceted social trends involving institutions, culture, and subjective well-being. Another two (O'Hara 1995; Figart 1997) provide strong, compelling expositions as to why gender and household issues are integral to understanding important macro/social phenonema, bringing them into focus for scholars who do not necessarily work in this field. A further two (McClintock 1999; Hayes 2006) tackle issues in international trade and investment having strong social-justice dimensions. Only two of the "big hits" (Arestis and Sawyer 2004; Lee and Keen 2004) specifically aimed at developing heterodox discourse and generated their citations in heterodox journals.

Two common themes uniting these pieces are as follows. First, they virtually all have a "logical fit" in a social economics journal. They cover issues squarely in the intersection between economics and social values. They have important implications for strategies to ameliorate social and/or individual well-being. Their analyses tend to be richer, more multifaceted, more narrative, and in some cases more directly relevant to policy problems than mainstream economic work. As such, these pieces embody and highlight the advantages of social-economics approaches. Second, most of the "big hits" are written with the ambition of changing the way people think—not just adding modestly and capably to existing knowledge, but really stirring up the pot. Their arguments are shaped so as to be highly compelling and accessible, not only to people who work on the issue in question—but also to social and heterodox economists more broadly, if not also open-minded mainstream economists, people working in other disciplines or in interdisciplinary fields, and/or policymakers. This suggests a potential for social and heterodox economists to increase the impact of their work by doing a better job of imagining who it could interest, and working hard to reach out to them in ways that will work.

Discussion and Concluding Thoughts

This article's analysis has three important implications for efforts to promote a vibrant, active heterodox discourse in the years ahead. First, while building a strong discourse amongst heterodox economists is a valuable project, *RoSE* experience suggests there are also potentially good benefits to forging links with people who work in other fields. The features of mainstream economic analysis to which many heterodox economists object are also those that make it inaccessible and/or of limited value to scholars working in other disciplines and/or in policy-oriented and applied work (e.g., excessive concern with expressing ideas in math; insistence on quantitative, "structural" empirical work; limited attention to institutions, history, culture, social values, and power; disinterest in intersections between economic trends and sociopolitical life, etc.). Thus, well-done heterodox work has potential to shape many research agendas besides "our own," especially if it is written to be interesting, intelligible, and important to people outside of heterodox circles as well as within.

A second and related point is that "exporting" the occasional idea or two to scholars in other fields may or may not give rise to sustained exchange, as illustrated by the fact that *RoSE* has lots of one-time exports but not much in the way of repeat business. This highlights issues of "barriers to trade" among discourses, as when one community expects those who contribute to its journals to relate their ideas to the theories, concepts, empirical methodologies, etc. that prevail in that field.[11] Thus, rather than exploring a wide range of ties to other fields, it would be more valuable to selectively cultivate alliances where good synergies can be expected (see Cronin 2010).

Third, it is important to make sure the open-mindedness of heterodox discourse works to its advantage and not its detriment. Heterodox scholarship values explorations of alternative approaches, does not throw out important "old" ideas just because they are "old," accepts narrative analysis as a valid way to make truth claims, etc. While this leads to an inclusive and pluralistic scholarly community, it also tends to create a terrain in which many interesting ideas are floated, but with many having little effect on how others do their work. Well-cited articles in *RoSE* suggest several ways of overcoming this, while keeping the range of topics and approaches considered broad. These include: writing papers to make sure their originality, importance, and implications stand out to a broad audience; placing related work together (as in special issues); making sure that papers wind up in outlets where they logically fit; and ensuring that journals' "aims and scopes" are clear, up-to-date, and well-known. Other possibly useful strategies could include increasing the attention given to current heterodox research in heterodox graduate programs, to position students to contribute to current research strands, rather than preparing them to reexplore classic heterodox works. It may, however, be necessary to face the reality that *some* of the things we like to write about are not in good demand.

Notes

1. The collection of articles in a recent issue of *On the Horizon* gives an excellent overview of issues. See Lee and Elsner (2008).

2. See Davis and Dolfsma (2008) and Lutz (2009) on varying interpretations of "social economics."

3. Note that, if an article in the "best of" issue was cited and the original article was published in 1993 or after, such citations were recorded in with the citations of the original work.

4. See Harzing and van der Wal (2008) for a comparison of Google Scholar versus ISI Web of Science as sources of data on citations.

5. An Appendix giving details of how journals were classified is available upon request.

6. See also Davis (2008) on the subject of dynamic interrelationships between heterodox and orthodox strands in economic research.

7. In cases when an article could fall under more than one category, I classified it according to the main contribution of the paper emphasized in its abstract and/or introduction. For example, an article that introduced the capabilities approach as a means of reinterpreting goals of economic development would be classified under "social theory" rather than development, on the grounds that its main innovation was the use of the capabilities approach, rather than advancing knowledge of economic development *per se.*

8. The ISI identifies all citations appearing in ISI journals in year t to articles published in that journal in years t-1 and t-2, and divides this by the number of articles published in that journal in those two years. The two-year citation measure used in the present article differs because analysis is not confined to citations in ISI journals and because we include citations in year t to articles published in year t, as well as those published in years t + 1 and

t + 2. (Note that concurrent citations are counted in the ISI's "immediacy factor," but not in its best-known "impact factor").

9. As discussed in Hicks (2004), bibliometric analysis suggests that the two- to three-year time horizon is appropriate for gauging the level of impact of articles in fast-moving scientific areas in which timely publication of specific empirical findings is central to the evolution of scholarly discourse—but less so for fields like math, psychology, and the social sciences, in which specific empirical findings constitute a smaller part of published research.

10. The difference is not significant, although that could reflect the relatively small number of papers in the category (14).

11. See Dymski (2009) for interesting discussion.

References

Colander, D. (2009). "Moving Beyond the Rhetoric of Pluralism: Suggestions for an 'Inside-the Mainstream' Heterodoxy." In *Economic Pluralism.* Eds. R. Garnett, E. Olsen, and M. Starr. London: Routledge, 36–47.

Cronin, B. (2010). "Boundary Influences in the Diffusion of Heterodox Economics." *American Journal of Economics and Sociology*—this issue.

Davis, J. (2008). "The Turn in Recent Economics and Return of Orthodoxy." *Cambridge Journal of Economics* 32(3): 349–366.

Davis, J., and W. Dolfsma, eds. (2008). *Elgar Companion to Social Economics.* Northhampton, MA: Edward Elgar.

Dolfsma, W., and L. Leydesdorff. (2008). "Journals as Constituents of Scientific Discourse: Economic Heterodoxy." *On the Horizon* 16(4): 214–225.

Dymski, G. (2009). "Afterward: Mortgage Markets and the Urban Problematic in the Global Transition." *International Journal of Urban and Regional Research* 33(2): 427–442.

Harzing, A-W., and R. van der Wal. (2008). "Google Scholar as a New Source for Citation Analysis." *Ethics in Science and Environmental Politics* 8(1): 62–71.

Hicks, D. (2004). "The Four Literatures of Social Science." In *Handbook of Quantitative Science and Technology Research.* Ed. Henk Moedd. Dordrecht, Netherlands, and Norwell, MA: Kluwer Academic, 473–496.

Lee, F. S. (2008). "A Case for Ranking Heterodox Journals and Departments." *On the Horizon* 16(4): 241–251.

———. (2010). "Research Quality Rankings of Heterodox Economic Journals in a Contested Discipline." *American Journal of Economics and Sociology*—this issue.

Lee, F. S., and W. Elsner. (2008). "Publishing, Ranking, and the Future of Heterodox Economics." *On the Horizon* 16(4): 176–184.

Kalaitzidakis, P., T. P. Mamuneas, and T. Stengos. (2003). "Rankings of Academic Journals and Institutions in Economics." *European Economic Association* 1(6): 1346–1366.

Lutz, M. (2009). "Social Economics." In *Handbook of Economics and Ethics.* Eds. J. Peil and I. Van Staveren. Northhampton, MA: Edward Elgar, 516–522.

Wall, Howard. (2009). "Journal Rankings in Economics: Handle with Care." Federal Reserve Bank of St. Louis Working Paper No. 2009-014A (April). Accessed electronically at: http://research.stlouisfed.org/wp/2009/2009-014.pdf.

Woolley, F. (2005). "The Citation Impact of Feminist Economics." *Feminist Economics* 11(3): 85–106.

The Diffusion of Heterodox Economics

By BRUCE CRONIN*

ABSTRACT. Heterodox economics is in part defined by exclusion from orthodox circles and there is an understandable tendency for heterodox economists to engage primarily with each other outside these circles. Yet the critique offered by heterodoxy speaks more widely. This study examines the diffusion of heterodox economic ideas beyond the immediate confines via an analysis of the citation of heterodox economic journals by other journals. The diffusion of heterodox economics across wider disciplines is traced utilizing data from Emerald, Wiley, and Sage bibliographic databases. Employing the techniques of social network analysis, key journals in the diffusion process are identified, with implications for heterodox economics publishing strategy and engagement in valuation processes.

The Diffusion of Heterodox Economics

The eruption of the latest in a long series of global financial crises underlines the stark contrast between the "normal science" of orthodox economics and the accumulating inconsistencies that, in Thomas Kuhn's well-known (1970) view, is the hallmark of a troubled paradigm. Yet, despite the extensive efforts of a growing heterodoxy since the late 1960s (Lee 2001, 2004; O'Hara 1995), there is little sign on the horizon of a "scientific revolution" in economics.

Heterodox economics is in part defined by exclusion from orthodox circles and so there is an understandable tendency for heterodox economists to engage primarily with each other outside these circles. At the same time orthodox economics is highly exclusionary itself (see Lee 2004). Yet the critique offered by heterodoxy speaks more widely, particularly to events such as these now and in the past, so it is perhaps surprising that there is not wider exchange with heterodox

*Department of International Business, University of Greenwich Business School, University of Greenwich, Park Row, London SE10 9LS, United Kingdom, E-mail: b.cronin@greenwich.ac.uk

American Journal of Economics and Sociology, Vol. 69, No. 5 (November, 2010).

views in mainstream economics. This study thus examines the diffusion of heterodox economic ideas beyond the immediate confines in an attempt to identify barriers to this process and potential strategies for change.

The diffusion process is examined via an analysis of the citation of heterodox economic journals by other journals. The diffusion of heterodox economics across wider disciplines is traced utilizing data from Emerald, Wiley, and Sage bibliographic databases. Employing the techniques of social network analysis, key journals in the diffusion process are identified, with implications for heterodox economics publishing strategy and engagement in valuation processes.

Literature

Kuhn's (1970) discussion of the emergence of scientific paradigms emphasizes the "normal science" of problem solving within the established parameters of a research community including associated methodological norms. But the process by which these norms are established and reproduced is considered only broadly, albeit the major significance attributed to their breakdown when inconsistencies accumulate within an established paradigm.

Kuhn defines a research community sociologically[1] as the product of similar education, careers, and social networks around a specialist canon of literature, together with a commitment to a particular professional community, normally among a group of overlapping identities. This shared activity underpins the distinctive values accorded to problems, discourse, relationships, and interpretations of common phenomena.[2] He argues that these only change with a gestalt shift that is very rare, citing Max Planck's (1949: 33–34) observation that,

> a new scientific truth does not triumph by convincing its opponents and making them see the light, but rather because its opponents eventually die, and a new generation grows up that is familiar with it.

Kuhn argues that an established paradigm remains established in large part because of the sunk costs of lifelong careers invested in the approach, in part due to the conservative nature of research communities, and in part because it remains more effective at solving a greater range of problems than any challenger, even in the face of accumulating anomalies. A new paradigm gains traction where it is able to solve those anomalies recognized by the established approach and when it promises to revisit earlier problems with more precision or open up a new set of problems that new adherents are interested in solving. Foucault (1980: 52), however, suggests the dynamic is not so much one of efficacy as of power: "the exercise of power itself creates and causes to emerge new objects of knowledge and accumulates new bodies of information . . . ."

Research on the sociology of social movements suggests that collection of adherents entails a process of differentiation (Merton 1973) and the contested, negotiated framing of collective identity (Gamson 1992; Goffman 1974). The strength of this framing varies in terms of interpretive scope, flexibility, inclusiveness, and resonance in terms of salience and credibility and the opportunities for framing provided by the social, cultural, and political environment[3] (Benford and Snow, 2000). Credibility is not only a product of internal consistency and empirical veracity but also of the credibility of frame articulators. Framing develops through discursive articulation and amplification of the salience of some aspect of the frame, through strategic alignment with other influential frames, by bridging, extending, or transforming the frame, and in contest with other frames (Benford and Snow 2000). Frames are contested internally in terms of interpretations, prescriptions, and strategies and externally by counterframing, more or less conscious attempts to rebut or undermine interpretative frameworks and core concepts, with institutional elites particularly influential (McAdam et al. 1996; Sabatier and Jenkins-Smith 1993; Welford 1997). And frames are contested by events, actions taken because of the framing transform understanding and thus the framing itself (Benford and Snow 2000).

Kuhn argues that the specific organization of modern research communities is simultaneously a source of immense productivity in the normal science of problem-solving and a source of orthodoxy. The key feature of such communities is individuals' commitment to research problems in detail and to find solutions to these problems acceptable by the community, that is, the arbiter of achievement is the community itself, albeit hierarchically organized on a paradigm-determined definition of professional competence. This community of self-arbitration is characterized by Whitley (1984), as "reputational work organization," supported by identities, participants, advocates, forums, and publicity (Fleck 1982; Hambrick and Chen 2008; Yoxen 1982).

Thus a research community is disciplinary; it disciplines behavior, both individual activity and interactions through the development of norms. For Foucault (1977), disciplinarity involves enclosing, partitioning, and ranking activity; a research community is legitimized by location in an academy with defined resources and procedures. Each member takes on a particular role within an established classification and the interactions between members are ordered by disciplinary norms, including classificatory systems. Thus a hierarchy is established among academic institutions, with those subscribing to the core of the discipline ranked most highly and most likely to interact and validate each others' activity, and those further away from the core most likely to be invalidated and excluded; in this way the capacity of the discipline is strengthened. Foucault emphasizes the role of formal examinations in determining individuals' position in a discipline, illustrated by the centrality of the peer-review publication process in academic communities. Similarly, Foucault's corrollorary of examination, confession, that is, the self-criticism necessary to discipline otherwise impenetrable motivations, operates through the mentoring and apprenticeship practices common in research communities.

A research community becomes established by mobilizing adherents to gain legitimacy, often around a claim of the social importance of the field (Merton 1973). Hambrick and Chen (2008: 34) suggest that a marker of academic legitimacy is when "a substantial number of major universities" designate staffing positions in the field to supervise graduate students, and resource allocations follow in terms of research funding and entry to academic journals and conferences. They argue that an important aspect in acceptance of a new field of study is its complementarity with the established fields, particularly adherence with "the norms, styles, and standards of adjacent established fields," though as Kuhn argues, research programs often develop in opposition to established norms (see also DiMaggio and Powell 1983; Meyer and Rowan 1977). This has resonance with Gramsci's (1971) concept of hegemonic alliances built from overlapping interests and with Sabatier and Jenkin-Smith's theory of policy advocacy coalitions built from overlapping secondary values alongside differing core values (Sabatier 1978; Sabatier and Jenkins-Smith 1993).

There is a structural element as well; a well-connected core and a heterogeneous periphery, providing novelty but also connection with accepted norms[4] (Marwell et al. 1988; Mizruchi and Stearns 2001; Reagans and Zuckerman 2001; Uzzi 1996). White (1992) suggests a hierarchy in the core-periphery relationship, indexing disciplines not just in terms of embeddness or density of ties but also qualitatively in terms of differentiation and dependence. In a study of junior faculty recruitment, Han (2003) finds such a hierarchy and to be particularly strongly defined in economics.

The pattern of core and peripheral interaction can be detected in interjournal citation. Journals are the key repository for academic output, distinctive journals central to the emerging identity of subdisciplines, and the hierarchy of journals underpinning the ordering of a discipline. A large body of work on the bibliometry of journal citation has helped delineate disciplines and subdisciplines and the hierarchy of journals within disciplines (e.g., Crane 1972; McCain 1984; Mullins 1973; Price 1965). While this work has traditionally centered on citation counts, recent efforts introducing the methods of social network analysis have begun to uncover more complex relationships that allow the detection of social order and hierarchy (e.g., Casey and McMillan 2008; Leydesdorff 2004; Rice et al. 1988).

The dynamics of disciplinary construction are particularly pertinent for sub- or emerging disciplines. As a field self-defined outside the disciplinary core of economics, heterodox economics faces the challenge of maintaining its own core while developing complementarity with the hierarchically ordered adjacent fields. This study therefore aims to extend existing research on the constitution of the heterodox economic community (Cronin 2008; Dolfsma and Leydesdorff 2008; Lee 2008) to explore its interactions with adjacent subdisciplines of economics, making use of the emergent bibliometric applications of social network analysis. By examining the borders of the subfield of heterodox economics formed by interjournal citation these techniques provide a means to identify adjacent or overlapping subfields. This offers the possibility of developing a strategy to increase recognition of the contributions of the heterodox approach in dealing with the accumulating anomalies encountered in the normal science of the established paradigm.

Data and Methods

Three major bibliographic databases, Wiley Interscience, Science Direct, and Sage, were searched for citations of articles from a list of journals categorized as heterodox economic by Lee (2008) over a common period of coverage, 1999–2007. Heterodox journals included in the database, such as the *Review of Radical Political Economics* published by Sage, were excluded from the citation data. So the dataset comprised citations of heterodox journals by nonheterodox journals.

Each citation of an article in a heterodox journal by an article in another journal was counted as an observation. The citation data were analyzed as a cumulative social network (for an examination of citation patterns among heterodox journals themselves, see Cronin 2008) using UCINET 6.0 and NETDRAW 2.1 software (Borgatti et al. 2002) to map the network of journal interrelationships formed by cross-journal citations. Clusters of closely and peripherally related journals were then identified, suggesting areas of primary or secondary disciplinarity commonality between heterodox and nonheterodox journals[5].

The core of journals most closely related to the group of heterodox journals through citation was identified by means of a k-core analysis (Seidman 1983). This allows the identification of the group of journals most closely interrelated at a particular density of connection, areas that contain clique-like structures. Within this core, particularly connected journals can be identified with the concepts of degree centrality and eigenvector centrality (Bonacich 1972; Freeman 1978). Degree centrality is simply a normalized count of the number of citations of articles in heterodox economics journals by articles in other journals; heterodox economics journals with the highest indegree are those most cited by other journals, while other journals with the highest outdegree are those that cite heterodox economics journals the most. Eigenvector centrality weights degree centrality by the centrality of each node connected; other journals with the highest eigenvector cite heterodox economic journals that are more highly cited by other journals, so it is a measure of intensity of engagement with heterodox economics. Betweenness centrality, a common indicator of brokerage in networks, is of limited value in this analysis because it would simply serve to highlight the given central intermediary position of the heterodox economics journals being cited.

Results

As presented in Table 1, the 20 identified heterodox economics journals were cited by other journals 2,618 times during the period, 327 times per year, with the *Cambridge Journal of Economics* and the *Journal of Economic Issues* the most cited. Because each database is constructed on the journals owned by the publisher, the data were examined for any distinctive citation patterns around each publisher. Journals in the Science Direct database were most likely to cite heterodox economics journals, particularly the *Cambridge Journal of Economics, Journal of Economic Issues,* and *Economy and Society.* Journals in the Sage database were more likely to cite a subset of heterodox journals, particularly *New Left Review, Feminist Economics,* and the *Review of Radical Political Economics.* With 262 citations over the eight-year period, Wiley journals rarely cited heterodox economics journals. This distinctiveness in citation activity by publisher suggests not only discipline specialism but also distinctive publishing agendas that may have strategic implications for heterodox publishing.

Figure 1 presents a visualization of the citation of heterodox economic journals by other journals listed in the three databases. Four clusters are apparent. *CC, ROAPE, RM,* and *NLR* are the core journals cited by the Sage group, with *NLR* being somewhat independent of the others. *FE, CNS, ES,* and *SS* are on the border of the Sage group and Science Direct journals. *ROSE, RBPE, ROPE, RIPE, CPE,* and *ME* are more to the center of the Science Direct and Wiley citations, but ME again somewhat independent. *JEI, IRAE, JPKE,* and *CJE* are on another border between Sage and Science Direct. Interestingly, among *CJE, RPE,* and *RORPE,* which are key intermediaries among heterodox

Table 1

Citations of Heterodox Journals by Database

	Sage	Science Direct	Wiley	All citations	Citations p.a.
Capital & Class (CC)	**76**	72	15	163	20.4
Cambridge Journal of Economics (CJE)	118	**167**	32	317	39.6
Capital, Nature Socialism (CNS)	**35**	29	6	70	8.8
Contributions to Political Economy (CPE)	8	**16**	2	26	3.3
Economy & Society (ES)	35	**120**	21	176	22.0
Feminist Economics (FE)	**85**	50	50	185	23.1
International Review of Applied Economics (IRAE)	33	**62**	8	103	12.9
Journal of Economic Issues (JEI)	125	**140**	32	297	37.1
Journal of Post Keynesian Economics (JPKE)	40	**64**	12	116	14.5
Metroeconomica (ME)	11	**100**	15	126	15.8
New Left Review (NLR)	**187**	91	19	297	37.1
Review of Black Political Economy (RBPE)	**53**	38	8	99	12.4
Review of International Political Economy (RIPE)	22	17	1	40	5.0
Rethinking Marxism (RM)	**53**	21	5	79	9.9
Review of African Political Economy (ROAPE)	**72**	52	15	139	17.4
Review of Political Economy (ROPE)	0	**45**	7	52	6.5
Review of Radical Political Economics (RORPE)	**81**	59	0	140	17.5
Review of Social Economics (ROSE)	**65**	59	14	138	17.3
Research in Political Economy (RPE)	**30**	0	0	30	3.8
Science & Society (SS)	**25**	0	0	25	3.1
Total	1,154	1,202	262	2,618	327.3

Note. Figures in bold indicate the database from which the journal received the most citations.

Figure 1

Citation of Heterodox Economic Journals by Sage, Science Direct, and
Wiley Journals

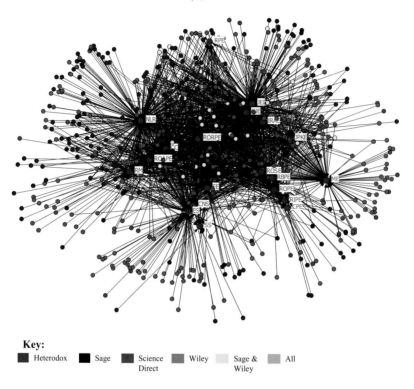

Key:

| ■ Heterodox | ■ Sage | ▨ Science Direct | ■ Wiley | ▨ Sage & Wiley | ▨ All |

journals themselves (Cronin 2008), it is *RORPE* that stands most
prominently at the center of external citation.

The network of 2,618 citations has a density of 0.192, with density
being the total of all ties divided by the number of possible ties (20
heterodox economic journals x 683 other journals = 13,660). The
mean citation by each other journal during the eight-year period is
3.83 and the mean citation of each heterodox economic journal by
each other journal is 0.19. So rather than a journal by journal analysis,
a group analysis of the pool of heterodox economic journals is more
appropriate.

The k-core analysis identified the most connected journals as those being connected by a path distance of 12 (k = 12). The other journals in this group, all with an outdegree centrality of 12 or more, are presented in Table 2, together with the normalized eigenvector centrality of each. The latter measure represents how intensively each journal engages with heterodox economic journals. As demonstrated in Table 3, this measure of reach is somewhat independent of the extensiveness of citation, as these journals cite less frequently than those in Table 2 but have greater eigenvector centrality than some.

As illustrated in Figure 1, heterodox economics is far from monolithic, with at least four distinct sets of relations with other journals evident. Social network analysis provides the means to delineate this clustering in detail via factional analysis. UCINET has a routine to undertake a tabu search to find a best fit of groups of related connections within a specified partition of a network (Borgatti et al. 2002). As discussed earlier, visual inspection of the network suggests the heterodox community is broadly partitioned into four, with three intermediary positions. But, as presented in Table 4, a seven-part partitioning using this routine essentially isolates only two groups of heterodox economic and related other journals, three clusters of other journals with one or two heterodox economic journals within them, and two clusters of other journals with no related heterodox economic journal. The main cluster encompasses half the journals and is mostly U.S.-based. The second cluster is arguably a more united, European-based, subdiscipline.[6] Figures 2 and 3 present the pattern of citation of heterodox economic journals by other journals within each of these two clusters within the 12-core. Finally, Figure 4 presents the next "ring" of slightly less connected journals, the 11-core.

Discussion

A social network approach to bibliographic analysis provides a number of insights that a traditional citation count approach does not. Citation counts highlight the journals most frequently citing another journal or a group of journals, as in Table 2. But it misses the clustering effect identified in the k-core analysis that highlights journals with lower raw counts but that cite the core of the heterodox set.

Table 2

Other Journals Within the Highest k-Core

Citing Journal	Degree Centrality	Normalized Eigenvector Centrality
Urban Studies	19	11.76
Progress in Human Geography	17	11.27
World Development	16	10.97
Geoforum	16	10.94
Critical Sociology	17	10.90
Futures	16	10.79
Journal of Socio-Economics	16	10.50
Social Science & Medicine	15	10.34
Journal of Development Economics	15	10.19
Economic and Industrial Democracy	14	10.15
Social Science Journal	15	9.90
Critical Perspectives on Accounting	14	9.82
International Sociology	13	9.69
Journal of Rural Studies	14	9.69
Journal of Economic Behavior & Organization	16	9.65
Political Geography	13	9.42
Ecological Economics	14	9.22
European Journal of Political Economy	14	9.18
Organization Environment	14	8.78
The Annals of the American Academy of Political and Social Science	14	8.69
Current Sociology	12	8.34
American Behavioral Scientist	13	8.30
Journal of Sociology	12	8.18
Journal of International Development	12	7.96

K = 12.

Table 3

Other Journals Outside the 12-Core with High
Eigenvector Centrality

Citing Journal	Degree Centrality	Normalized Eigenvector Centrality
Work Employment Society	14	10.06
Journal of Industrial Relations	14	10.03
Human Relations	12	9.54
Progress in Development Studies	12	9.14
Journal of Management	10	9.11
Organization Studies	13	9.02
Structural Change and Economic Dynamics	13	8.96
Journal of Economic Psychology	12	8.73
Accounting, Organizations and Society	11	8.64
Critical Social Policy	11	8.49
Organization	11	8.39
Women's Studies International Forum	10	8.22
Land Use Policy	11	8.20
Media Culture Society	11	8.08
Journal of Family Issues	9	8.04
Acta Sociologica	10	8.02

As shown in Table 2, *Current Sociology, American Behavioral Scientist, Journal of Sociology,* and *Journal of International Development* are of this type, that is, key intermediaries in the external field. The traditional approach also overlooks journals that may have lower citation counts but cite journals that themselves are highly cited, that is, the more prominent journals in the heterodox set, as presented in Table 3. The network approach thus can highlight engagement with the mainstream conversation between different schools of thought.

The pattern of interjournal citations displays the core-periphery structure indicative of a distinctive subdiscipline, confirming the sampling strategy. The k-core analysis demonstrates an ordering of relationships beyond that discipline, a hierarchy in White's and

Table 4

Clustering of Heterodox Economics Journals Within a
Seven-Part Partition

Cluster 1

Cambridge Journal of Economics (CJE)
Contributions to Political Economy (CPE)
International Review of Applied Economics (IRAE)
Journal of Post Keynesian Economics (JPKE)
Metroeconomica (ME)

Cluster 2

Review of Black Political Economy (RBPE)

Cluster 3

Capital, Nature Socialism (CNS)
Review of Political Economy (ROPE)

Cluster 4

Capital & Class (CC)
Feminist Economics (FE)
Journal of Economic Issues (JEI)
New Left Review (NLR)
Review of International Political Economy (RIPE)
Rethinking Marxism (RM)
Review of African Political Economy (ROAPE)
Review of Radical Political Economics (RORPE)
Review of Social Economics (ROSE)
Research in Political Economy (RPE)
Science & Society (SS)

Cluster 5

Economy & Society (ES)

Foucault's terms, with overlapping secondary interests characteristic of complementarity with adjacent fields.

The characteristics of this pattern of interaction offer the possibility of a strategy to increase the influence of the subdiscipline through enhanced framing; amplifying the salience of some aspect of the frame in alignment with adjacent frames. This engages the aligned frames in

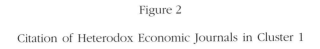

Figure 2

Citation of Heterodox Economic Journals in Cluster 1

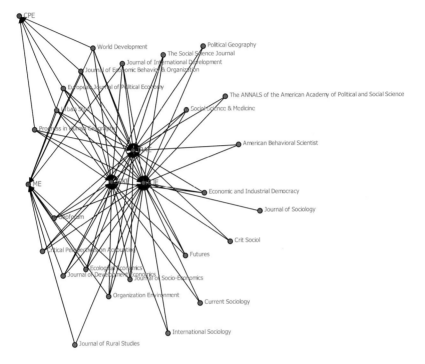

shared discourse that demarcates the distinctive values underpinning the alignment, important to the growth of a Kuhnian paradigm. In practical terms, such a strategy would involve publication of salient aspects of the heterodox discourse in the journals most closely aligned with the heterodox frame; those in the 12-core and those most closely clustered with the particular subgroups of the heterodox set. Publication of heterodox approaches in key intermediary journals also provides opportunities to bridge frames.

Identification of the salient aspects of the heterodox discourse is important. While changes in the social, cultural, and political environment provide environment, Benford and Snow (2000) argue that framing is strengthened not only by salience but also interpretive

Figure 3

Citation of Heterodox Economic Journals in Cluster 4

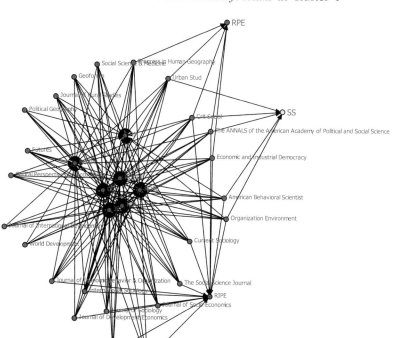

scope, flexibility, inclusiveness, and credibility. Likewise, Kuhn emphasizes that a new paradigm gains traction where it solves anomalies recognized in the mainstream and treats these with more precision or opens issues that aligned frames are interested in.

As Merton, Foucault, and White argue, differentiation is key to mobilization. Perhaps, controversially, this suggests that the emergence of salient aspects of the discourse can be accelerated by enclosing, partitioning, and ranking activity. White, in fact, suggests this can be measured both qualitatively in terms of differentiation and dependence and quantitatively in terms of embeddness or density of ties, as employed in this study.

Figure 4

Citation of Heterodox Economic Journals in the 11-Core

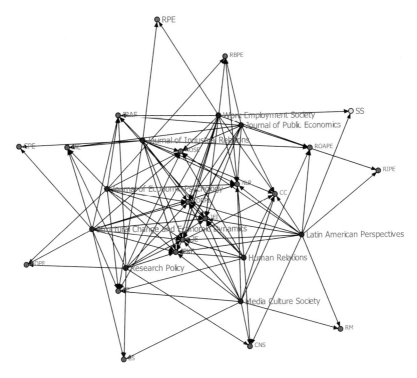

Conclusion

The entrenched orthodoxy that characterizes economics and cripples its ability to anticipate major events emerging outside its paradigm is often portrayed as monolithic and impenetrable by outsiders and the natural order of things by its practitioners. There is an understandable tendency for subdisciplines, particularly heterodox perspectives, to stick to their own. But this study has demonstrated that there is an ordering to the different perspectives within economics, with some perspectives more engaged with some than others. This provides the basis for strategy, the alignment of interests, and the strengthening of a counter-paradigm.

The pattern of interjournal citation detected by applying social network analytic methods to bibliographic data fits the expectations of disciplinary ordering of theorists from Kuhn to Merton, Foucault, and White. It is thus reasonable to expect that the strategies suggested by related theorists as to how cognitive frames and social coalitions are developed are applicable to the diffusion of heterodox ideas. Certainly, the political-economic bases of the power of orthodox economics is a large part of the story and need careful examination in the development of strategy but part of the exclusion of heterodox perspectives from the mainstream also lies in the limited attempts at systematic engagement with complementary perspectives.

A central part of this Gramscian "war of position" is to differentiate the salient parts of heterodox perspectives that have both explanatory power and resonate with the concerns of adjacent frames. This involves deepening the rigor and explanatory power of the core ideas while aligning with other frames on secondary values. Strengthening the core frame, then, implies enhancing its disciplinarity through Foucauldian examination and confession, while maintaining the flexibility and resonance to mobilize widely. While heterodox discourse has recently broadened, explicit advocacy of pluralism pointing to the recognition of the need for flexibility (Cronin 2008), it is less clear whether the core disciplinarity is being strengthened, which is necessary to maintain the credible side of resonance. White's method of disciplinary indexing offers a potential test of this for future exploration.

Notes

1. Cf. Kuhn (1962), which defined it tautologically as those who share a paradigm, a paradigm being what the community shares.

2. Later specified as symbolic generalizations, relational beliefs, values, and exemplars.

3. For example, Operations Research had its origins in the logistical needs of the U.K. and U.S. armies during World War II (Kirby 2000).

4. Examining the differentiation within management studies from the 1980s into subfields of strategic management, international business, and business and society, Hambrick and Chen (2008) identify the more unified elite Harvard-based core underpinning the rapid growth of the first.

5. The network was visualized using a default spring-embedded algorithm, utilizing geodesic distances, a distance between components of 5 and 100 iterations, calculating Distances + N.R. + Equal Edge Lengths and starting with a Gower scaling.

6. I am grateful to Carlo D'Oppoliti for the observation of the geographical distinction in this clustering.

References

Benford, R., and D. Snow. (2000). "Framing Processes and Social Movements: An Overview and Assessment." *Annual Review of Sociology* 26: 611–639.

Bonacich, P. (1972). "Factoring and Weighting Approaches to Status Scores and Clique Identification." *Journal of Mathematical Sociology* 2: 113–120.

Borgatti, S. P., M. G. Everett, and L. C. Freeman. (2002). UCINET *for Windows: Software for Social Network Analysis.* Harvard, MA: Analytic Technologies.

Casey, D., and G. S. McMillan. (2008). "Identifying the 'Invisible Colleges' of the Industrial and Labour Relations Review: A Bibliometric Approach." *Industrial and Labour Relations Review* 62(1): 126–132.

Crane, D. (1972). *Invisible Colleges: Diffusion of Information in Scientific Communities.* Chicago: University of Chicago Press.

Cronin, B. (2008). "Journal Citation Among Heterodox Economists 1995–2007: Dynamics of Community Emergence." *On the Horizon* 16(4): 226–240.

DiMaggio, P. J., and W. W. Powell. (1983). "The Iron Cage Revisited: Institutional Isomorphism and Collective Rationality in Organisational Fields." *American Sociological Review* 48(2): 147–160.

Dolfsma, W., and L. Leydesdorff. (2008). "Journals as Constituents of Scientific Discourse: Economic Heterodoxy." *On the Horizon* 16(4): 214–225.

Fleck, J. (1982). "On the Autonomy of Pure Science: The Construction and Maintenance of Barriers Between Scientific Establishments and Popular Culture." In *Scientific Establishments and Hierarchies.* Eds. N. Elias and R. Whitley, pp. 267–292. Dordrecht: Reidel.

Foucault, M. (1977). *Discipline and Punish: The Birth of the Prison.* London: Penguin.

——. (1980). *Power/Knowledge: Selected Interviews and Other Writings by Michel Foucault, 1972–77* (C. Gordon, Ed.). Brighton: Harvester.

Freeman, L. C. (1978). "Centrality in Social Networks: Conceptual Clarification." *Social Networks* 1(1): 215–239.

Gamson, W. A. (1992). *Talking Politics.* New York: Cambridge University Press.

Goffman, E. (1974). *Frame Analysis: An Essay on the Organization of Experience.* Garden City, NY: Anchor Books.

Gramsci, A. (1971). *Selections from Prison Notebooks.* New York: International Publishers.

Hambrick, D. C., and M.-J. Chen. (2008). "New Academic Fields as Admittance-Seeking Social Movements: The Case of Strategic Management." *Academy of Management Review* 33(1): 32–54.

Han, S.-K. (2003). "Tribal Regimes in Academia: A Comparative Analysis of Market Structure Across Disciplines." *Social Networks* 25(3): 251–280.

Kirby, M. W. (2000). "Operations Research Trajectories: The Anglo-American Experience from the 1940s to the 1990s." *Operations Research* 48(5): 661–670.

Kuhn, T. S. (1962). *The Structure of Scientific Resolutions*. Chicago: University of Chicago Press.

———. (1970). *The Structure of Scientific Resolutions*. 2nd Enlarged. Chicago: University of Chicago Press.

Lee, F. S. (2001). "Conference of Socialist Economists and the Emergence of Heterodox Economics in Post-War Britain." *Capital and Class* 75: 15–39.

———. (2004). "To be a Heterodox Economist: The Contested Landscape of American Economics, 1960s and 1970s." *Journal of Economic Issues* 38(3): 747–763.

———. (2008). "A Case for Ranking Heterodox Journals and Departments." *On the Horizon* 16(4): 241–251.

Leydesdorff, L. (2004). "Clusters and Maps of Science Journals Based on Bi-Connected Graphs in Journal Citation Reports." *Journal of Documentation* 60(4): 371–427.

Marwell, G., P. E. Oliver, and R. Prahl. (1988). "Social Networks and Collective Action: A Theory of the Critical Mass. III." *American Journal of Sociology* 94(3): 502–534.

McAdam, D., J. D. McCarthy, and M. N. Zald, eds. (1996). *Comparative Perspectives on Social Movements Opportunities, Mobilizing Structures, and Framing*. Cambridge: Cambridge University Press.

McCain, K. W. (1984). "Longitudinal Author Cocitation Mapping: The Changing Structure of Macroeconomics." *Journal of the American Society for Information Science* 35(6): 332–343.

Merton, R. K. (1973). "Social Conflict Over Styles of Sociological Work." In *The Sociology of Science: The Theoretical and Empirical Investigations*. Ed. R. K. Merton, pp. 47–69. Chicago: University of Chicago Press.

Meyer, J. W., and B. Rowan. (1977). "Institutionalized Organizations: Formal Structure as Myth and Ceremony." *American Journal of Sociology* 83(2): 340–363.

Mizruchi, M. S., and L. B. Stearns. (2001). "Getting Deals Done: The Use of Social Networks in Bank Decision-Making." *American Sociological Review* 66(5): 647–671.

Mullins, N. C. (1973). *Theories and Theory Groups in Contemporary American Sociology*. New York: Harper & Row.

O'Hara, P. A. (1995). "The Association for Evolutionary Economics and the Union for Radical Political Economics: General Issues of Continuity and Integration." *Journal of Economic Issues* 29(1): 137–159.

Planck, M. (1949). *Scientific Autobiography and Other Papers.* New York: Philosophical Library.

Price, J. D. d. S. (1965). "Networks of Scientific Papers." *Science,* 149(3683): 510–515.

Reagans, R., and E. W. Zuckerman. (2001). "Networks, Diversity, and Productivity: The Social Capital of Corporate R&D Teams." *Organization Science* 12(4): 502–517.

Rice, R. E., C. L. Borgman, and B. Reeves. (1988). "Citation Networks of Communication Journals, 1977–1985: Cliques and Positions, Citations Made and Citations Received." *Human Communication Research* 15(2): 256–283.

Sabatier, P. (1978). "The Acquisition and Utilization of Technical Information by Administrative Agencies." *Administrative Science Quarterly* 23(3): 396–417.

Sabatier, P. A., and H. C. Jenkins-Smith, eds. (1993). *Policy Change and Learning: An Advocacy Coalition Approach.* Boulder, CO.: Westview.

Seidman, S. (1983). "Network Structure and Minimum Degree." *Social Networks* 5(3): 269–287.

Uzzi, B. (1996). "The Sources and Consequences of Embeddedness for the Economic Performance of Organizations: The Network Effect." *American Sociological Review* 61(4): 674–698.

Welford, R. (1997). "From Green to Golden: The Hijacking of Environmentalism." In *Hijacking Environmentalism: Corporate Responses to Sustainable Development.* Ed. R. Welford, pp. 16–39. London: Earthscan.

White, H. C. (1992). *Identity and Control: A Structural Theory of Social Action.* Princeton, NJ: Princeton University Press.

Whitley, R. (1984). *The Intellectual and Social Organization of the Sciences.* Oxford: Clarendon Press.

Yoxen, E. (1982). "Giving Life in a New Meaning: The Rise of the Molecular Biology Establishment." In *Scientific Establishments and Hierarchies.* Eds. N. Elias and R. Whitley, pp. 123–144. Dordrecht: Reidel.

Pluralism at Risk? Heterodox Economic Approaches and the Evaluation of Economic Research in Italy

By Marcella Corsi, Carlo D'Ippoliti, and Federico Lucidi*

ABSTRACT. We analyze Italy's recent research evaluation exercise (VTR) as a salient example in discussing some internationally relevant issues emerging from the evaluation of research in economics. We claim that evaluation and its criteria, together with its linkage to research institutions' financing, are likely to affect the direction of research in a problematic way. As the Italian case documents, it is specifically economists who adopt unorthodox paradigms or pursue less diffused topics of research that should be concerned about research evaluation and its criteria. After outlining the recent practice of economic research in Italy and highlighting the relevant scope for pluralism that traditionally characterizes it, we analyze the publications submitted for evaluation to the VTR. By comparing these publications to all the entries in the EconLit database authored by economists located in Italy, we find a risk that the adopted ranking criteria may lead to disregarding historical methods in favor of quantitative and econometric methods, and heterodox schools in favor of mainstream approaches. Finally, by summarizing the current debate in Italy, we claim that evaluation should not be refused by heterodox economists, but rather that a reflection on the criteria of evaluation should be put forward at an international level in order to establish fair

*Marcella Corsi and Carlo D'Ippoliti are at the Department of Social, Economic, Actuarial and Demographic Studies of the University of Rome "La Sapienza," Viale Regina Elena 295/E, 00161 Rome, Italy. Federico Lucidi is at the Fondazione Giacomo Brodolini, Viale di Villa Massimo 21, 00161 Rome, Italy. Contacts: marcella.corsi@uniroma1.it, carlo.dippoliti@uniroma1.it, lucidi@fondazionebrodolini.it.

This work is part of the project "*La valutazione della ricerca nelle Università italiane: criticità dei metodi adottati e proposte alternative*" (coordinator: Marcella Corsi), financed by the Sapienza University of Rome. We are grateful to the other members of the research team for their fruitful comments and to Andrea Salvatori for his constructive criticism. Usual disclaimers apply.

American Journal of Economics and Sociology, Vol. 69, No. 5 (November, 2010).
© 2010 American Journal of Economics and Sociology, Inc.

competition among research paradigms, thus, preserving pluralism in the discipline.

Introduction

This article aims at presenting the recent experience of Italy's first research assessment exercise (VTR, *valutazione triennale della ricerca*) as an internationally relevant example in highlighting a neglected aspect of the evaluation of economic research, that is, the impact of research evaluation on research practice itself.

It will be shown that particularly (but not exclusively) when financial resources are linked to the outcome of the evaluation, procedures and criteria of assessment may create strong incentives for researchers and research institutions to modify their original aims and strategies. Thus, it is crucial to set clear principles and objectives for economic research and to conduct any research assessment on the basis of these objectives. As the case of Italy shows, when pluralism is not explicitly among these goals, the assessment exercise may result in a marginalization of minority approaches, which instead, may be deemed worthy of survival and cultivation, both by policymakers and the scientific community.

The case of Italy is especially suited for our aims for two reasons: on one hand, pluralism of methods and topics within economics is traditionally well established in the Italian academia (if not in absolute terms, in an international comparison). Therefore, Italy's case is convenient for exemplification but is also relevant *per se*, at least from the perspective of certain economic approaches. On the other hand, the recent research assessment exercise in Italy (VTR) exhibits certain characteristics that clearly highlight the risks as well as the potentiality of research evaluation, with the aim of preserving and developing heterodox economic approaches, along with providing the *stimulus* for a lively and healthy debate within the mainstream.

Our findings support the view that if research institutions are encouraged to engage only in the lines of research that are likely to receive the highest rating according to the evaluation criteria adopted within the VTR, a convergence process is to be expected within economics, resulting in a potential disregard of heterodox schools and historical methods, and in favor of mainstream "Anglo-Saxon" approaches and quantitative methods. Ultimately, research pluralism may be harmed. These objections have been highlighted by Lee and Harley (1998), Lee (2007), and Lee and Elsner (2008) with reference to the U.K. Research Assessment Exercise. These works show that evaluations based on the criteria of closeness to mainstream economics, by means of the subsequent allocation of funds, may shape economic research in the middle-to-long run toward the disappearance of non-mainstream research fields. Thus, a critical reflection about the rating and ranking criteria adopted in the evaluation exercise is necessary.

Specifically, we conduct a statistical analysis of the publications evaluated within the VTR, contrasting them to a comparable subsample of the EconLit dataset. Our aim is to highlight systematic patterns in the selection of the publications submitted for evaluation. The underlying hypothesis, attaching relevance to this analysis, is that research institutions in the future will discourage the development of research topics (or approaches) that they deem unsuitable for evaluation because they are less likely to be positively ranked and thus, given the link between evaluation and funding, to contribute to the institutions' budgets.

Our main point is that, if evaluation is implicitly based on the criterion of proximity to the mainstream, as it was done in Italy's case, such behavior on the side of institutions may negatively affect the financing of research projects by nonmainstream economists as well as their hiring and career prospects. On the contrary, we claim that it is advisable and indeed possible to conduct research assessments that prove rigorous in assessing quality and at the same time are respectful of pluralism. For these purposes, evaluation should be based on the principles of accountability of the evaluators, transparency of aims and processes, and fair competition of research approaches and of institutions.

This article is organized as follows: the next section briefly outlines the scope and relevance of pluralism in economic research in Italy, highlighting the historical origin and the current diffusion of "heterodox" approaches to economics in Italy. The following section describes the mechanism and procedures of the VTR. The fourth section presents the results of our statistical analysis, and our conclusions summarize the ongoing debate on the evaluation of economic research in Italy and place our contribution in this context.

On Pluralism in Economic Research

Italian Context

It would be well beyond the aim of the present work to provide a complete picture of all the topics and approaches to economic research currently pursued in Italy. However, it appears possible to highlight their variety and scope, in terms of a lively competition between geographical locations, public and private sector, single research centers and institutions, and most notably among alternative methodological and theoretical approaches and research fields.

As Pasinetti and Roncaglia (2006) highlight, this plurality may be considered partly as a result, and partly as a reaction, to the long period of dictatorship that Italy experienced in the 20th century.

Indeed, Italy has been at the frontier of economic research since its inception. As Roncaglia (2005) points out, we could even date it back to the Middle Ages with the Scholastic writers, or the 17th century with Bernardo Davanzati and Antonio Serra. Since the tradition of moral philosophy and humanistic studies (which political economy was a part of) was largely fostered during the Enlightenment period, it should not come as a surprise that between the end of the 18th and the beginning of the 19th century, Italian writers heavily contributed to the early development of the marginalist approach to economics, for example, with Vilfredo Pareto, Maffeo Pantaleoni, and Enrico Barone.

The advent of fascism affected the development of economic research in Italy in three ways: a) it required academics to make a vow of loyalty to the Fascist Party; b) it imposed autarchy and a corporatist philosophy of the economic system; c) it promulgated racial laws. As a consequence, eminent economists (such as Piero Sraffa) decided to move out of the country, not to be involved in the totalitarian regime, or they were forced to move to avoid persecution because of their faith (as Franco Modigliani was).

The economists who stayed in Italy were isolated from the international debate and frequently focused on narrow topics such as monetary issues or business cycles, or applied issues, which afforded greater intellectual freedom from the cultural yoke of the regime. After World War II, it was rightfully decided to avoid a cleansing of these scholars, limiting the democratic reaction to the dismissal only of those few academics who were most actively involved with the dictatorship.

The survival of the old school generated a favorable environment for further development of applied economics within and outside universities. This development occurred in governmental agencies aimed at forecasting (ISCO, the Istituto di Studi sulla Congiuntura), planning (ISPE, the Istituto di Studi per la Programmazione Economica), and/or supporting policy making, for example, within ministries (as in the case of the SVIMEZ, the agency for the development of the *Mezzogiorno*) or the Bank of Italy. These agencies gained a certain reputation in the cultural and political debate, as did private research centers such as that of Confindustria (Italy's largest entrepreneurs' association), and within trade unions.

Overall, this institutional plurality corresponded to a certain plurality of points of view, especially concerning policy implications.

However, a crucial boost to the reprise of internationally relevant economic research came from the many scholarships and grants aimed at allowing brilliant students to spend periods of study and research abroad. Partly due to the presence of the mentioned personalities of Sraffa and Modigliani, and partly because these were already attractive gravitation centers for Italian researchers, Cambridge (U.K.) and the Massachusetts Institute of Technology (MIT) became crucial learning centers for Italian economists, along with Oxford with John Hicks, and to some extent Harvard with J. A. Schumpeter.

The youngest generations were thus confronted with approaches rather different than that of Friedman's Chicago and the Monetarist School, being that they were more acquainted with the Austrian School and the neoclassical synthesis *à la* Hicks and Modigliani, or with more radical critiques and alternatives to static marginalism, especially the Keynesian and Sraffian approaches in Cambridge, and Schumpeter's evolutionary approach.

Along these lines, with the crucial contribution of students and researchers returning from periods abroad, the largest universities became autonomous centers of research and training, which developed a lively and even heated debate, though they usually did not develop their own "schools."[1]

The wide scope of methods and topics pursued by these masters determined the variety and pluralism of the subsequent generations of scholars working in Italy today. Without any pretensions to completeness and without specifying the affiliation of any scholar to a certain school of thought, it is possible to identify peculiar traits, foreign to the mainstream, and rather close to post-Keynesian and Sraffian traditions (as practiced, for example, by Luigi Pasinetti, Pierangelo Garegnani, Augusto Graziani, Claudio Napoleoni, Sergio Parrinello, Alessandro Roncaglia, Neri Salvadori, Luigi Spaventa, Mario Tonveronachi, or by international scholars who worked in Italy for certain periods, such as Jan Kregel among others); to the feminists (Tindara Addabbo, Elisabetta Addis, Francesca Bettio, Marcella Corsi, Daniela Del Boca, Antonella Picchio, Annamaria Simonazzi, Paola Villa); as well as to the evolutionists, experimentalists, and behavioralists (Giovanni Dosi, Massimo Egidi, Mauro Gallegati, or eminent foreign scholars who work—also—in Italy, such as John Hey, Samuel Bowles, and Axel Leijonhufvud).

As above mentioned, these approaches flourished side by side with the cultivation of the neoclassical paradigm, more or less related to its neoclassical synthesis variant, by authors such as Tito Boeri, Francesco Giavazzi, Tullio Jappelli, Marco Pagano, Pietro Reichlin, and Guido Tabellini (to mention a few), and the Italian economists who after their studies kept working abroad (mostly in the United States and the United Kingdom): Alberto Alesina and Orazio Attanasio, for example, who frequently participate in Italy's academic and political debate.

The plurality of points of view determined in Italy a habit and openness to the debate on the foundations of our discipline, greater than in Anglo-Saxon countries, in Austria and Germany, and in some sense closer (for example) to the atmosphere emerging in France, India, or Japan.

These fundamental debates are also related to, and the cause of, a widespread cultivation of the history of economic thought (with such authors as Giancarlo De Vivo, Maria Cristina Marcuzzo, and Annalisa Rosselli), a discipline that was already considered by the older tradition of economics in Italy not as a distinct field of inquiry, but as a fundamental tool of core economic analysis.

At the same time, the survival of the old applied tradition, largely flexible concerning the underlying theory for the reasons hinted at above, and the preservation of pluralism of topics and methods within it, was particularly encouraged by the specific economic vicissitudes of Italy's reconstruction and Italy's subsequent role "at the frontier" of the Cold War. We can thus find diverse fields of research such as the studies on *Mezzogiorno* and on unbalanced local development, on international monetary systems, distribution of income, division of labor and international trade, industrial districts, and the construction of structural econometric models. Partly linked to these streams of research is the research on econometrics and quantitative methods, carried on by internationally visible scholars such as Marco Lippi or Franco Peracchi.

These applied themes are often dealt with in a perspective that is "not fully mainstream," although their characterization as "heterodox" is not obvious, for example, when looking at simple quantitative parameters (such as keywords, cited literature, JEL codes). Nonetheless, a quantitative outlook of the current composition of Italy's research practice, outlined in the next section, may help define the peculiarity of the case under study.

A Quantitative View

Beside the problems of identification mentioned in the previous paragraph, it should be remarked that the very definition of "heterodox" approaches is problematic and controversial: some authors or schools may perceive themselves as mainstream, while being considered unorthodox by others, or vice versa. For this reason, lacking an *ad hoc* sample on researchers' identification and self-identification (as was done by Axarloglou and Theoharakis, 2003), in the remainder of the article we will define *mainstream* and *heterodox* approaches according to publications' JEL codes.

This method entails a conservative bias, since authors may opportunistically choose "theory-neutral" JEL codes in order to maximize their chances of publication in mainstream journals, and because the

Journal of Economic Literature classification system exhibits a very basic aggregate classification, providing little detail on nonmainstream approaches and themes, and possibly lacking some relevant descriptors.[2]

Thus, in order to classify a product as "heterodox," we require it to be characterized by at least one of the following JEL codes:

B5—Current Heterodox Approaches
  B50—General
  B51—Socialist; Marxian; Sraffian
  B52—Institutional; Evolutionary
  B53—Austrian
  B54—Feminist Economics
  B59—Other
E1—General Aggregative Models
  E11—Marxian; Sraffian; Institutional; Evolutionary
  E12—Keynes; Keynesian; Post-Keynesian

On this basis, it is possible to consider a rough classification of Italian economists. Specifically, we consider a dataset composed by the entries in the EconLit database authored in the period 2001–2003 by economists located in Italy (thus, not necessarily of Italian nationality), in order to ensure consistency with Italy's research assessment exercise, as explained in the following section. While the dataset cannot provide a definitive answer on the number of active researchers working on certain topics, it can help to identify at least the relative dimensions of different subgroups or "schools."

First, we classified products into eight very broad subdisciplines (fields) of economics on the basis of their JEL code(s) according to the criteria described in Appendix A. These categories are: *applied economics; economic policy; heterodox economics; econometrics and quantitative methods; economic history; history of economic thought; corporate finance and management;* and *other.* "*Other*" is here to be intended as a residual category, including all products whose JEL codes do not precisely fall into one of the previous categories. Thus, given our classification, it mainly includes field-specific theoretical works (for example, theoretical models of health economics, economic geography, and so on).

We then classified authors according to the subfields in which they have published. Specifically, we assigned an author to a field if he or she had published at least one product in the relevant subdiscipline in the considered period. To our aims, this criterion is superior to others equally available because it implies a convenient definition of "heterodox" economics. For example, an economist is classified as a heterodox economist if he or she manifested the nonmainstream nature of her/his work by authoring at least one publication that explicitly declares, through its JEL codes, a nonmainstream perspective.[3]

Figure 1 exhibits the resulting distribution of researchers and of products, for example, showing under the header "heterodox economics" the proportion of products authored by a heterodox economist (though not necessarily the number of heterodox publications, which we will deal with later). The distribution of researchers can be

Figure 1

Distribution of Italy's Researchers and Their Publications on EconLit, Years 2001–2003

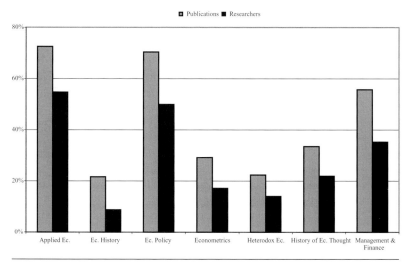

Note: Figures do not sum up to one: both publications and researchers may be classified under several categories simultaneously. The residual category "other" is not plotted to improve clarity of the Figure.

Source: our elaboration from EconLit, average values for years 2001, 2002, 2003.

used to compare the relative diffusion of certain approaches or topics in Italy, while the distribution of products is indicative of the international visibility of their publications (defined as the inclusion in the EconLit dataset).[4]

While it is likely that the EconLit dataset underrepresents the heterodox output of Italian heterodox economists, as we will discuss below, and despite the mentioned conservative bias of our method, a 23 percent share of publications and 14 percent of scholars classified as "heterodox" appear as relatively high figures when compared to other countries.[5] Similarly, as many as 22 percent of Italian economists also write on the history of economic thought, collectively authoring more than a third of all the products in our EconLit dataset.

It should be mentioned that a quantitative analysis based on the entries recorded by EconLit (as will be carried out in the remainder of the article) bears a second conservative bias, as many relevant contributions by leading Italian heterodox economists (as well as by historians of thought) are frequently published in the form of books and book chapters, which are hardly collected by EconLit. Furthermore, heterodox economists have traditionally been very involved in local and national policy making, comparatively more than in other countries and in some periods possibly more than mainstream economists. This led many heterodox economists to focus their research on Italy-specific themes and frequently to write in Italian in order to better address the national public opinion (some examples are provided by the last two chapters of Roncaglia 2005). These factors further contribute to the underrepresentation of heterodox economics located in Italy within the EconLit dataset we employ, and thus characterize our estimates as prudential or even conservative.

Italy's Research Assessment Exercise (VTR)

The first official evaluation of Italian universities and research institutions (VTR), sponsored by the Ministry for Research and managed by an ad-hoc governmental committee, Comitato di Indirizzo per la Valutazione della Ricerca (CIVR), was set up in 2005 for the evaluation of the research output produced between 2001 and 2003. In the case of economics, this exercise focused exclusively on publications, as authoritatively suggested by a special issue of the *Journal of the European Economic Association* published in 2003 that contained the results of a project on evaluating economic research in Europe (the project was initiated by the Council of the association in 1999). In their introduction to the issue, Neary et al. (2003) even state that "only published journal articles undergo a widely accepted process of peer review which is the essence of quality control in any scientific discipline." However, in the Italian case, books and book chapters were considered as well.

The CIVR assessment was conducted through a qualitative peer-review process on a sample of research output selected by participating research institutions. The selection of products occurred in a "top-down" fashion, as heads of departments (and, at higher levels, of faculties) were delegated to choose which publications to submit to the evaluation (in the Italian university system, faculties are administrative units in charge of planning and managing the activities related to teaching, whereas departments organize research activities). Products' ratings were then summed up at the level of institutions (universities or other research institutions) with the aim to construct disciplinary rankings of public research centers. The rationale of a publication's selection, being a matter of crucial importance for the preservation of pluralism in economics, will be analyzed in detail in the next section.

The exercise proceeded as follows (see Lippi and Peracchi 2007, for details): 14 "research areas" were recognized, which represented the units of analysis. Economics, statistics, management, and business studies were grouped into Area 13, though some margins of overlapping across areas remained as the classification of products is not always straightforward (for example, in the field of statistics). As a result, neither faculties nor departments were evaluated directly, since, for example, economists may be employed in several different departments of one university, which would be evaluated for the area as a whole.

Research centers were asked to submit a number of research products equal to at least one half of the number of full-time equivalent academic staff (full professors, associate professors, and research fellows). However, this proportion was to be respected at the level of the whole institution, not of each research area. Thus, universities were free to submit relatively more products in their specific areas of perceived excellence.

For each area, a panel of national and international experts was nominated, and submitted products were distributed among the panel's members according to their specific expertise. Each member of the panel was responsible for proposing a *rating* of the products assigned to her/him; in turn, the ratings were formulated on the basis of two or more independent referees' reports of each product. Finally, the whole panel voted on the member's proposals.

According to the norms established for all disciplines, research products were rated according to several criteria, the most prominent being the ranking of the product with respect to scientific excellence in "a value scale shared by the international scientific community." As we will discuss in the next section, the vagueness of this definition of research quality is the origin of a substantial bias in the selection of products to be submitted for evaluation.

The average of products' ratings constituted the rating of the institution itself: no consideration was taken for other variables measuring quality of research management, governance, and fund raising. Thus, it was implicit in the methodology that a unique process (leading to a single indicator) could evaluate publications, research output, research staff, and research institutions.

For each research area, universities were partitioned in four size classes according to the number of submitted products, and rankings of institutions were presented separately for each size class. In order to appear at the top of the disciplinary rankings, it was optimal for research centers to submit as few publications as possible, namely, only those they could expect to be judged as excellent by the referees, and possibly by the same authors (thus introducing a conservative and conformist bias in the process).

The introduction of size classes to partition the rankings, by preventing a direct comparison of institutions submitting very different number of publications, was an expedient to counterbalance this distortion. A crucial ambiguity characterized the rest of the process: Was the exercise meant to measure the average achievements of research in Italy by analyzing a representative sample of the research output, or was it meant to recognize and single out excellence by assessing only the best publications? This ambiguity was never solved during the process, highlighting a fundamental lack of transparency that resulted in each institution behaving on the basis of its perceived convenience. Thus, the study of the institutions' selection of publications to be submitted is highly indicative of the *a priori* perception of a publication's or a paradigm's quality.

This issue appears to be the most relevant, since the communication of results in terms of disciplinary rankings, often with little emphasis on the methodology adopted for rating and ranking, risks being perceived as an overarching answer for whatever question concerning the quality of research institutions, as noted by Lee (2007). Due to their one-dimensional quantitative nature, rankings very easily lend themselves to many other uses beyond their original rationale, without reference to the fact that they were built on the basis of specific indicators constructed to measure some variables and not others.[6]

This lack of transparency may descend from the nature of the exercise, officially characterized as being only a pilot.[7] However, as a consequence of the rhetoric strength of rankings, right after the exercise and until a recent decision by the central government, claims were frequently made that the resulting rankings should affect the future allocation of public funds, despite the fact that the VTR exercise was conducted as a typically ex-post assessment (for example, by Checchi and Jappelli 2008; Giavazzi 2008; Jappelli 2008).[8]

The results of the first evaluation of public research in Italy are undoubtedly positive, in general terms. The CIVR assessment represented a first step toward a change in the attitude of universities and researchers, introducing the principles of accountability and merit, hopefully with positive offspring in terms of research quality, competitiveness, and attractiveness of Italian universities. The outcomes of this first assessment also provide some food for thought. Its implementation brought about some criticality, concerning both the methodology and its application to the human and social sciences, economics in particular. The next section will introduce some issues by means of a statistical analysis of the products submitted for evaluation; we then draw some conclusions in light of the debate that the VTR stimulated among Italian economists.

A Statistical Analysis

Some Descriptive Statistics

The VTR evaluation exercise constitutes a good case study to highlight an issue often neglected: the impact that research evaluation may have on the development of research itself. This section argues that Italy's VTR embodied incentives for research institutions to highlight their mainstream economic research, while submitting for evaluation a small number of heterodox economic publications. This trend is particularly worrying because if an institution's budgets directly or indirectly depend on the results of the evaluation exercise, it will inevitably lead to disregard and prevent the development of research paradigms that are not likely to receive a positive evaluation. It is, therefore, of prime importance, for the sake of pluralism in economics, that these paradigms are not systematically identified with the heterodox approaches.

In order to investigate the selection of products submitted to the VTR, we will compare two datasets: one is composed of the products submitted for the fields of economics and statistics (Area 13); the other is a subsample of the EconLit dataset, containing the publications authored in the years 2001–2003 by economists located in Italy.[9]

Preliminary to the analysis, it is crucial to note that as none of the datasets is representative of the whole production of economists located in Italian research institutions, it is difficult to inquire into how they relate to the actual scientific output. The broader picture provided by the EconLit dataset, compared to the self-selected nature of the VTR dataset, allows us to consider the EconLit dataset as a benchmark to understand how faculties decided to attend the evaluation exercise.[10]

Our EconLit dataset exhibits 2,709 entries, authored or co-authored by 1,347 authors in the 2001–2003 period. Almost all of the products (2,509) in the EconLit database exhibit at least one JEL code. Conversely, 1,007 products are included in the VTR dataset, by a total of 842 authors. Since Area 13 of the VTR includes publications belonging to either economics or statistics, when considering only economics the dataset collapses to 597 products (22 percent of the EconLit corresponding figure). By matching the datasets, we were able to assign one or more JEL codes to 361 of them.

As shown in Figure 2a, the composition of publications in the two datasets, by typology of publication, is significantly different. It emerges that research institutions decided to submit books proportionally more than their appearance in the EconLit dataset (15 percent of submitted products, *vis-à-vis* 4 percent in EconLit), while submitting book chapters in a smaller proportion (24 percent in EconLit, 12 percent in VTR). Journal articles represent more than 70 percent of both datasets.

A major source of this difference may be the partly different disciplinary scope of the two datasets, with the VTR extending over a larger number of subdisciplines within social sciences. Thus, according to Peracchi (2007), the president of the panel of experts for Area 13 (economics and statistics), Italian researchers in the fields of financial and business economics and management studies—who constitute a large share of the VTR dataset—have a higher propensity (with respect to the other researchers included in Area 13) to publish

Figure 2

Composition of the Datasets by Publication Typology: a: Composition
of the Datasets; b: Composition of the Subsamples of Publications
Exhibiting at Least One JEL Code

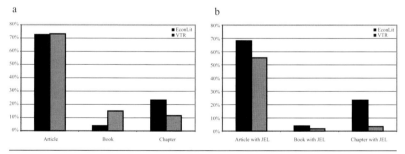

Note: a: the EconLit sample is composed of 2,709 products. For the VTR sample, only the 597 products in economics are considered; b: the EconLit subsample of products with JEL codes contains 2,509 products (92.6 percent of the sample). The VTR subsample includes 361 products (60.5 percent of products in economics). Percentage values refer to the whole sample.

books and book chapters, frequently in Italian.[11] It is thus likely that these typologies of publication are not overrepresented in the VTR but rather underrepresented in the EconLit dataset. Indeed, the latter exhibits a lower coverage also of interdisciplinary journals and journals focusing on subjects less related to the traditionally-defined (mainstream) topics of economics, including management and business studies journals.

In what follows, we will focus on the subsamples of products that exhibit at least one JEL code: Figure 2b shows the relative composition of these subsamples. By comparing Figures 2a and 2b, it is evident that, when looking only at products exhibiting a JEL code, most books, as well as a considerable number of book chapters, submitted to the VTR are ignored by the analysis. There is a presumption that these are mostly the above-mentioned publications written in Italian. As a matter of fact, our sample of products denoted by JEL codes includes most products that were classified by the Area 13 panel of experts as belonging to "economics." Conversely, more than two-thirds of products without a JEL code were submitted for the disciplines "statistics and operational research" or "business administration."

Bearing these caveats in mind, we compare the composition of the two datasets employing the eight field categories defined above. As already noted, allocation of the same publication across several subdisciplines is allowed for products that exhibit more than one JEL code: the results are displayed in Figure 3.

As shown in Figure 3, substantial differences emerge between the two subsamples. In a number of fields, products appear in a considerable proportion in the EconLit dataset, while being drastically underrepresented in the VTR dataset: it is the case of applied economics (−5.1 percent absolute difference between the EconLit and the VTR, or −20.5 percent relative to the proportion in EconLit), history of economic thought (−4.8 percent, or −34.3 percent in relative terms), economic policy (−4.1 percent, or −23 percent), economic history (−1 percent, or −44.3 percent), and heterodox approaches (−1.8 percent or −35.4 percent). By contrast, two fields are more represented in the VTR dataset than in EconLit: financial and business economics (+3.9 percent or 26 percent of the EconLit proportion), and econometrics and quantitative methods (+6,6 percent, or +174.2 percent).

Figure 3

Composition of the Datasets by Field

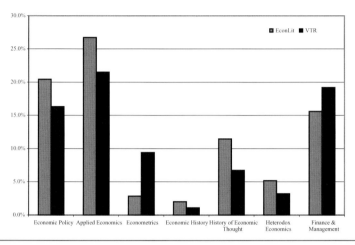

Note: the field of each product is assigned on the basis of the respective JEL code(s). The EconLit subsample of products with a JEL code contains 2,509 products; the VTR subsample includes 361 products. Products with more than one JEL code are assigned simultaneously to all the relevant fields. To improve clarity, the figure does not include the category "other" (87.8 percent of entries in the EconLit subsample and 83.7 percent in the VTR one).

At a more disaggregated level, this corresponds to a reduction of the frequent (in the EconLit dataset) JEL codes A—General Economics, F—International Economics, J—Labor Economics, L—Industrial Organization, and R—Regional Economics in favor of publications denoted by JEL codes C—Quantitative Methods, D—Microeconomics, and G—Financial Economics.

The Selection of Products Submitted to the VTR

Assuming that research institutions decided to comply with the aims of the evaluation and there was no opportunistic behavior on their side, the selection of products submitted for evaluation can be studied with respect to two main hypotheses. As a matter of fact, institutions' choice somehow reveals their degree of understanding of the aims of the VTR, which were characterized by a substantial uncertainty and lack of transparency, as mentioned above. Thus, we consider two alternatives:

> H.1) Institutions may have chosen to submit a *representative* sample of their staff's publications, if they believed the VTR was aimed at fairly representing the state-of-the-art of research in Italy; or
>
> H.2) Institutions may have chosen to submit their best publications, if they believed that the VTR was aimed at signaling and rewarding *excellence.*

In the absence of a clear consensus on what the criteria are to define scientific excellence in economics, the latter hypothesis is equivalent to affirm that institutions tried to maximize their expected rating, according to the definition of excellence, that, in their opinion, the evaluating panel would adopt. As suggested in the introduction, it is the widespread adoption of the latter criterion that implies a concrete risk for the survival and development of any heterodox approach to economics.

Given the absence of a complete dataset of the whole scientific production by Italian economists, it is virtually impossible to test hypothesis H.1.

However, it is at least possible to investigate the extent to which the distribution of product typologies reflects the distribution of academic staff (whose total number is known), and/or differences in the staff's average productivity. To this aim, we employ the classification of staff proposed above, based on researchers having published at least one product in a certain field in the relevant period. The composition of the research staff in the two datasets is displayed in Figure 4.[12]

Since in the VTR dataset the vast majority of authors are recorded with only one publication, the scope of each author's fields of publication is reduced, with respect to EconLit.[13] Accordingly, in the VTR dataset all fields exhibit a lower number of active researchers recorded. However, it is clear from Figure 3 that some fields exhibit a larger drop than others. Thus, if the EconLit dataset records a 54.7 percent of authors who in the relevant period published at least once on applied issues, they are reduced to 28.4 percent in the VTR dataset. The respective figures for the other fields are: economic history 8.8 percent as opposed to 1.3 percent, economic policy 49.9 percent and 18.7 percent, econometrics 17.1 percent and 11.3 percent, financial

Figure 4

Distribution of Authors in the Two Datasets

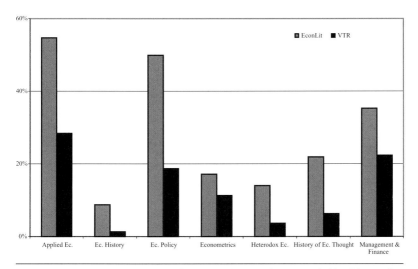

Note: Each author is assigned a field according to the JEL code(s) of his or her publications recorded in the relevant dataset. The EconLit subsample of products with a JEL code contains 2,509 products; the VTR subsample includes 361 products. Publications with more than one JEL code are assigned simultaneously to all the relevant fields; authors are consequently assigned to more than one field. For the sake of clarity, the figure does not include the category "other" (87.8 percent of entries in the EconLit subsample and 83.7 percent in the VTR one).

and business economics 35.3 percent and 22.4 percent. After economic history, the history of economic thought, and heterodox approaches, exhibit the largest differences (relative to their value in EconLit): respectively from 21.9 percent to 6.3 percent and from 14 percent to 3.7 percent.

It is, indeed, possible that the work of these economists was less frequently selected for the evaluation because they are less productive, if they publish a smaller number of visible products with respect to their colleagues. This hypothesis is easily rejected. As shown in Table B1 in Appendix B, the average productivity of Italian economists, measured by the unweighted number of products recorded in the EconLit dataset, is not significantly different across subfields.[14]

Since (in total, and for each subfield) the number of researchers, times their average productivity, equals their output, under the hypothesis that the EconLit dataset provides a closer picture of reality than the self-selected sample of products submitted for evaluation, we can affirm that the allocation of products submitted to the VTR does not match the distribution of researchers' output by subfield; products were not selected with the aim to constitute a representative sample of economic research in Italy.

We are thus left with our second hypothesis, according to which research institutions tried to maximize their expected rating. The rationale of this assumption is magnified by the fact that—as was expected—results were presented in the forms of institutions' rankings. The use of "football league" rankings is relevant because evidently if someone comes before, someone else must come next. Thus, rankings introduce, beside the financial incentive to be highly ranked (not being subject to budget cuts from the central government), a further argument related to institutions' reputation (and indirectly a new financial incentive, if students' enrollment choices are affected by public rankings).

Unfortunately, by investigating the visibility of the submitted publications, we are able to collect some evidence that may corroborate this hypothesis, but not to falsify it (or to show under what conditions it would be falsified).

Our hypothesis H.2 respects the principle of parsimony, as it allows us to explain the observed patterns both in terms of publication typology, and of field classification simultaneously. In fact, given the *ex ante* uncertainty on the definition of "research quality," it would have been rational for research institutions, if they wanted to maximize their expected rating, to submit the most internationally visible products, preferably already "legitimated" by previous peer-review processes (mainly journal articles) and possibly by an impact factor (IF), as a means to signaling quality. In light of the characteristics of economic research in Italy (though there is a presumption that this observation applies elsewhere), this criterion of selection ostensibly favors mainstream journals and quantitative approaches over heterodox and historical research, as well as publications written in English over any other language.

Both "demand" and "supply" reasons may explain the different publication habits across subdisciplines and between different schools and approaches. On one hand, mainstream economics enjoys larger audiences, leading to a higher demand for research products in this area. On the other hand, a nonexclusive reliance on journal articles as the best means for dissemination of results is typical of many heterodox schools, interdisciplinary approaches, and, specifically, of historians of economic thought, as mentioned above.

As it appears from Figure 5, researchers in the latter fields, indeed, exhibit a higher propensity to write books and book chapters. According to the Econlit dataset, these typologies account for more than 40 percent of the total publications in the categories history of economic thought and heterodox approaches. Beyond the quantitative dimension, there is also a qualitative argument, since these publication typologies were frequently selected for evaluation in the two subfields, according to hypothesis H.2, this means that they were perceived as being good pieces of research, liable of being positively evaluated. Indeed, although the high proportion of books and book

Figure 5

Comparison of Datasets, Product Typology by Field

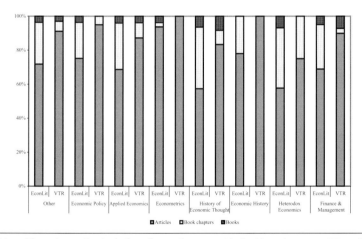

Note: The subsamples include only products provided with at least one JEL code.

chapters is not perfectly respected in the VTR dataset, the history of economic thought is the only field exhibiting (relatively) more books than in the EconLit dataset, while heterodox economics is the field exhibiting the highest proportion of book chapters among the products submitted for evaluation (3.6 times the average).

The Visibility of Research Output

Thus, it appears that, under the hypothesis that institutions tried to maximize their rating, different choice rules appear to have been applied for different subfields. At the same time, institutions seem to have selected subdisciplines according to the rationale of maximizing their prospective rating, acting on the presumption that certain publications (or certain paradigms) are of less quality than others.

It appears, therefore, a sensible question to analyze the extent to which certain publication typologies, and—at the macro level—certain approaches and subfields, actually exhibit a higher international visibility than others; for example, to what extent the institutions' presumptions are correct.

However, initially, it should be stressed that even if the mentioned criteria (peer review and IF) could be good signals of publications' international *visibility*, they would still not necessarily denote research *quality*. The rationale of using visibility as a proxy for quality only rests on the uncertainty over what the quality of economic research is, and on how to measure it. Only under this uncertainty it appears rational to rest on majority, or mainstream, criteria.

We investigate publications' visibility by counting the number of citations they received, as recorded by the Google Scholar search engine (as of August 2007): we label this indicator as the publications' Google Factor (GF). Although not as precise,[15] this measure conveys more information for our purposes than the usual ISI—Web of Sciences database, insofar as product typologies other than articles are thereby considered (most books and book chapters).

Figures 6a and 6b compare the distributions of GF and IF associated with the publications submitted to the VTR. As it appears from Figure 6b, the number of individual citations as measured by the Google Factor exhibits a power-law form of distribution, which is

Figure 6

Distribution of Products Submitted to VTR, by Impact Factor and
Google Factor

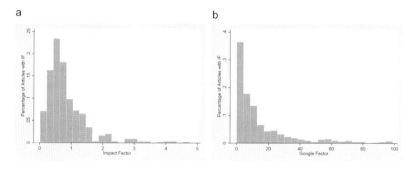

a   b

typical of the bibliometrics literature (compare, for example, Redner
1998; Van Raan 2005). By contrast, the distribution of the IF (for those
articles published in journals that have one) exhibits a peculiar
log-normal shape: with modal and median values significantly higher,
and very few observations at low values of IF (which instead characterize most journals in economics). Although not conclusive, this piece
of evidence suggests that the VTR sample is not random with respect
to the impact factor, while being biased toward articles exhibiting high
impact factors.

In our sample, the IF and the GF are indeed mildly correlated (the
Pearson correlation coefficient is 0.48), although this correlation
explains only a small fraction of the total variance. In other words, the
presumption that an article's visibility can be predicted by the IF of the
journal in which it is published is true on average, but is not very
robust (it is frequently false in individual cases) and not substantiated
by a strong correlation.

In Appendix B (Table B2) we collect some descriptive statistics on
publications' GF and journals' IF by subfield. In general, it is found
that there are relevant differences in the average and median IFs and
GFs across subfields, as well as a relevant variance within each field.

The large variability of individual citations around the subfields'
average values appears even more clearly when considering the

Figure 7

Products Submitted to VTR: Google Factor Plotted Against
Impact Factor

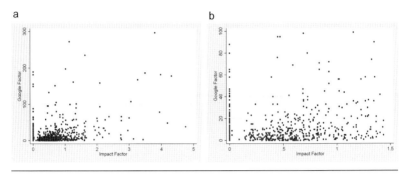

Note: a: The whole VTR sample is considered; b: VTR sample, products with
GF < 100.

totality of publications by not limiting the analysis to journal articles.
As shown in Figures 7a and 7b (where a "zero" IF was assigned to
books, book chapters, and articles published in journals without an
IF), a cloud of individual citations prevents us from identifying a
strong correlation between the IF and the GF. Moreover, it is worth
noting that many articles published in journals with an IF (37 out of
552) received no citations even after four years (the issue was emphasized also by Oswald 2007). Vice versa, we find that several books and
articles published in journals without an IF were largely cited on
Google Scholar.

Thus, our analysis suggests that the nonexclusive reliance on the
two mentioned criteria of publications' selection that we found as
strongly present in the subfields of history of economic thought and
heterodox economics are not suboptimal behavior on the side of
research institutions. Instead, even if research quality could be proxied
by international visibility, the criteria of peer review and IF do not
appear as adequate measures of it.

Conclusions: The Current Debate in Italy

While the introduction of the principles of accountability and merit
has been identified as the main improvement brought about by the

VTR, above we pointed out the following as its main drawbacks: lack of transparency on the aims and methodology of the exercise, use of "football league" rankings to disseminate its results, insufficient reference to researchers' productivity, application of the same method indifferently for the evaluation of publications, researchers, and institutions, and finally a foggy definition of research quality.

As the analysis suggests, the last mentioned aspect—the reference to "a value scale shared by the international scientific community"— appears as crucial from the point of view of the preservation of pluralism in economics, and specifically for the survival of heterodox approaches. Luigi Pasinetti, a member of the panel of experts in charge of evaluating the publications submitted for the field of economics, deemed the topic so important to obtain the right to attach a minority report (titled "A note on points of dissent") to the final report of the panel. He denounced that the words "shared" and "international scientific community" have been interpreted by the majority of the other members of the panel (and the majority of referees) as substantially availing the adoption of closeness to the mainstream as a fundamental criterion of judgment.[16] Guido Tabellini, the chairman of the subgroup of the panel of experts with specific competence in economics, replied to Pasinetti with a further attachment to the final report. After denying that the mainstream of economic research constitutes a unique research paradigm, he stressed that reference to international standards is fundamental, and that "the real risk is that, in order to protect some sects of researchers that are dying out, we will avoid comparisons and we will abstain from discriminating the excellent research, which really moves the frontiers of knowledge, from low-quality research. Or, even worse, that by *a priori* refusing to refer to the international scientific community, we will end up evaluating according to arbitrary criteria, that represent the idiosyncrasies and the prejudices of the members of the panel" (Annex 4, p. 32, our translation).

As Pasinetti points out, the activity of this panel has been characterized by a number of points of dissent, as the members of the panel did not reach a consensus agreement on the rating of about one-third of total products (whose merit grade was decided by majority voting),[17] while in some cases they decided to consult further external experts in addition to the two referees assigned to each product. A public discussion emerged as a consequence of this disagreement, which involved economists' associations and single researchers, and took place on the Internet as well as in a number of conferences and workshops.

As of May 2009, 128 economists signed an open letter petitioning that pluralism should become a fundamental criterion of research evaluation. The open letter forcefully puts forward the argument that the evaluation of publications should be separated from that of researchers, which in turn should be different from that of institutions. Specifically, it would be necessary to evaluate publications looking at their intrinsic quality, according to the specific standards of each subdiscipline and without considering the typology (journal article, book, book chapter), language, and place of publication.[18]

On the other hand, considering the evaluation of institutions, it seems important to come to an agreement about what the final rankings are expected to assess, for example, if they should award the average quality of research, or if they should compare only the best research products (the "excellence"). While the second criterion could be effective in allocating funds to the most promising lines of research, it may also bring about an asymmetric information problem: in fact, if funds are allocated to faculties (and not to single researchers, nor to research projects) those unproductive researchers who work in top-ranked faculties will be awarded without merit. Conversely, if the former criterion is applied, top researchers working with mediocre colleagues could be harmed, but rankings will probably be more indicative to the stakeholders (students, academics, and government, for example) of the average quality of institutions.[19] According to this criterion, the participation of all the academic personnel in the evaluation exercises should be required.[20]

The present work contributes to this debate, while highlighting Italy as an internationally relevant case study. Beyond the interest *per se*, being the host country of a relevant number of heterodox economists, the case of Italy suggests, then, that heterodox economists in every country should not refuse the evaluation of their research and the award of merit (Tabellini clearly made the point). Moreover, both within the mainstream and within heterodox approaches it should be clear that some pieces of research or some institutions are—from some points of view, to be strictly defined—better than others. And that the reward of merit is fundamental to set up the right incentives to researchers, as well as to provide the best environment to work in.

However, what our empirical analysis shows is that the rules governing the evaluation of research quality should respect a principle of fair competition. Specifically, although rankings were provided for research institutions as a whole, Italy's VTR did not respect a principle of fair competition among research paradigms, by providing conditions for better awarding research of distinctly mainstream character. Indeed, in the context of an ever-increasing process of multi-authorship across several "competing" research institutions, one could question the idea that only competition (rather than cooperation) takes place among institutions, while it could be claimed that competition among paradigms is more relevant for pluralism, and thus for the development of our discipline. It is, therefore, of prime importance that the criteria and the practice of evaluation do not *a priori* favor any specific paradigm or approach. The case of Italy shows that if such evaluation criteria are not explicitly stated, the large numeric majority currently enjoyed by the mainstream (even in an atypical country as Italy) risks producing a bias against minority stances.

It is consequently fundamental that minority groups (heterodox economists, as well as non Anglo-Saxon writers, and mainstream scholars specializing in less diffused topics or research areas) do not ignore the theory and practice of research evaluation, but engage in the explicit and fair *ex-ante* definition of clear rules. Only transparency and accountability of evaluation criteria and bodies can solve the century-long issue of who judges the judges.

Notes

1. However, we should recall at least Federico Caffè (whose main research fields were economic policy and public finance) and Paolo Sylos Labini (market forms, development, and technical change) in Rome, Giorgio Fuà in Ancona (development), Franco Momigliano in Turin (international economics), Siro Lombardini in Milan (monetary theory), Giacomo Becattini in Florence (industrial organization and local development).

2. Furthermore, our selection of JEL descriptors is affected by the fact that some, potentially relevant, JEL codes (for example, G01—Financial crises)

were only recently added, and are not considered here, since the publications considered in this study only refer to the period 2001–2003, in order to match the period considered by the VTR research assessment exercise.

3. When considering the single field of research in which authors have more extensively written, the following pattern emerges: researchers writing on field theoretical topics (in our classification, frequently falling into the category "other") account for 84 percent of Italy's academic staff, while researchers writing mostly on applied topics account for 11.5 percent and historians of thought for 7.3 percent. The rest is represented by minorities accounting for between 0.1 percent (heterodox economists, similarly to economic historians) and 5 percent (financial and business economists). Figures do not sum up to one because in the relevant period several researchers used the same number of JEL codes for different fields. This piece of evidence descends from researchers' habit to denote their papers with an equal number of "methodological" and "theoretical" descriptors, or of "historical" and "applied" ones, in order not to qualify the paper (and themselves) as belonging to a single specialist field.

4. The differences between the two distributions cannot be imputed to differences in productivity (number of publications per author) because neither distributions sum up to one. Authors typically use more than a unique JEL code category; therefore, they are classified under more than one field; publications themselves usually exhibit more than one JEL code. Moreover, publications are often authored by two or more authors, who may not belong to the same category in our classification.

5. For example, Axarloglou and Theoharakis (2003) report that in 2002, among members of the AEA, roughly the same figure (14 percent) of their respondents self-identified with one of the schools of thought identified by the JEL codes we selected as "heterodox" (with the difference that they included all institutionalist schools, but excluded feminists). However, beside the conservative bias of our estimate, which does not include certain heterodox schools such as the experimentalists or the behavioralists, it should be noted that their respondents were (anonymously) faced with a general question on one's overall preanalytical vision, for example, not implying as strict of a requirement as our definition does, by demanding to publicly report their vision by selecting a JEL code for at least one publication during the 2001–2003 period.

6. A typical example in the scientific literature, applied to the evaluation of Europe's research institutions, is the well-known paper by Kalaitzidakis et al. (1999), providing for the first time a comprehensive ranking of European universities in economics, though "based on publications in a core set of highly ranked, *mainstream*, economic journals" (italics added). Astonishingly, throughout the paper the authors themselves seem to perceive their rankings as measures of unconditional research quality, thus ignoring that nonmainstream readers may embrace a different point of view (compare, for example,

the authors' conclusions: "the London School of Economics, Tel-Aviv University, and Oxford University are the three leading economic schools in Europe. . . . These results are independent of the metrics used. . . . This finding raises concerns about the current state and impact of economic research in Europe relative to North-America").

7. Formally, the CIVR was requested to assess progress toward the achievement of the political goals stated in the National Plan for Research, but it actually took the form of an internal evaluation, with little or no attention to the external impact of research, in terms of the impact of research on society.

8. Recently, the government approved a decree mandating that from 2010 up to 7 percent of the state funds yearly transferred to universities will be allocated according to the quality of institutions' teaching, research, and infrastructure (this share should subsequently increase up to 30 percent). For year 2010, 60 percent of this share was determined employing the VTR rankings.

9. In order to maintain comparability, we excluded from our analysis the few Ph.D. theses, working papers, and review articles recorded in the EconLit database because none of these typologies of products were submitted to the VTR exercise for Area 13.

10. It should be noted that a high number of scholarly economics journals published in Italy (almost 40) are included in the Econlit dataset.

11. While the VTR dataset does not entail information on products' language, we can actually confirm that the distribution by product typology of the "financial and business economics" subarea is very peculiar with respect to the other two, exhibiting as many books as 49 percent of the total, and as few journal articles as 39 percent.

12. When considering authors, the EconLit sample comes much closer to the universe than when considering publications: as Marcuzzo and Zacchia (2007) document, more than 70 percent of Italy's economists authored at least one publication recorded by EconLit.

13. For the same reason the possible second definition referred to in note 5, classifying researchers according to the field in which they have published more intensively, is unfit to analyze the VTR dataset.

14. Instead, a high variance is found within groups, significantly higher than the variance across groups. The substantially large skewness of the distributions within groups implies that, in general, average values lie far above median values, for example, within-group averages are heavily affected by single, very productive researchers. It should be recalled that the EconLit dataset encompasses all researchers working in Italy's institutions, but not all their publications.

15. In particular, it does not correct for self-citations and it does not weigh citations according to the visibility of the citing publication.

16. For example, Pasinetti reported that several referees explicitly indicated the IF as a signal of the quality of the evaluated products: "It is first hand documentary evidence from the referees' reports I had read, before offering (or denying) my cross-panelist consensus. The referees (two for each product) had to fill in answers to 4 different questions concerning: quality, relevance, originality, and internationalization. Cases like the following were the first cause of my denying consensus (without any effect, being always in a minority). Quality of the product: 'This paper is published in a top field journal, the IF of the journal is high, hence the paper is excellent' or conversely (always on quality of the paper) 'this paper is published in my opinion in a non serious journal [in the specific case of this quotation it was the *Journal of Post Keynesian Economics*], hence the quality is limited'. Notice that the evaluation I am referring to is on *quality*, not on *internationalization* of the product!" (p. 6 of Annex 4, italics in original). This is but one example for the argument for the need of a greater transparency of the process, including the publication of referees' reports, as a fundamental requirement for keeping the evaluators accountable.

17. The Final Report of the Panel for the Area 13 (*Relazione finale di Area*), is available online (only in Italian) at http://vtr2006.cineca.it/rel_area/panel_13.pdf.

18. The petition is available online: http://www.letteraapertavalutazioneri cerca.it. The arguments that emerged in the context of the subsequent public discussion are not completely new in the literature: we refer to the introduction to this special issue and to the other articles collected here for a review of this literature. In our opinion, it is worth noting that in the specific context of peer-review processes, these critiques assume a relevant dimension even within mainstream approaches. Indeed, while the anonymity of peer-review processes is threatened, nowadays, by the availability of research databases and Internet search engines, it is likely that within specific streams of research real experts are competitors, so that referees may be subject to conflicts of interests. Moreover, reliance on evaluation criteria based mainly on international visibility may disproportionately favor consolidated research areas (Geuna 2001; Frey 2003), hindering the development of new fields by young researchers. More generally, a serious threat is posed for "periphery" countries, where such criteria may undermine the diffusion of country-specific analyses, thus reducing the (external) relevance of research in terms of impact on society and the economy (Colander 2008).

19. Two corollaries emerge from this reasoning. First, research excellence should be evaluated separately from overall university rankings (for instance, by granting funds to specific research projects, submitted to ad-hoc evaluating commissions). Second, only the application of an "average" evaluation criterion could encourage a healthy competition among universities in attracting

the best researchers in each field, rather than favoring the mobility of "top" researchers with the only purpose of maximizing expected rankings.

20. The drawbacks of such an approach, when applied to a peer-review evaluation, stand in the costs and in the complexity of the procedure, which in the long run may even outweigh benefits (Geuna and Martin 2003).

References

Axarloglou, K., and V. Theoharakis. (2003). "Diversity in Economics: An Analysis of Journal Quality Perceptions." *Journal of the European Economic Association* 1: 1346–1366.

Checchi, D., and T. Jappelli. (2008). "Come dare risorse ai migliori". www.lavoce.info, September 4, 2008.

Colander, D. (2008). "Can European Economics Compete with U.S. Economics? And Should It?" Paper presented at the "IZA Workshop on Research in Economics: Rewards, Evaluation and Funding," Bonn (DE), May 26 and 27, 2008.

Frey, B. S. (2003). "Publishing as Prostitution? Choosing Between One's Own Ideas and Academic success." *Public Choice* 116: 205–223.

Geuna, A. (2001). "The Changing Rationale for European University Research Funding: Are there Negative Unintended Consequences?" *Journal of Economic Issues* 35(3): 607–632.

Geuna, A., and B. Martin. (2003). "University Research Evaluation and Funding: An International Comparison." *Minerva* 41: 277–304.

Giavazzi, F. (2008). L'inizio della fine dei concorsi. www.lavoce.info, November 18, 2008.

Jappelli, T. (2008). Largo al merito! Ma è solo l'inizio. www.lavoce.info, December 3, 2008.

Kalaitzidakis, P., T. P. Mamuneas, and T. Stengos. (1999). "European Economics: An Analysis Based on Publications in the Core Journals." *European Economic Review* 43: 1150–1168.

Lee, F. S. (2007). "The Research Assessment Exercise, the State and the Dominance of Mainstream Economics in British Universities." *Cambridge Journal of Economics* 31: 309–325.

Lee, F. S., and W. Elsner. (2008). "Publishing, Ranking, and the Future of Heterodox Economics." *On the Borizon* 16(4): 176–184.

Lee, F. S., and S. Harley. (1998). "Peer Review, the Research Assessment Exercise and the Demise of Non-Mainstream Economics." *Capital and Class* 66: 23–51.

Lippi, M., and F. Peracchi. (2007). "Il primo esercizio italiano di valutazione della ricerca: una prima valutazione." *Rivista italiana degli economisti* 2: 267–276.

Marcuzzo, M. C., and G. Zacchia. (2007). "L'ECONLIT e gli strumenti per la valutazione della ricerca economica in Italia." *Rivista italiana degli economisti* 2: 277–306.

Neary et al. (2003). "Evaluating Economics Research in Europe: An Introduction" *Journal of the European Economic Association* 1: 1239–1249.

Oswald, A. J. (2007). "An Examination of the Reliability of Prestigious Scholarly Journals: Evidence and Implications for Decision-Makers." *Economica* 74(293): 21–31.

Pasinetti, L. L., and A. Roncaglia. (2006). "Le scienze umane in Italia: il caso dell'economia politica." *Rivista Italiana degli Economisti* 11: 461–499.

Peracchi, F. (2007). Closing session of the conference "Funziona! Ricetta per Riformare un Sistema Universitario Pubblico. Dal Regno Unito all'Italia." Rome, November 25, 2007, Fondazione IRI.

Redner, S. (1998). "How Popular Is Your Paper? An Empirical Study of the Citation Distribution." *European Physical Journal B* 4: 131–134.

Roncaglia, A. (2005). *The Wealth of Ideas*. Cambridge: Cambridge University Press.

Van Raan, A. F. J. (2005). "Statistical Properties of Bibliometric Indicators: Research Group Indicator Distributions and Correlations." *Journal of the American Society for Information Science and Technology* 57(3): 408–430.

Appendix A

Research products were classified according to the following criteria, based on the JEL classification system.

Applied Economics: C9, C90, C91, C92, C93, C99, L6, L60, L61, L62, L63, L64, L65, L66, L67, L68, L69, L7, L70, L71, L72, L73, L74, L78, L79, L8, L80, L81, L82, L83, L84, L85, L86, L87, L88, L89, L9, L90, L91, L92, L93, L94, L95, L96, L97, L98, L99, O5, O50, O51, O52, O53, O54, O55, and the whole categories R and P.

Corporate Finance and Management: all the JEL codes included under the letters G and M.

Economic History: all the JEL codes included under the letter N.

Econometrics and Quantitative Methods: all the JEL codes included under the letter C, with the exception of C7, C70, C71, C72, C73, C78.

Economic Policy: D18, E5, E50, E51, E52, E58, E59, E6, E60, E61, E62, E63, E64, E65, E66, E69, F13, F33, F34, F35, F42, I18, I28, I38, J18, J28, J38, J48, J58, J68, J78, J88, L4, L40, L41, L42, L43, L44, L49, L5, L50, L51, L52, L53, L59, O2, O20, O21, O22, O23, O24, O29, O38, Q18, Q28, Q38, Q48.

Heterodox Economics: B5, B50, B51, B52, B53, B59, D57, E11, E12.

History of Economic Thought: all the JEL codes included under the letter B, excluding B5, B50, B51, B52, B53, B59.

The residual category **Other**: C7, C70, C71, C72, C73, C78, L1, L10, L11, L12, L13, L14, L15, L16, L17, L18, L19, L20, L21, L22, L23, L24, L25, L26, L27, L28, L29, L2, L30, L31, L32, L33, L34, L35, L36, L37, L38, L39, L3, O10, O11, O12, O13, O14, O15, O16, O17, O18, O19, O1, O3, O30, O31, O32, O33, O34, O35, O36, O37, O38, O39, O4, O40, O41, O42, O43, O44, O45, O46, O47, O48, O49, as well as the whole categories A, D, E, F, H, I, J, K, and Z.

Appendix B

Table B1

Output of Researchers in Economics: Number of Publications Recorded in EconLit, 2001–2003

	Applied Ec.	Ec. Policy	Other	Heterodox Ec.	Econometrics	History of Thought	Ec. History	Finance Manag.
				All Publications				
Mean	6.6	6.6	5.8	7	7.1	6.9	9.1	7.3
Median	5	5	4	6	5	6	8	6
Std. Var.	5.5	5.3	5.1	5.3	5.7	5.3	5.4	5.8
Skewness	1.6	1.6	1.9	1.4	1.4	1.2	0.6	1.5
Min	1	1	1	1	1	1	1	1
Max	27	27	27	22	22	22	22	27
5%	1	1	1	1	1	1	2	1
95%	18	17	17	20	20	20	22	20
				Journal Articles				
Mean	4.1	4.3	3.7	3.6	4.3	3.4	5	4.6
Median	3	3	3	3	4	3	4	4
Std. Var.	3.7	3.8	3.4	2.6	2.7	2.5	3.4	3.9
Skewness	2.4	2.3	2.5	0.7	0.9	0.7	0.7	2.3
Min	0	0	0	0	0	0	0	0
Max	22	22	22	10	12	10	13	22
5%	0	1	0	0	1	0	1	1
95%	11	11	10	8	8	8	12	11
				Book Chapters				
Mean	2	1.9	1.7	2.9	2.5	2.9	3.6	2.3
Median	1	1	1	2	1	2	4	1
Std. Var.	2.8	2.4	2.5	3.4	3.7	3.2	3.4	2.9
Skewness	2	1.6	2.3	1.8	1.8	1.6	1.5	1.9
Min	0	0	0	0	0	0	0	0
Max	14	10	14	14	14	14	14	14
5%	0	0	0	0	0	0	0	0
95%	8	8	2	10	10	10	14	8
				Books				
Mean	0.4	0.4	0.4	0.5	0.4	0.6	0.5	0.5
Median	0	0	0	0	0	0	0	0
Std. Var.	1	1	0.9	1.3	0.9	1.2	0.7	1.1
Skewness	3.8	3.8	4.1	4.2	2.3	3.7	1.1	3.6
Min	0	0	0	0	0	0	0	0
Max	8	8	8	8	3	8	2	8
5%	0	0	0	0	0	0	0	0
95%	2	2	2	3	3	3	2	2

Source: Our elaboration on EconLit dataset, years 2001–2003.

Table B2

Impact Factor and Google Factor: Descriptive Statistics

	Publications	Mean	Median	Std.Dev.	Skewness	Min	Max	5%	95%
Impact Factor									
Applied Economics	56	0.875	0.6865	0.643	3.051	0.217	4.312	0.236	2.087
Economic Policy	47	0.898	0.723	0.757	2.165	0.089	3.795	0.2	3
Economic Theory	230	0.887	0.7045	0.716	2.344	0.089	4.756	0.2	2.196
Heterodox Economics	5	0.501	0.444	0.124	0.699	0.403	0.688	0.403	0.688
Econometrics	27	0.78	0.62	0.531	1.995	0.222	1.315	0.24	1.315
Economic History	4	0.644	0.674	0.264	0.373	0.297	0.929	0.297	0.929
History of Ec. Thought	10	0.48	0.301	0.477	1.111	0.022	1.333	0.022	1.333
Finance & Management	49	1.101	0.806	0.823	1.443	0.135	3	0.272	3.494
Google Factor									
Applied Economics	78	25.846	9	43.138	3.431	0	272	0	93
Economic Policy	59	27.203	10	47.764	3.808	0	296	0	80
Economic Theory	302	23.139	9	40.431	3.704	0	296	0	93
Heterodox Economics	12	3.25	2.5	2.8	1.134	0	10	0	10
Econometrics	34	17.206	7.5	20.095	1.475	0	69	1	69
Economic History	4	12.75	4.5	18.209	1.138	2	40	2	40
History of Ec. Thought	24	3.5	1.5	6.84	3.551	0	33	0	9
Finance & Management	69	27.623	12	39.149	2.356	0	186	0	101
Google Factor—Articles Only									
Applied Economics	68	27.132	10.5	44.817	3.41	0	272	0	93
Economic Policy	56	28.464	11	48.719	3.714	0	296	0	80
Economic Theory	275	23.96	10	40.959	3.729	0	296	0	95
Heterodox Economics	9	3.333	2	3	1.339	1	10	1	10
Econometrics	34	17.206	7.5	20.095	1.475	0	69	1	69
Economic History	4	12.75	4.5	18.209	1.138	2	40	2	40
History of Ec. Thought	20	2.5	2	2.856	1.147	0	9	0	9
Finance & Management	62	27.258	12	37.232	2.449	0	186	0	98
Google Factor—Articles with Impact Factor Only									
Applied Economics	56	31.179	14	48.237	3.103	0	272	0	151
Economic Policy	47	29.404	12	46.478	4.187	0	296	1	76
Economic Theory	230	26.504	11	42.542	3.567	0	296	1	95
Heterodox Economics	5	3.2	3	1.924	0.396	1	6	1	6
Econometrics	27	19.593	8	21.855	1.16	0	69	1	69
Economic History	4	12.75	4.5	18.209	1.138	2	40	2	40
History of Ec. Thought	10	3.7	3	3.268	0.664	0	9	0	9
Finance & Management	49	33.327	19	39.68	2.169	0	101	1	186

Note: Only publications provided with at least one JEL code are considered.

Research Evaluation Down Under: An Outsider's View from the Inside of the Australian Approach*

By Harry Bloch

Abstract. Australia is currently undertaking its first national evaluation of university research, which is being performed by the Australian Research Council (ARC) at the request of the Australian government. The Australian approach to evaluation has some unique characteristics, especially a focus on evaluating research quantity and quality by the field of the research activity rather than by individual academic or administrative unit. This raises issues of the classification of areas of research, which has already caused controversy for Australian heterodox economists. There is also controversy about the quality rankings

*Harry Bloch has been Professor of Economics at Curtin University of Technology in Perth, Australia since 1997. He has previously held academic positions at the University of Tasmania (Australia), University of Denver (USA), University of Manitoba (Canada), University of British Columbia (Canada), and Illinois Institute of Technology (USA) and has also been a visiting faculty member at Queen's University (Canada), the University of Warwick (UK), University of East Anglia (UK), Australian National University, University of Lancaster (UK), University of Liverpool (UK), and the University of California at Santa Barbara (USA). His main research interests are industrial pricing, international trade, economic development, productivity analysis, and dynamic competition. His recent work has concentrated on the movement of real prices of primary commodities in the long run and on the development of a theory of the firm that encompasses evolutionary change. The author has benefitted from the comments of three anonymous referees and from participants at the workshop, Assessing Heterodox Economics in a European Context. Helpful comments on an earlier version and help in researching the topic were also received from John King, Peter Kriesler, Fred Lee, Stan Metcalfe, Paul Miller, and Alex Millmow, but they bear no responsibility for any errors or omissions. The views expressed in this article are those of the author alone and do not represent those of the Australian Research Council or any other organization with which the author is affiliated. Professor Bloch may be contacted at the Centre for Research in Applied Economics, School of Economics and Finance, Curtin University of Technology, GPO Box U1987, Perth WA 6845, Australia, E-mail: h.bloch@curtin.edu.au

of economics journals. This article provides a critical review of the Australian approach to research evaluation and discusses the implications for heterodox economists.

Introduction

Australia is conducting its first national evaluation of university research. It has been a rocky start. Preparations began in earnest in 2005 with the establishment of an administrative group within the Commonwealth (national government) bureaucracy to carry out assessment under the Research Quality Framework (RQF). The RQF details were never finalized, but the proposals sent out for consultation with the university sector suggested assessment along lines similar to the U.K. Research Assessment Exercise. Specifically, the end result was to provide a quality ranking by discipline-based units for each university determined by an expert panel in that academic discipline. The nascent scheme had Australian heterodox economists extremely worried that the RQF would speed the decline of heterodox research and teaching "down under" (see King 2007).

There was relief among heterodox economists when the Liberal-National Party Coalition (conservative) government was defeated by the Australian Labor Party (ALP) (center-left) at elections in November 2007 and the RQF was abandoned. However, the policy of conducting a research assessment was not abandoned in totality. Instead, the new government replaced the RQF with Excellence in Research in Australia (ERA). This has left substantial concerns about the likely impact on heterodox economists (see King and Kriesler 2008).

The intention of ERA is to provide an evaluation of the research performance by academics in Australia within discipline and subdiscipline groupings.[1] The evaluation will be informed by quantitative information on the amount and quality of activity (publications, funded expenditure, and applied outcomes) per researcher within each discipline classification over the period 2003–2008. The quantitative information together with qualitative information is to be assessed by expert discipline panels to place the research performance of each discipline at each university into a performance band from one to five, representing a level of performance relative to world performance benchmarks.

The Labor government has indicated that the results of ERA will only be published as a distribution of outcomes across universities. No results for individual universities are to be published (no league table), although each university will be given the results of its own performance evaluation in each discipline along with comments from the expert review panel. Further, the results are not to be used in determining funding allocations for universities. Nonetheless, universities can be expected to use the results in hiring and promotion decisions of individuals and in determining areas for expansion or closure. Periodic repeats of the exercise are intended and no commitment has been made regarding continuing the exclusion of funding consequences or the ban on publishing results for ranking universities by discipline. King and Kriesler (2008) provide examples of how Australian university economics departments are dealing with heterodox economists in anticipation of the implementation of ERA. While the experiences cited are diverse, there are clearly some warning signs for heterodox economists.

This article reviews several aspects of the proposed Australian research evaluation exercise as it relates to heterodox economics. The section below contains a discussion of the approach to research evaluation planned for ERA. This is followed by an account of the revision of the research code classification that was undertaken in 2007, which led to substantial controversy regarding the positioning of economic history and the history of economic thought. The fourth section reviews the recently completed journal ranking exercise, while the fifth discusses other elements of the research evaluation exercise. The article concludes with personal observations and words of advice.

In discussing the development and potential effects of ERA, the author draws on his involvement in peer-review processes connected to research evaluation. He was a member of the executive committee of the Economic Society of Australia (ESA) when the ESA designed and carried out a survey of Australian economics professors to provide advice to the government on the ranking of economics journals. He also was previously editor of *The Economic Record*, the ESA's flagship academic journal. Currently, he is a member of the College of Experts, a panel that advises the ARC on applications for competitive research grants. These experiences, along with participation in the Society for Heterodox Economists and the History of Economic Thought Society of Australia, provide a broad exposure to the research activities, mainstream and heterodox, of Australian economists.

Background on the Australian University System and Excellence in Research for Australia

There are 37 public and two small private universities in the Australian system.[2] In 1974 the Commonwealth (federal) government took over primary responsibility for funding universities from state governments and also abolished tuition fees. Subsequently, tuition fees were reinstated. The government now regulates the maximum fee and maximum enrollments for domestic undergraduate students, but allows universities to set their own enrollment and fee levels for international students and domestic higher degree students.[3] In addition to the tuition fees received from students, the Commonwealth provides funding for domestic undergraduate and higher degrees by research students (doctorates and research master degrees) on the basis of an annually determined amount per full-time equivalent student, as long as the enrollment is within an institution's regulated enrollment target.[4]

Tuition fees from the unregulated portion of the total student load for public universities, namely, international undergraduate students and all coursework master degree students, account for an increasing share of total funding of universities.[5] Further, the government has set in place a progressive removal of caps on enrollment levels for domestic undergraduates starting from 2012, which may lead to shifts in load across institutions. Thus, the public universities are faced with increasing uncertainty about their future tuition income streams.

In addition to funding related to student enrollments, universities receive funding from the Commonwealth specifically for research purposes. This funding is partly from competitive research grants awarded to individuals and research centers and partly from block grants designed to support research infrastructure. The block grants are determined by a formula related to the amount of competitive research funding received, the number of higher degree students completing, and the number of publications in the categories of books, book chapters, articles in refereed journals, and refereed conference publications. The block grant funding for research is the component of funding likely to be first affected by outcomes of the ERA performance evaluation. A minor fraction of university funding comes from contract research for governments and businesses, while an even smaller fraction comes from gifts from individuals and businesses.

The publication data used in determining the block grants are quantity measures. With regard to the quantity of publications, Williams (2010) notes that the fastest growth in publications over the period 2004 to 2008 is from "new universities," institutions that have only been officially recognized as universities since a reorganization of the university system in 1987.[6] Growth in publications, and hence in the amount of funding received from the block research grants, has been slower at the long-established universities.

The push for evaluating the research performance of Australian universities has come against the background of increasing competition for research funding and increasing uncertainty about student enrollments and resulting income. The evaluation conducted under Excellence in Research for Australia (ERA) is designed to build on the quantitative information that is already collected for determining research infrastructure block grants. The quantity information is to be supplemented by quality information regarding publications and other research outputs, and then all the information is to be subjected to evaluation by committees of discipline experts.

Responsibility for administration of the research evaluation under ERA has been given to the Australian Research Council (ARC), the statutory authority that administers the Commonwealth's program for funding research in universities and other research organizations through competitive grants. The quality measures being developed by the ARC for ERA include rankings of academic journals into four quality bands, similar rankings for conferences in some disciplines, and either citation analysis or peer review of selected individual publications.[7] The mix of quality measures to be used in each discipline is designed to match normal practices of the discipline. For the economics discipline, peer review of a sample of publications will be used rather than citation analysis, which recognizes the long lags in citations common for economics publications.

All of the quantity and quality data for a discipline are to be provided to a Research Evaluation Committee (REC) consisting of discipline experts (not necessarily all academics) covering the related disciplines within each of eight clusters. The cluster within which economics is included for the purposes of the ERA performance evaluation is the Social, Behavioural and Economic (SBE) cluster, which covers most social science disciplines along with business and education. Members of the RECs will be drawn from Australia and overseas, representing the various different disciplines included in each cluster. Mainstream economists are likely to dominate those positions on the SBE REC that are allocated for economics.

Each REC will provide a score for each university in each discipline classification within its cluster. The scores are to be in five quality bands indicating whether the research performance is well above average, above average, average, below average and well below average as compared to a world benchmark. There is no prescription provided as to how the RECs are to combine the information from the various quantity and quality measures; rather, the RECs are expected to use their expert opinion on the relevance of various measures to the determination of performance in the particular discipline.

Universities are to provide a coding for each item of research output into four-digit classifications of the field of research (FoR) classification scheme provided in the Australian Bureau of Statistics (see Australian Bureau of Statistics (ABS), 2008a for details). Likewise, each individual researcher will have his or her research effort allocated across up to three four-digit FoR codes. The RECs will then provide an evaluation score for each two-digit and four-digit FoR clasification at each university, based on the output and effort coded to that classification.[8] The structure of the FoR classification scheme and the controversies associated with it are discussed in the next section.

It is important to note that the ERA scores are to be for the research conducted within a discipline or subdiscipline rather than within an administrative unit or for a nominated group of individuals. This represents a departure from standard practice in research evaluations overseas. Also, the evaluation is meant to be comprehensive, covering all academic staff employed in positions that have at least some research activity as part of their job description. There is no discretion for universities to opt out some individuals.

Research Classification Codes for Economics

The Australian Bureau of Statistics (ABS) reports biennially on research activity in higher education (almost exclusively in universities). The information includes the amount of expenditure and number of individuals (including academic, other staff, and research students). Published data are broken down by type of activity (pure, basic, applied, and experimental), by location (state or territory within the Australian Commonwealth), by source of funding, and by research field. Economics is at the finest level of disaggregation for which data are published and accounted for some AUD$134 million of expenditure in 2006, which was approximately 2.5 percent of total research expenditure in the higher education sector in that year (see ABS 2008b, Table 2.4).

In 2007 the ABS undertook a review of its classification system for reporting research activity. According to the preface to the document explaining the revised system: "The Australian and New Zealand Standard Research Classification (ANZSRC) has been developed for use in the collection, analysis and dissemination of research and experimental development statistics in Australia and New Zealand" (ABS 2008a: v). The preface goes on to explain that the revision is a response to changes in the R&D sector in Australia and New Zealand as well as changes in user requirements for R&D data. This reclassification occurred during the early stages of preparations for research assessment of Australian universities, although there is no explicit mention of the forthcoming assessment as a rationale for reclassification.

The classification scheme put out for consultation in 2007 listed the history of economic thought (HET) and economic history (EH) within the two-digit classification "philosophy and religious studies" (FoR 22), specifically they were included as six-digit classifications within the four-digit classification "history and philosophy of specific fields" (FoR 2202), Previously, they had jointly constituted one of five subdisciplines of economics. At the time, historians of economic thought (a group that includes many heterodox economists) and economic historians (more mainstream, but often viewed as methodologically deviant because of their ambivalence toward mathematical theorizing) strenuously objected to their separation from economics. At the end of the consultation, the new classification scheme retained "history of economic thought" within economics as a six-digit classification within the four-digit classification "economic theory" (FoR 1401), while "economic history" was retained as a six-digit classification within the four-digit classification "applied economics" (FoR 1402).[9]

As noted in the section above, the ERA evaluation of research performance is to be based on FoR classifications. In preparation universities are now asking academics to allocate their research activity (both effort and outputs) over fields of research (FoR) codes as defined in the ABS research classification scheme. Effort and each individual output is to be assigned in terms of percentages to between one and three classifications at the four-digit level of the FoR classification, with the allocated percentages adding up to 100 percent. Within the two-digit FoR classification for "economics" (FoR 14) there are four-digit FoR codes: "economic theory" (FoR 1401), "applied economics" (FoR 1402), "econometrics" (FoR 1403), and "other economics" (FoR 1499). "Heterodox economics" is the heading for one six-digit code within FoR 1499, while the other six-digit codes in 1499 are for "ecological economics," "comparative economics," and "economics not elsewhere classified."[10]

The classification system and allocation process is certain to lead to understatement of the amount of activity classified as heterodox economics. Heterodox economists who classify their full research effort as belonging to FoR 1499 are stating that they do not devote effort to economic theory (including history of economic thought), applied economics (including economic history and other standard subject areas, such as health, international, and labor), or econometrics. A choice is required between the heterodox orientation of the research and the method or subject matter; theory, applied, or econometric. Of course, a compromise of sorts is possible with classifying part of effort and part of each output to more than one four-digit FoR code, but even here the attribution to heterodox economics is a fraction of the whole.

The severity of the understatement of research output in heterodox economics will be particularly severe with regard to journal articles. Here, the output will be allocated to the FoR code that has been assigned to that journal for the purposes of ERA. Originally, it was decided that each journal would have only a single two-digit or four-digit code. However, after consultation the final journal assignments list up to three FoR codes for each journal. Where a journal has multiple FoR codes, a choice can be made of any of the included codes or percentages of the output can be allocated over more than one code. There is also a list of multidisciplinary journals, for which articles can be allocated to any FoR code. Most economics journals have only a single FoR code assigned, implying that all articles in that journal are automatically allocated to the FoR code for the journal.

Table 1 lists the FoR codes assigned to the 62 heterodox journals identified by Lee and Cronin (2010) in their contribution to this special issue.[11] Notably, only six are assigned in whole or in part to FoR 1499. The six are two journals in ecological economics, *Ecological Economics* and *International Journal of Green Economics*, two political economy journals, *Australian Journal of Political Economy* and *Rethinking Marxism*, one comparative economics journal, *Economic Systems Research*, and one journal, *International Journal of Social*

Table 1

Distribution of 62 Heterodox Economics Journals by Field of Research (FoR) code

FoR code	number of journals
14—economics	6
1401—economic theory	16
1402—applied economics	22
1403—econometrics	1
1499—other economics	6
FoR codes other than 14, 1401, 1402, 1403, or 1499	33
not ranked	2

Source: http://www.arc.gov.au/era/era_journal_list.htm (accessed April 29, 2010).

Economics, that is presumably deemed either to be heterodox economics or economics not elsewhere classified. It seems heterodoxy is
pretty much an empty box as far as journal classifications are concerned.[12] The only four-digit economics code to which fewer heterodox journals have been assigned is "econometrics" (FoR 1403). Thus,
under ERA articles in heterodox economics journals will not be
attributed to heterodox economics in terms of being counted in the
broader classification "other economics" into which heterodox economics has been classified.

Ranking of Journals

The journal rankings that have been developed for use in the Excellence in Research for Australia (ERA) evaluation have been derived in
a consultation process with universities, academic societies, and individual academics. A preliminary ranking developed by the Australian
Research Council (ARC) ERA team put out for consultation with the
academic community listed over 400 economics journals, that is,
journals assigned to FoR 14, 1401, 1402, 1403, or 1499, along with
thousands of journals classified in other FoR codes. The preliminary
rankings were based on submissions from academic societies and
other peak academic groups, with the economics rankings largely
based on a submission from the Economic Society of Australia (ESA).

The ESA ranking of journals was based on a survey of professors of
economics and econometrics working in Australian universities.[13] Each
respondent was asked to rank a list of journals into four bands, A*, A,
B, and C, with A* journals representing the top 5 percent, A the next
15 percent, B the next 30 percent, and C the bottom half. Respondents
were not required to rank all journals, but neither were they disquali-
fied from ranking journals with which they had limited familiarity. The
overall ESA ranking was determined by a simple average of individual
respondent rankings, with A* given a value of 1, A given 2, B given
3, and C given 4. The numerical averages were then grouped into
letter ranks by designating the top 5 percent of journals as A*, etc. The
rankings of the individual respondents were far from uniform, with
the standard deviation of the numerical scores generally being greater
than 0.5 (more than half way between adjacent letter ranks).

The preliminary ranking of journals for ERA was released for consultation in mid 2008. Comments were invited from universities, academic societies, and individuals. Many issues were identified, including the same journal being ranked in more than one discipline, sometimes with different ranks. The ARC utilized committees of experts from the various discipline groupings to move towards consistent classifications and rankings, which took account of the responses to the preliminary rankings. During this process the ESA made strong representations that the results of its survey should determine the ranking of journals assigned to the economics FoR codes (14, 1401, 1402, 1403, and 1499).[14]

Table 2 presents the distribution of ranks for the group of 62 heterodox journals identified by Lee and Cronin (2010) in their contribution to this special issue. The first three columns show the ranking category, the target percentage that was set for journals to be included at this rank, and the actual distribution of ranks for the 62 heterodox economics journals. Also shown in Table 2 is the distribution of ranks for the same journals based on the ESA survey of economics and econometrics professors.

On first glance the ERA rankings seem to have treated heterodox journals reasonably well. While there is only one heterodox journal

Table 2

Distribution of Rankings of 62 Heterodox Economics Journals
(% of Total in Parentheses)

Rank	Target percentage	ERA rankings	ESA survey rankings
A*	5%	1 (2%)	0 (0%)
A	15%	16 (26%)	13 (21%)
B	30%	25 (40%)	25 (40%)
C	50%	18 (29%)	17 (28%)
Not Ranked		2 (3%)	7 (11%)

Sources: ERA rankings: http://www.arc.gov.au/era/era_journal_list.htm (accessed April 29, 2010).

ESA rankings: http://www.ecosoc.org.au/cc/publications (accessed April 29, 2010).

ranked A* journal, A* are targeted to account for only 5 percent of total ranked journals. Sixteen of the 62 ranked journals (26 percent) are in the A category for ERA, which compares to a target of 15 percent for the full sample. The journals ranked to category B are also higher for ERA (40 percent) than the 30 percent target for the full sample, while the C ranked journals are only 18 percent for ERA compared to a target of 50 percent for the full sample. If the 62 heterodox journals were separated as a group and required to have a distribution matching the targets set for ERA, there would be perhaps one or two more A* journals but many fewer A and B journals than in the ERA rankings.

There are three important caveats to the apparently favorable ranking of the heterodox journals. First, they are not based on a like for like comparison. Based on their analysis of journal quality equivalence, Lee and Cronin (2010) conclude that "the Australian rankings systematically undervalues the heterodox journals that are included." This reflects both the low number of heterodox journals that are highly ranked in the ERA ranking and the variable scores on the Lee and Cronin ranking scale for the top tier mainstream journals.

Second, as also shown by Lee and Cronin, the relative position of the heterodox journals differs from their relative ranking based on their quality from the perspective of heterodox economics. For example, according to the ERA targets approximately 20 percent of journals should be ranked A* or A, but among the top 12 out of 62 heterodox journals based on the scoring of Lee and Cronin none are ranked as A* in the ERA rankings, five are ranked as A, six are ranked as B, and one is ranked as C. Further, the one heterodox journal ranked as A* for ERA, *History of Political Economy*, is only number 23 in the Lee and Cronin ranking.

It is arguable that the heterodox economics journals with higher rankings for ERA are not those most important and attractive to heterodox economists. Rather, the heterodox journals with high rankings are those important and attractive to mainstream economists, as the ERA rankings have been determined largely by the ESA survey of economics and econometrics professors. Of the 55 heterodox journals in both the ERA and ESA rankings, the ranks are identical for all but six. The six journals with different ranks include five that are one rank higher for ERA than in the ESA survey, which can be attributed to the influence of specialist interests related to, but separate from, heterodox economics.[15] The one case where a heterodox journal has a lower ranking for ERA (rank C) than in the ESA survey (rank A), *Journal of Economic Issues*, appears to have been the result of an administrative error and breakdown in communications in the intent by the ARC to implement the results of the ESA survey.[16]

A third important caveat required in regarding the ERA rankings as favorable to heterodox economics is that most of the 60 ranked heterodox economics journals are not recognized as relevant to heterodox economics for purposes of the ERA performance evaluation. As noted in the previous section only six journals are classified into the category "other economics" (FoR 1499). Of these six, only one is ranked A, two are ranked B, and three are ranked C. Thus, the discipline-based classification scheme for research output in ERA means that most articles in high-ranking heterodox journals will not contribute to a high quality ranking for the four-digit classification "other economics" that includes heterodox economics.

Other Evaluation Metrics

The small number of journal articles in heterodox economics likely to be classified in the category "other economics" (FoR 1499), and the relatively low quality rankings assigned to the journals in which these articles, appear to argue against a good performance evaluation for the category including heterodox economics. Of course, journal article quantity and quality are only two of the metrics that will be assessed by the Research Evaluation Committee (REC) for the Social, Behavioural and Economics (SBE) cluster evaluating the economics discipline (FoR 14 and its component four-digit codes). Also included are publications of research books, book chapters, papers, and presentations at refereed academic conferences. Further, there are data on external research income (excluding Commonwealth block grants to universities, but including Commonwealth funded competitive research grant schemes). However, heterodox economics is unlikely to score well in any of these other metrics, further contributing to a poor showing for the "other economics" classification in the performance evaluation score.

The problem for the "other economics" classification in achieving high scores on evaluation metrics beside journal articles can be illustrated by examining data from the Australian Research Council (ARC) on research funding provided through two major grant funding schemes that are available to individual researchers or research teams in universities. Applications for funding require the applicant to specify one or more discipline classification codes relevant to the application, along with a percentage weighting if more than one code is chosen. This coding is done at the six-digit level of the classification, which would separate heterodox economics in the current classification scheme, but the most disaggregated data published is at the level of four-digit FoR code. Table 3 shows the number of grants and total funding tabulated by the four-digit codes for economics.

The classification of grants in Table 3 is according to the new ANZSRC classification scheme, but the classification scheme available to applicants at the time that the grants were submitted was the preexisting ASRC. The grants have been reclassified based on a concordance between the classification schemes. As explained above, the change in classifications removed economic history and history of economic thought as a subdiscipline, so grants in that subdiscipline have been redistributed. Also changed were the groupings within the "other economics" classification, with the grouping "political economy" removed and the groupings "heterodox

Table 3

ARC Funding Grants in Economics by FoR Classification 2002–2008 (% of Total in Parentheses)

FoR classification	Number of grants	Amount of ARC funding
1401—economic theory	28 (10.3%)	8,727,463 (13.4%)
1402—applied economics	194 (71.1%)	45,637,948 (70.1%)
1403—econometrics	47 (15.5%)	10,060,042 (15.5%)
1499—other economics	4 (1.5%)	637,216 (1.0%)

Source: http://www.arc.gov.au/xls/WebData_RFCD_to_FAO.xls (accessed on April 29, 2010).

economics" and "ecological economics" added to the prior groupings of "comparative economic systems" and "economics not elsewhere classified."

According to the data in Table 3, "other economics" (FoR 1499) accounts for a miniscule portion of grant-funded economics research at 1.5 percent of grants and 1 percent of funding. The implication is that heterodox economics, as part of this classification, is unimportant in terms of funded research. Of course, there was no coding for heterodox economics in ASRC, so any such implication is unwarranted. However, this finer point is unlikely to be noticed when the evaluation metrics are considered by the Social, Behaviourial and Economic Research Evaluation Committee (SBE REC) in providing a score for "other economics" at the various universities.

In addition to the impact of the historical conversion of research categories, there is the previously noted fundamental problem inherent in the structure of both the old and new classification schemes that will lead to heterodox economics activity being understated in the ERA evaluation. Both schemes distinguish classifications within economics by method and subject, which leads to the four-digit FoR classifications of "economic theory," "applied economics," "econometrics," and "other economics." However, there is no distinction between mainstream and nonmainstream approaches within any of the categories, other than placing heterodox economics as a six-digit classification within "other economics." Much funding of research that is heterodox in approach is likely to have been classified into four-digit FoR codes for "economic theory" and "applied economics," or even "econometrics," just as Table 1 shows has occurred with the assignment of heterodox economics journals to FoR codes.

Universities have discretion in assigning FoR codes for publication outputs other than journal articles, which includes books, book chapters, and conference papers.[17] Although the choice of coding is the responsibility of the university, they can be expected to generally follow the advice of the author where the author is willing and able to participate. Here, heterodox economists have the opportunity to designate their work as belonging to the classification "other economics" (FoR 1499). However, there are reasons to expect that even here the output of heterodox economics will be underreported.

First, the assignment of any particular output will need to deal with the fundamental problem of the overlapping nature of the FoR codes in economics. For most heterodox economics this creates a conflict between classification by subject and approach. For example, it will be tempting to assign a book containing a heterodox treatment of macroeconomics wholly or partially to "economic theory" (FoR 1401) or to "applied economics" (FoR 1402) rather than assigning wholly to "other economics" (FoR 1499).

A second deterrent facing authors in classifying heterodox publications as belonging to "other economics" is that output in this classification at their university may be insufficient to reach the minimum threshold required for a performance score. For disciplines such as economics where peer review of publications is utilized a minimum of 30 items of assessable output is required. Given the small number of journals for which articles will be classified as belonging to "other economics," a large number of books, book chapters, and conference publications will be required before a performance score is possible. Further, for any publication that is designated as belonging partially to "other economics" and partially to another FoR code, only that portion designated as "other economics" counts towards satisfying the 30-item threshold.

A final deterrent likely to affect classifying publications as belonging to the "other economics" is the results in a trial of the ERA performance evaluation conducted in 2009. This trial only involved the clusters for Physical, Chemical and Earth Sciences (PCE) and the Humanities and Creative Arts (HCA), but each of the two-digit FoR classifications involved in the trial includes a four-digit code for other research in the discipline. These "other" codes are designated by the last two digits of the code being 99. The published results show generally poor results for "other" FoR codes.[18]

The published results provide only a maximum score and an average score over all reporting institutions, as is consistent with the intention not to publish results for individual universities. Across the eight different two-digit FoR classifications in HCA, there is not one in which the average score for the "other" code (FoR xx99) is above average for the world standard and in each two-digit classification the "other" code has the lowest score of any of the four-digit codes. No such clear pattern emerges in the results for the three two-digit FoR classifications included in PCE, but it is telling that there is no institution that reached the minimum output threshold for the "other" code in the earth sciences (FoR 0499). No information is provided on the number of institutions scored in each FoR classification, but the earth sciences result is suggestive that generally only a small number of institutions met the minimum threshold in for the "other" codes.

Likely Outcomes and Lessons for Heterodox Economists

The ERA evaluation of university research performance being undertaken in Australia is somewhat unique in that the evaluation is being done by discipline rather than by individual or organizational unit. As outlined above, the classification system to be used for measuring research output relegates heterodox economics, economic history, and the history of economic thought to classifications of "other economics," "applied economics," and "economic theory," respectively. This seems sure to lead to hiding the magnitude of nonmainstream research activity. There are also likely to be negative implications in terms of the quality evaluation of heterodox economics research, at least judging from the scores awarded to work in the "other" codes within those disciplines included in a 2009 trial of the ERA (economics was not included in this trial).

I am among the many economists who are self-taught when it comes to economic analysis that is outside the mainstream. My education as an undergraduate at the University of Michigan (mainstream—left) and postgraduate at the University of Chicago (mainstream—right) provided limited pluralism in either ideas or method. It is largely due to colleagues, particularly at the University of Denver in the mid 1970s to the mid 1980s, that I was exposed to alternative approaches to economics. I had already established a publication track record in mainstream applied economics (industrial economics and international trade) before beginning to publish in heterodox journals. I continue to engage with both heterodox and mainstream research, publishing in both mainstream and heterodox journals and participating in both mainstream and heterodox organizations.

From the perspective of an outsider, I've experienced referees and grant assessors who view research in heterodox economics with indifference or even open hostility. As an insider, particularly as a former editor of a mainstream journal and as a current member of a panel advising government on funding research grants, I know that such reactions aren't universal and that a substantial group of mainstream economists provide fair reports on heterodox research and grant applications. Further, at least in the case of Australia, I am reasonably confident that journal editors and national research funding bodies make efforts to limit the impact of unfair assessments on the selection of papers for publication and the recommendation of grant proposals for funding.

As an outsider on the inside, I see growing vitality of heterodox economics research in Australia over recent decades. There is a large and growing community of heterodox economic scholars producing a substantial body of interesting and important research.[19] Yet, the advent of a national research evaluation under ERA poses great challenges to this community. The output of heterodox economics research will be woefully understated and heterodox economists are likely to be undercounted. When the output is counted it will be as part of the "other economics" classification, which is likely to achieve a poor performance score. Thus, heterodox economics will be further marginalized and tarnished with a low quality reputation.

For heterodox economists already employed in universities the individual consequences are not likely to be quite so severe. All of their research funding and publications will be attributed to them as individuals regardless of the field of research (FoR) code to which the metrics have been assigned. The quality of their work will not be individually evaluated by a research evaluation committee, which will most likely be dominated by mainstream economists. Even where some of their research output is sent for peer review, the results of the review will not be available to their employing university. They can survive in the guise of pluralist economists, which is an apposite characterization for individuals whose research output and effort is spread over a number of research classifications. However, the marginalization of heterodoxy will still matter in terms of diminishing the likelihood of hiring like-minded colleagues. What university will want to build up its staff profile in an obscure and low quality specialization within economics?

Let me close by applying some ideas generated from my work in evolutionary economics (a sometimes neglected branch of heterodox economics). In analyzing the relationship between innovation and dynamic competition in industry it is noted that there is resistance to new products, processes, and ways of doing business. Progress requires overcoming this resistance. Scientific discourse is a social construction and, as such, has built-in biases favoring the status quo. This puts resistance in the way of those wanting to pursue careers in heterodox economics.

Will resistance from the mainstream prevent the further development of heterodox economics? Not likely, but challenging orthodoxy will not be any easier in economic science than is challenging established practices in industry. Fortunately or unfortunately, the rewards to success in making progress in economics are different than in industry. Instead of generating enormous fortunes for successful entrepreneurs, the payoffs to innovative scholarship are more akin to those in noncommercial artistic endeavors. Thus, the circumstances facing heterodox economists might be described by the old saying, you have to suffer if you want to sing the blues.[20]

There are some things Australian heterodox economists can do collectively to improve the outcomes for heterodox economics in future research evaluations. First, they can emulate the behavior of historians of economic thought. Not only was this group able to restore its classification as part of a core field of research within economics, namely, economic theory, but three journals in the history of economic thought have been ranked higher in the ERA rankings than they were in the survey of economics and econometrics professors. As noted above, only two other heterodox journals had a similar achievement. Perhaps the relatively young Society of Heterodox Economists (Australian based but not necessarily Australian focused) can emulate the pattern of behavior of its more established counterpart, the History of Economic Thought Society of Australia.

A second collective project that might improve the evaluation outcomes for heterodox economics would be to push for better placement of heterodox economics within the research classification scheme used by ERA. The key objective would be to achieve placement outside the "other economics" field of research. The experience of the trial evaluation in humanities and creative arts demonstrates that placement in the "other" code within a discipline is deadly in terms of the evaluation of research performance. Ideal for heterodox economics would be to be grouped with fellow travelers, history of economic thought and ecological economics, under a heading such as alternative economic analysis. However, even a placement within the "applied economics" or "economic theory" classifications would be preferable to being left on the outers in "other economics."

Notes

1. Current details of the purposes and procedures for ERA can be viewed at: http://www.arc.gov.au/era/default.htm.

2. The two private universities, Bond University in Queensland and the University of Notre Dame in Western Australia, collectively accounted for approximately 1 percent of the total student load in the university system in 2008 (source: *Students, Selected Higher Education Statistics, Private Universities*, Australian Department of Education, Employment and Workplace Reform, http://www.DEEWR.gov.au, accessed April 19, 2010).

3. Most domestic undergraduate students pay their tuition fees using the Higher Education Contribution Scheme (HECS), which provides loans from the Commonwealth government repayable through future tax liability.

4. The amount per student varies across each discipline cluster and level of study. Economics is within the cluster with the lowest funding per student.

5. Overseas students accounted for 27 percent of the total student load of public universities in 2008, while postgraduate course work students (including overseas students) accounted for 22.5 percent (source: *Students, Selected Higher Education Statistics, Public Universities*, Australian Department of Education, Employment and Workplace Reform, http://www.DEEWR.gov.au, accessed April 19, 2010). The revenue per student for international and postgraduate students is generally substantially higher than for domestic undergraduate students. Universities also receive revenue from offshore delivery of their courses and from licensing their courses to both offshore and onshore private providers.

6. This reorganization led to former colleges of advanced education and institutes of technology becoming universities and also led to a number of mergers of smaller institutions.

7. There are also research output categories for the creative arts, including original creative work, live and recorded performances, and certain exhibitions.

8. There are minimum levels of research output required before an evaluation will be undertaken for a particular four-digit discipline classification at a particular university. Otherwise, the output will be used in evaluating the university at the two-digit FoR code level, but no score will be provided at the four-digit level. It is likely that at some smaller universities the amount of output at even the two-digit level might be insufficient for a scoring to be undertaken.

9. The struggle to maintain the classification of history of economic thought and economic history as part of economics is discussed in Kates and Millmow (2008).

10. Heterodox economics was not recognized in the ABS research classification prior to the latest revision. Instead, there was a category of political economics, which presumably is now meant to be included within heterodox economics.

11. The number of journals in Table 1 adds up to more than 62 because some journals have more than one FoR code assigned. One journal, *Journal of Economic Methodology*, is assigned to both FoR 1401 and 1403. Another journal, *Intervention: European Journal of Economics and Economic Policy*, is assigned to both FoR 1401 and 1402. Nine journals with four-digit economics codes also have four-digit codes outside economics. These are mostly history of economic thought journals, which are also assigned to the code for "history and philosophy of specific scientific" fields (FoR 2202), and political economy journals, which are also assigned to the code for "political science" (FoR 1606).

12. There are also six journals from the Lee and Cronin (2010) listing that are assigned to the "economics" two-digit FoR code, 14, without being assigned to any component four-digit code. These are *Cambridge Journal of Economics, Metroeconomica, Review of Austrian Economics, Econ Journal Watch, Quarterly Journal of Austrian Economics*, and *Journal of Interdisciplinary Economics*. Articles published in these journals may be assigned to any of the four-digit codes with the 14 code.

13. Details of the design and implementation of the survey are reported in Abelson (2009).

14. See Abelson (2009) for a discussion of the ESA's efforts to resolve in its own favor the differences between the ARC preliminary rankings and the rankings in the ESA survey.

15. The specialists whose interests have been served are historians of economic thought, with three history of thought journals being ranked higher in the ERA rankings than in the ESA survey (two journals going from B to A rank and one going from A to A*), and political scientists, with two political

economy journals that are solely or jointly assigned to the "political science" classification (FoR 1606) upgraded from B in the ESA survey to A in the ERA rankings.

16. Correspondence regarding the *Journal of Economic Issues*, from Margaret Sheil, CEO of the Australian Research Council, dated March 12, 2010 notes that "the ARC has worked closely with the Economic Society of Australia (ESA) to develop the journal rankings for Economics disciplines. I can confirm that this journal was considered by the ESA through several iterations who maintained their recommended C ranking." Peter Abelson, who acted as liaison for the ESA with the ARC over the iterations referred to by Margaret Sheil, notes the following in regard to the *Journal of Economic Issues*: "ARC downgraded this from ESA recommended A to C. Regrettably this change appears to be due to confusion between this journal and another, possibly the Journal of Environmental Informatics."

17. In some disciplines FoR codes have been assigned by the ARC to a list of conferences, but this has not occurred in economics.

18. For results of the trial evaluations, see http://www.arc.gov.au/era/ HCA09_trial.htm and http://www.arc.gov.au/era/PCE09_trial.htm (accessed April 30, 2010).

19. The Society for Heterodox Economics, an Australian-based group, currently has over 200 subscribers to its mailing list and its annual conference regularly has over 100 attendees.

20. In this context, Butler et al. (2009) provide an illuminating history of heterodox economics at the University of Sydney.

References

Abelson, Peter. (2009). "The Ranking of Economics Journals by the Economic Society of Australia." *Economic Papers* 28(2): 176–180.

Australian Bureau of Statistics (ABS). (2008a). *Australian and New Zealand Standard Research Classification (ANZSRC)*. Catalogue 1297. Canberra: Australian Bureau of Statistics.

——. (2008b). *Research and Experimental Development, Higher Education Organisations, Australia, 2006*. Catalogue 8111. Canberra: Australian Bureau of Statistics.

Butler, Gavan, Evan Jones, and Frank Stilwell. (2009). *Political Economy Now*. Sydney: Darlington Press.

Kates, Steven, and Alex Millmow. (2008). "The History Wars of Economics: The Classification Struggle in the History of Economic Thought." *History of Economics Review* 47: 110–124.

King, J. E. (2007). "RQF and HET: Assassin and Corpse?" *History of Economics Review* 45: 106–111.

King, J. E., and Peter Kriesler. (2008). "News from Down Under." *On the Horizon* 16(4): 289–292.

Lee, Frederic, and Bruce Cronin. (2010). "Research Quality Rankings of Heterodox Economic Journals in a Contested Discipline." *American Journal of Economics and Sociology*, this issue.

Williams, Ross. (2010). "Research Output of Australian Universities: Are the Newer Universities Catching Up?" *Australian Universities Review* 52(1): 32–36.

Economics Performance and Institutional Economics in Poland After 1989

By Agnieszka Ziomek

Introduction

Institutional economics is a unique way of looking at the economy and the processes that influence its development. The uniqueness refers mostly to its difference from neoclassical economics. Starting from the mid-1990s, Poland witnessed an active interest in heterodox economics, including many other economic trends, apart from mainstream economics. The reasons behind this interest are related to the practical economics on the macroeconomic level. One of the reasons for the development of heterodox economic research was that the theses about the end of the transformation process in Poland, which appeared before the end of the 1990s, were inconsistent with the statistical data illustrating the state of the Polish economy. The development of a few branches of economy and of a few markets does not equal the development of social institutions, better welfare of people, or better access to social services. The state of the Polish economy after 20 years of transformation brought an increased interest in the alternative approaches of the economy that could be useful in explaining economic phenomena and pointing to the proper changes in economic policy.

Apart from a number of trends in heterodox economics, currents in institutional economics (IE) are also of great interest. After 1989, orthodox economics was dominant in Poland both in teaching and practical economics. During the late 1990s, the renewed interest in IE turned out to be essential for the understanding and explanation of the current socioeconomic situation, as it exerted a strong influence on the market and on the implementation of new economic reforms. The socioeconomic situation of that time involved the privatization of State Treasury assets, and its consequences, illegal employment and the development of the gray economy. Papers, published mostly in Poland, explained economic processes by the means of the methods

American Journal of Economics and Sociology, Vol. 69, No. 5 (November, 2010).

of institutional economics. However, it has to be noted that those papers presented the methods of new institutional economics (NIE). A number of them failed to include the historical context and descriptive studies that are characteristics of traditional institutionalists. NIE is an attempt to fuse mainstream economic theory with the traditional institutional economics (TIE) and shows several trends. Those trends include: the new theory of the firm (Coase 1990, 1992, 1998), social and public choice theory (Buchanan and Yoon 2003, 2008), the theory of international regimes, a new economic history, and the theory of transaction costs (North 1994, 2003). What seems to be important is that NIE always seeks to set economic phenomena within the institutional environment. Due to the fact that NIE has an exploitative attitude toward institutions, one can postulate that it does not refer to IE at all. Moreover, it does not fully resemble neoclassical economics, as it almost entirely rejects the neoclassical theory of the firm, the neoclassical perception of market mechanism, and the construction of the *homo oeconomicus* model.

Still, taking into consideration its explanatory values, the IE, with its holistic character and historical and evolutionary outlook on socio-economic phenomena, was overlooked in scholarly works. NIE, on the other hand, is still dominant in the published theses and articles.

Due to the fact that IE, and especially NIE, have been the fields of scholarly interest for a relatively short time, the works published in Poland point to the application of the selected institutional arguments, rather than to the full and complete implementation of the institutionalist method of traditional institutionalism and NIE. Many authors[1] make occasional and indirect references to institutionalism, not wishing to implement the theory in its entirety.

The aim of the article is to present a number of selected social and economic phenomena that are of great interest to the scholars investigating the TIE and NIE. However, the article does not seek to provide a complete record of the scholars and their writings grouped according to the above criteria. As mentioned above, IE has only recently (after 1989) become a popular research subject, which makes it impossible to create an all-encompassing and clear-cut division of academic ideas and Polish schools that teach economics, with certain exceptions to this rule. So, the small number of papers being published on IE[2] makes it impossible to single it out as a separate category that can be subject to assessment in Polish scientific journals. Moreover, it is difficult to speak of the integration of the IE environment in light of a few and rarely published papers on IE. However, it is worthwhile to investigate a selection of papers on IE and especially their way of interpreting socioeconomic phenomena. Among the chosen examples, numerous instances of applying theories to different areas of the economy and law can be identified. This approach is present in the research of a group of Polish economists.

Institutionalism in Polish Economics—Main Aspects of Research

This article highlights many aspects of economics, including institutionalist methodology and institutionalism's place in the theory of economic thought. Case studies show how IE can be applied. However, because of the nature of Polish economics and areas of contemporary study, the specific thematic fields can be identified, namely: economic transformation, that is, shock transformation, institutional theories of the state, including the role of the state in the economy, and social and economic changes on the job market. In general, one has to remember that most of the issues discussed in this article have been based on NIE.

Authors of papers mentioned below devoted to economic transformation processes and their problems focus on the following: the reasons behind the change of the system and its inevitability, the description of the transformation process, the order of the reform changes, the role of the state and the market in this process, the phenomena accompanying the transformation (that is, the creation and the role of interest groups), and the phenomenon of rent-seeking and redistribution coalitions.

It is worth referring to a few selected theses on the subject. One of such papers is an article by B. Fiedor[3] titled "New Institutional Economics as a Basis of Theoretical Reflection on the Transformation Process from the Planned Economy to the Market Economy" and A. Wojtyna's paper "If the Traditional Economics Let Us Understand the New Economy?" (2000a). The authors define NIE as having a rather large scope, including new political economy, which (together with transaction cost theory, the theory of property rights, and formal as well as informal institutional analysis in historical perspective) investigates political phenomena, the functioning of the state, and non-economic aspects of social life. Other economists stress the fact that the transformation process at its preconstitutive stage is characterized by an excessive demand for public regulation (compared to a mature market economy) and underdevelopment, or development of regulatory power in the wrong direction. On the one hand, this can lead to numerous regulatory mistakes in public regulations by the state. On the other hand, it may lead to an inadequate supply of good regulatory solutions. In fact, the rapid, whimsical changes in the system of regulation created complexity. Regulatory changes intentionally and unintentionally largely reduced the value of economic initiatives. The biggest problem was not that the enterprises were faced with too many constraints, but rather that it was unknown to them what exactly the constraints were (Swaan and Lisowska 1996). However, the approach of IE towards public regulation is used to explain the process of creating institutional market foundations in "emerging market economies" (Wilkin 2008; Szabolcs 2007).[4]

The Role of the State in the Transformed Economy

Poland was liberalized with one "big bang" freeing 90 percent of prices, eliminating most trade barriers, abolishing state trading monopolies, and making its currency convertible for current transactions all at once in January 1990 (World Development Report 1996). Parallel to that, at the very beginning of the transformation process, the state had to establish preconstitutive property rights along with the corresponding formal institutions to decrease general uncertainty in the economy and to exclude (or to considerably limit) the possibility of gaining economic profits by way of "robbery" (Hockuba 1995; Besler and Persson 2009).[5] So, the state also needed to create new "rules of the game," and the informal and formal institutions that would make sure that those rules are followed (Wojtyna 2000a, 2000b; Staniszkis 2007). What is more important is that the environment and governance structures complement each other in any sector of industrial production (Rossiaud and Locatelli 2009).[6]

The market and the state are parts of the institutional structure within which people function. The construction of the theories of the state need to be interdisciplinary. The central bank as an institution is also interpreted on such a level. Noga (2008) reminds the readers that currency circulation may be disrupted by different factors. To ensure a sufficient supply of liquidity enabling the exchange of goods and services, the central bank enters the market as a market governance institution. Apart from creating or strengthening institutions in the country, the deliberations about Poland's transformation model are also of interest. In a number of papers we find that authors emphasize that transformation should not be a shock transformation because it would exclude a considerable group of people from benefiting from the new rules of the market system. Legiędź's study (2008) is worth noting. One of his main claims is the argument that basing the transition of the Chinese economy on institutional changes was a success from an economic as well as social point of view because many citizens did not experience the negative effects of the reforms like those experienced in the Central and Eastern European countries. The Chinese reforms were gradual, but it is impossible to create a universal solution for a successful transformation drawing on their experiences. Every country needs to choose its own way toward transformation. As Swaan and Lisowska (1996) argue, the "economic performance depends upon the interplay between incentives, institutions, and capabilities. Changes in incentives alone, for instance through price liberalization, financial stabilization, and ownership changes, will be unable to bring about immediate, radical improvements in performance."

Hausner (1995) presents an interesting explanation based on institutional methodology. He describes the strategy of systemic change. The negotiated strategy as an alternative to the liberal approach is based on an interactive approach. Implementing this strategy calls for minimum changes in habitual patterns of behavior. The implementation of a liberal approach based on an imperative method of social change has created an interaction crisis. One of the major symptoms of this crisis is the contradiction between political articulation and institutionalization. It seems, as Hausner points out, that the only effective pro-transformation way of overcoming this contradiction would be to create structures that could bridge the gap between society and the authorities and to mediate conflicts between them (Hausner 1995).

Consequently, as a response to this crisis, a Committee for Community Dialogue was created in 1994 at the central government level, as well as other industry committees and committees at the regional level.

Institutional Unemployment and Job Market Institutions

The unemployment revealed in 1989 is a phenomenon that evolved both in the sense of its character and causes. Amongst the causes of unemployment investigated from the standpoint of institutional labor economics, some statements about legal regulations and socially accepted norms of behavior, considered as informal institutions influencing unemployment, can be found Kinnear's work (1999). In Poland, a considerable number of informal institutions appeared as a result of repeating patterns of human behavior. Some of these institutions have their own names, such as the "roller coaster effect," while others refer to a particular situation, including the case of an employer who was made to sign an untruthful refusal of employment. The influence of these institutions on the process of economic growth in the country is investigated as partly relating to IE. It is difficult to perceive elements of the institutional order, such as formal and informal institutions, or the degree to which the accepted rules are observed, as determinants of economic growth (Boni 2002, and Ziomek 2009). The influence of a social institution on economic growth is difficult to estimate due to the fact that the institution can be characterized by fleeting and unstable actions or as being focused on supporting concrete measures. We also need to remember that the aim of an institution is not to support the economic growth processes because an institution is usually established to facilitate a concrete process. Studies of a few chosen institutions show that their influence is unstable, hence, they can either be pro- or anti-growth.

Unemployment can be analyzed according to the relationships between some selected institutions (Jarmołowicz and Woźniak 2008). Part of the unemployment can be blamed on the dominant institutions in a given economy. Jarmołowicz and Woźniak (2008) explain the existence of institutional unemployment as an effect of the behavior of three groups of subjects such as employees, employers, and the state. The actions of these subjects can lead to unemployment due to adverse effects caused by the law or by excessive economic policy intervention. The above mentioned causes of unemployment are also cited by Baccaro and Rei (2007), who claim, at least according to the pooled data, that the impact of labor market institutions is, for the most part, not robust and that high unemployment is mostly caused by high real interest rates and independent central banks. Clearly, there could be more fine-grained institutionals effects that are not captured by these models. For example, labor market institutions may affect different demographic groups in different ways, so that even though there is no average effect on unemployment, there are distinct effects on group-specific employment and unemployment rates, such as those for women and youth. We cannot assess these more nuanced effects with our specification (Baccaro and Rei 2007). The explanation of the determinants of unemployment needs to be completed. Solow's remark provides an insightful comment for this part of the article: "It does not follow from any of this that the ordinary forces of supply and demand are irrelevant to the labour market, or that we can do without textbook apparatus altogether. It only follows that they are incomplete and need completing" (Solow 1990).

Interest Groups (Gray Economy)

An important aspect of the process of creating institutional market foundations in "emerging market economies" is that economic reforms lead to rapid growth in the private sector. However, when reforms are too slow, informal shadow economies of private firms will emerge accompanied by spontaneous privatization (World Development Report 1996). Therefore, some argue that a rapid and transparent privatization, liberalization, and demonopolization of the economy is needed to reduce the scope for corruption. In an economy that is undergoing such transformation, due to an unstable system, fledging institutions, slow privatization,[7] and the fraternization of power, one witnesses a drive toward profit through skimming. One common phenomena that appears in transition economies is the emergence of a considerable number of big interest groups. The big interest groups run business based on income redistribution. Very often they are referred to as "redistribution coalitions." The activity of those groups is visible through the creation of new patterns of behavior that become informal behavioral rules. Such behaviors consist of lobbying and clientelism used by the managerial elite. As Staniszkis (2007) indicates, the postcommunist managerial elite occupy the commanding positions of the economy but do not have exclusive political power. This phenomenon has materialized itself from a bargain with "humanistic intellectuals," needed by the managerial elite to legitimize their social capital and to co-opt civil society. The new power elite is a broad-based class alliance. The nomenclature has not consolidated their function because market institutions, private ownership, foreign capital, and the inability to pass on power to their children have maintained the fluidity of postcommunist class structure (Staniszkis 1991). The issue to be considered using NIE is the role of such coalitions in diminishing economic and political transparency, increasing public regulation, and improving the significance of state bureaucracy.

What is interesting in Poland is to analyze positive response of trade unions to system breakdown. For example, the trade unions have been key components of the neoliberal project of system transformation. Neither of the two main unions, Solidarity and the All-Polish Trade Union Alliance (OPZZ), has prevented market reforms. During the initial phase of the transition process, the independent trade union Solidarity was strongly aligned to anti-communism and the political parties that adopted a pro-market stance. Thus, labor organizations have often supported policies such as privatization (Shields 2004).

Institutionalism in the Structure of Polish Scientific Institutions

There are few very important academic centers where IE and NEI are developing. They are the Polish Academy of Sciences in Warsaw, which publishes scientific papers where one can read about applying heterodox theories, Wrocław University of Economics, specifically the

Chair of Microeconomics and Institutional Economics, and the Warsaw University Chair of Political Economy.

The research activities of the Chair of Microeconomics and Institutional Economics focuses, among other things, on IE. This is visible in the activities of its faculty who strive to popularize the ideas of IE. The papers by Klimczak serve as a good example, especially his 2006 paper entitled "Application of Institutional Economics and its Chosen Problems." In the introduction, Klimczak writes that "investigating how in Poland private property becomes constituted, how markets and different forms of entrepreneurship are created and developed, required using theoretical microeconomic reflection, which is Institutional Economics" (Klimczak 2006, 2008). The author focused on institutional/contractual economics by referring to the ideas of J. R. Commons. The Chair of Microeconomics and Institutional Economics was the first organizer of the first, and so far the only, conference in Poland devoted to IE.[8] Among public high schools in Poland, the Chair of Political Economy is also worth mentioning as it applies the IE approach in its research. The research concerns the issues of national income, inflation, the transformation process, property transformation, social services, economic problems of agricultural development and agricultural policy, comparative studies of economic systems, statistical methods, and the social policy of the state. This institution offers as a part of its didactic activities the following lectures: 30 hours of lectures (6 ETCS points) for graduate economics students specializing in the field of developmental economics; the lecture is entitled IE and is delivered in English. The chairman of the Department of Microeconomics and Institutional Economics, J. Wilkin, explains that his aim five years ago, when the lectures were first delivered, was to diversify the economics curriculum in Poland. This diversification marks, to a certain extent, a progress in the teaching of economics. After 1989 nonorthodox elements of economics were excluded from the curriculum; though the situation has changed, still many universities only teach classical and neoclassical economics. Warsaw University can serve as an example of changes in the curriculum but it should not be treated as a stable trend in the country.

Apart from the Polish schools mentioned above, there are also some that have failed to introduce IE ideas into their curriculum. However, even those scientific institutions offer research, projects, and publications on this subject. Those include: Poznan University of Economics, Poznan University of Adam Mickiewicz, and the University of Economics in Cracow. These academic institutions are a springboard for the development of IE in Poland and have a chance of becoming important academic centers encouraging the development of institutionalism in economics on a large scale.

Summary

Institutionalism in economic research in Poland is developed and applied in various forms. It is useful for explaining the truth rather than being popular. The prevalent movement in heterodox economics is NIE. Papers in IE mostly refer to the process and phenomena of the transformation period in Poland.

The interest in IE in Poland is visible in the increasing number of publications on the topic. Institutionalism has become relevant in science. According to the traditional school of IE and NIE, a great need to interpret phenomena from a more holistic, evolutionary, and historical perspective has been currently created. IE can broaden its field of research and encompass many other phenomena occurring in society and in transition economies.

The European Union (EU) cohesion policy points to the need of implementing the "good governance" principle. This law is addressed to countries (mostly in Central-Eastern Europe) where per capita income is less than 75 percent of the average per capita income in the EU. The law is based on the following rules: openness, participation, accountability, effectiveness, and coherence. Each rule is important for establishing a more democratic governance system. They underpin democracy and the rule of law in the member states, but they apply to all levels of government—global, European, national, regional, and local.[9]

The issue of popularizing heterodox economics in Poland is worth examining since there is an inadequate number of research and educational centers that are dedicated to heterodox economics. The dominant orthodox trend in economic thought and literature calls for the need to popularize IE. For the popularization of this concept one could recommend introducing workshops, seminars, and conferences (preferably in this order). At the same time, we should strive to introduce heterodox economics into the curriculum. This, however, may prove to be more difficult than the previously recommended measures. Nevertheless, it is only through continuous education that we can guarantee an interest in heterodox economics.

Notes

1. M. Lisowska and J. Hauser are exceptions to this.

2. The term institutional economic is used to define some of the discussed issues of the traditional institutional economics and new institutional economics (NIE). The reason behind this is to avoid the segregation of scholars' writings according to the criterion of the economic views.

3. B. Fiedor (2008).

4. In Hungary, there are various names given to the part of the economy that eludes and avoids paying taxes. It is called the black economy (crime), the gray economy (moonlight jobs), or the light gray economy (hidden employment) depending on which segment or form is being addressed (Szabolcs 2007).

5. The current experience of today's poor nations indicates that state capacity cannot be taken for granted. Cited authors analyze investment in state capacity as purposeful decisions reflecting circumstances and institutional structure. Our theoretical analysis highlights the factors that shape these decisions and points to a basic complementarity between fiscal and legal capacity. The analysis brings together ideas from economic history, finance, development economics, and political economics (Besler and Persson 2009).

6. This issue is highlighted in an article by Rossiaud and Locatelli (2009), who deal with the current change of the institutional and organizational framework of the Russian oil industry. Regarding this evolution, the main characteristic is the increasing involvement of national oil companies in upstream activities. The reorganization of the industry is explained by relying on the NIE framework. The authors argue that the current reorganization is an attempt to increase the coherence of the institutional arrangements governing transactions between the Russian state and private oil companies.

7. An in-depth study of the development of the privatized companies was carried out by Angelucci, Estrin, Saul, Konings, and Zolkiewski (2001). According to the authors, domestic competitive pressure as measured by market structure, and increased import penetration are associated with higher firm performance in Poland, irrespective of the ownership structure of the firm. Hence, the development of the companies did not actually depend on the privatization, but rather on the amount of foreign capital.

8. The conference "Institutional Economics in Poland, Experiences and the Future" took place in Wrocław, Poland, November 17–18, 2008, at which 33 papers were presented. This scientific event was one of the first open forums for changing opinions on the relevance of institutional economics. Most of the presented opinions were close to the neoclassical institutional economics.

9. European Governance (2001: 10).

References

Angelucci, M., S. Estrin, J. Saul, J. Konings, and Z. Zolkiewski. (2001). The Effect of Ownership and Competitive Pressure on Firm Performance in Transition Countries: Micro Evidence from Bulgaria, Romania and Poland. CEPR Discussion Papers 2985.

Baccaro, L., and D. Rei. (2007). "Institutional Determinants of Unemployment in OECD Countries: Does the Deregulatory View Hold Water?" *International Organization* 61(3): 527–569.

Besler, T., and T. Persson. (2009). "The Origins of State Capacity: Property Rights, Taxation, and Politics." *American Economic Review* 99(44): 1218–1244.

Boni, M. (2002). "The Labor Market in Poland: Current Trends and Challenges." In *Labor, Employment, and Social Policies in the EU Enlargement Process: Changing Perspectives and Policy Options*, World Bank, 57–77.

Buchanan, J. M., and Y. J. Yoon. (2003). "A Correction in Elementary Public Choice Geometry." *Public Choice* 115(3–4): 285–298.

——. (2008). "Public Choice and the Extent of the Market." *Kyklos* 61(2): 177–188.

Coase, R. (1992). "An Institutional Structure of Production." *American Economic Review* 82(4): 713–719.

——. (1998). "A New Institutional Economics." *American Economic Review* 88(2): 72–74.

——. (1990). "Accounting and Theory of Firm." *Journal of Accounting and Economics* 12(1–3): 3–13.

Commission of the European Communities. (2001). European Governance, White Paper. Brussels: Commission of the European Communities.

Fiedor, B. (2008). "New Institutional Economics as a Basis of Theoretical Reflection on the Transformation Process from the Planned Economy to the Market Economy."

Hausner, J., T. Kudłacz, and J. Szlachta. (2005). *Institutional Conditions of Regional Restructuring of Poland.* Warsaw: KPZK PAN.

Hockuba, Z. (1995). *The Way to the Spontaneous Order.* Warsaw: PWN.

Jarmołowicz, W., and B. Woźniak. (2008). "Institutional Unemployment – Theoretical Aspects."

Kinnear, D. (1999). "The Compulsive Shift to Institutional Concerns in Recent Labor Economics." *Journal of Economic Issues* XXXI: 169–181.

Klimczak, B. (2006). "The Chosen Problems and Practical Applications of Institutional Economics." AE: Wroclaw, 7.

———. (2008). "Institutional Paradox of Transformation," Conference of Institutional Economics in Poland—Experiences and the Future, Wroclaw, Poland.

Legiędź, T. (2008). "Transformation in People's Republic of China from the Perspective of Institutional Economics," Conference of Institutional Economics in Poland, Experiences and the Future, Wrocław, Poland.

Noga, M. (2008). "Institutional Economics and the Functioning of the Central Bank," Conference of Institutional Economics in Poland—Experiences and the Future, Wrocław, Poland.

North, D. C. (1994). Institutional Change: A Framework of Analysis, http://ideas.repec.org.

———. (2003). The Role of Institutions in Economic Development. Discussion Paper Series, No. 2003.2.

Rossiaud, S., and C. Catherine Locatelli. (2009). "The Obstacles in the Way of Stabilising the Russian Oil Model." *Post-Communist Economies* 21(4): 425–438.

Shields, S. (2004). "Global Restructuring and the Polish State: Transition, Transformation, or Transnationalization?" *Review of International Political Economy* 11(1): 132–154.

Solow, R. (1990). *The Labour Market as the Social Institution.* Oxford: Basil Blackwell Inc.

Staniszkis, J. (1991). "Political Capitalism in Poland." *East European Politics and Societies* 5(1): 127–141.

———. (2007). "Dilemmas of Transition Period." In M. Bałtowski, M. Miszewski, *Economic Transition in Poland.* Warsaw: PWN.

Swaan, W., and M. Lisowska. (1996). "Capabilities, Routines, and East European Economic Reform: Hungary and Poland Before and After the 1989 Revolutions." *Journal of Economic Issue* XXX(4): 1031–1055.

Szabolcs, Vamosi-Nagy. (2007). *Quarterly Hungarian Economic Review* 2: 46–52.

Wilkin, J. (2008). "Institutional Theories of the State—Chosen Concepts," Conference of Institutional Economics in Poland—Experiences and the Future, Wrocław, Poland.

Wojtyna, A. (2000a). "If the Traditional Economics Let Us Understand the New Economy?" TIGER.

———. (2000b). "The New Studies on the Role of Institutions in the Economy Growth and Transition Process." *National Economy* 10.

Ziomek, A. (2009). "Institutions of Labour Market as the Condition of Economic growth." In W. Jarmolowicz (ed.), *Economic and Social Determinants of Economic Growth, Working Papers vol. 121*, Poznan University of Economics, 71–87.

From Heterodoxy to Orthodoxy and Vice Versa: Economics and Social Sciences in the Division of Academic Work

By Dieter Bögenhold*

ABSTRACT. The term "heterodox economics" has been in existence for several decades. Recent revival of heterodox economics can be regarded as a growing criticism of economists within the own profession of economics. Modern economics is designed as a one-world-capitalism without history and without regional specifications, without institutions, and without real human agents. Heterodox approaches have the aim to underline that different institutions matter, including religion, language, family structures and networks, systems of education, and industrial relations. Taking the discussion within a broader framework of the history of science acknowleges divergencies and convergencies between different approaches in economics that are also in permanent recomposition. The discussion comes up with the interpretation that recent academic developments provide chances for new modes of intellectual reintegration of formerly disparate areas.

The Rise of Economics and Orthodoxy and Heterodoxy[1]

The article addresses some questions about the development of economics. Where is economics coming from and where is it going to, what is the domain of economics and in how far coexist different approaches in economics? We observe dichotomic labeling in economics that distinguishes between mainstream and heterodox economics but these opposed monoliths are both diverse themselves. The attempt to define both camps clearly is especially difficult

*The author teaches as contract-professor at the Free University of Bolzano, Department of Economics and Management, Via Sernesi 1, 39100 Bolzano, Italy, dboegenhold@unibz.it

American Journal of Economics and Sociology, Vol. 69, No. 5 (November, 2010).

since both concepts have vague borders and both are embedded in overall changing contexts of scientific changes for decades. The thesis of the article is that mainstream economics does not remain the same mainstream economics when acknowledging historical changes and the same is valid for heterodox economics. Changes occur permanently that modify boundaries of the two camps and that affect also potential convergencies. Orthodox economics is a synonym for mainstream economics. Heterodox economics seems to be a counter project to orthodox economics and it seems to be in itself a loose coupling of different approaches with the common denominator of being *non*-mainstream (Lee 2009). In a situation that orthodox and heterodox economics are moving forward and claiming new areas of positions, orthodox positions can partially converge with those being formerly heterodox. The argumentation is concerned with the organization and development of modern economics. The evolution of tendencies may bring up new fields of research and may also foster some new bridges between orthodoxy, heterodoxy, and further fields of social sciences. The discussion takes two examples (out of possibly many more) to highlight interdisciplinary links for the benefit of a holistic integration. It will be shown that an increasing integration of the history of economic thought will provide methodological tools that must serve as necessary background for recent activity in economics. Finally, the article argues in favor of an integration of network analysis, which may be a reasonable strategy to fill the micro-macro gap.

The question of what is the matter of economics has a long tradition. The often quoted statement by Jacob Viner, "economics is what economists do" (quoted in Barber 1997: 87), was completed already by Frank Knight when he added "and economists are those who do economics" (quoted in Buchanan 1964: 213). Looking at activities of economists shows that the domain of economics is always in transition. Since no clear borders exist that provide rational marks for the area of economics even such current understanding is not much further than it was at times of Viner or Knight.

The divisional order of economics is characterized by practice that mirrors the multiplicity of academic production and a somehow occidental development rather than a systematic reasoning how to design an academic subject. With respect to the definition of what economics is and how it is organized into different subfolders two trends overlap each other. (i) We have a long-term trend of the development of economics in which the discipline increasingly gained firm ground and recognition and in which a process of differentiation started to evolve. This trend took part within the last one and a half centuries. The field of economics also started to become a professional system with clear curricula, degrees, academic societies, and university departments with an increasing number of publications and related journals. (ii) Parallel to the consolidation process of economics the subject formed borderlines with neighboring fields that were formerly an ultimate part of economics. Looking over the course of the last hundred years topics of economics have modified and multiplied.

One of Max Weber's book titles was *Wirtschaft und Gesellschaft* ([1921] 1972), which was later repeated by Parsons and Smelser in their study "Economy and Society" (1956), indicating the ultimate link between both items. However, since the middle of the 20th century a point of development was reached when the broad scenario including different academic domains of social sciences, especially those of economics, history, and sociology, was not practiced and studied anymore. Specialization has occurred by which specific aspects of economy or society became subject of further investigation. "Few persons competent in sociological theory," Parsons and Smelser explained, "have any working knowledge of economics, and conversely . . . few economists have much knowledge of sociology" (Parsons and Smelser 1956: xviii). Earlier, classic authors had practiced interdisciplinary investigation working as a matter of course, without specific methodological explanation and without knowing that they did interdisciplinary work by a view of later times.

Historically, the rise of modern economics was closely connected to the rise of neoclassical *theory*, which had its foundations in the marginal utility theory. Related economists tried to establish a kind of economics that was defined as being theoretical and—in this sense—universal and general. "Pure" economics (Walras [1874] 1954) was a credo trying to do economics in a way like other natural sciences were practicing too, having clear procedures and the aim to arrive at laws.

In order to apply economic discussion to modern capitalism in general statements, formulated relationships had to be abstract in an understanding that they could be used for all modern capitalist economies independently of concrete time and space. Getting a level of abstraction was seen as closely connected to the utilization of mathematics. Due to this understanding the rise of neoclassical economics was very much a rising import of mathematics as a tool to formalize statements. This mathematization of economics was clearly expressed when, e.g., looking at Jevons, who wrote in his introduction: "It is clear that Economics, if it is to be a science at all, must be a mathematical science" (Jevons 1871: introduction).

Bringing a complex development to a very brief denominator, much of 20th-century development in economics is the establishment of neoclassic thought, which is taught as textbook knowledge to undergraduate students and that dominates wide parts of the nonuniversity public and public policy (Freeman 2009). Clear relationships concerning many items like growth, prices, trade, or employment are done at very general levels as if economies exist in a vacuum having no institutions and no contextual framing of time and space. "Pure economics" served to be a program of abstractness that had problems when confronted with competing empirical material since pure economics was related to an economy in a vacuum. This type of thought emerged and became a predominant paradigm of thought during the 20th century, which in its nucleus served to be a kind of academic religion (Nelson 2001).

Simultanously, a variety of new special fields of economics were founded that did not exist decades before, among them were, for example, industrial economics, labor economics, small business economics, household economics, and economics of aging. Many further new areas evolved and served as impressive examples of the general trend of academic specialization and differentiation. The more complex economics became, the smaller the real terrain of neoclassical theory remained, although the general image of economics, especially when looking from the outside *at* the field, is still neoclassical orthodoxy. Talking about the mainstream economics overlaps somewhat with general ideas of neoclassical thought that we find even today in textbooks for undergraduate courses.

From Abstract to Concrete Economies:
Revival of Institutionalist Thought and Heterodox Economics

Multiplying economics in a sense of widening the horizont and of pluralization of perspectives is devoted to a small share of pioneers whereas the majority is working steadily with conventional issues in traditional ways doing research and teaching as they always did. Doing academic routines in "convoy" (Bögenhold 1995) is a topic that we find carefully described in philosophy of science as a systematic organizing principle where competing styles of thought are formed into camps of thought (Fleck 1980; Kuhn 1962; Collins 2002). For economics, Lee and Harley (1998) and Lee (2010) showed that these camps survive through diverse subtle methods of reciprocal reverence systems.

Principally speaking, theoretical economics became increasingly an abstract science during the 20th century, trying to bring the complexity of economic life into formulas. Abstractness is combined with sterility in order to arrive at universal statements (or laws) that apply universally. The German Historical School and the Institutional School, especially in North America, went down in the course of the 20th century (Dorfman 1955) but seemingly major ideas are going to become recovered in recent times since many ideas of those schools converge with ideas of heterodox economics and arguments for economic institutionalism (Lee 2009). Although institutionalism was practiced by well-known names during the first half of the 20th century (Dorfman 1946–1959), mainstream economics was closely related to neoclassical thought and its variations.

Especially in the last 10 or 20 years, an increasing number of voices started to criticize the assumptions of the type of thought connected to the abstract modeling (Lee 2004). Among these assumptions the concept of the human actor seemed to be the most problematic one since the *homo oeconomicus* serves to be a function rather than a living human body. Also ideas of symmetric information and of economic equilibrium were not taken for granted by a growing number of economists. Hodgson (1994) summarizes the basic premises that proved to become more and more problematic: "(1). The assumption of rational, maximizing behavior by agents with given and stable preference function; (2.) a focus on attained, or movements toward, equilibrium states; and (3.) the absence of chronic information problems (there is, at most, a focus on probabilistic risk: excluding severe ignorance, radical uncertainty, or divergent perceptions of a given reality" (Hodgson 1994: 60).

What many mainstream economists took for granted for a long time started now to be questioned at an increasing scale: Who is the actor, does the actor have gender, biography, emotions, religion, location, and preferences and why does the actor what he or she does? Hodgson (1994) lists eight different items of critique that formed different zones of critique: 1. Institutionalism eschews atomism and reductionism in economic analysis, typically positing holistic or organistic alternatives. 2. Instead of the rational, calculating agent of neoclassical theory, institutionalism sees human behavior as normally driven by habit and routine, but occasionally punctuated by acts of creativity and novelty. 3. Instead of an exclusive focus on individuals as units of analysis, institutionalism regards self-reinforcing institutions as additional or even alternative analytical units. 4. The conception of the economy is of an evolving, open system in historical time, subject to processes of cumulative causation—instead of approaches to theorizing that focus exclusively on mechanical equilibria. 5. Institutionalism sees individuals as situated in and molded by an evolving social culture, so that their preference functions are not given and fixed but in a process of continuous adaptation and change. 6. Likewise, technology is regarded evolving, and as a primary motivating force in socioeconomic development—in contrast to a theoretical framework that takes technology as fixed and exogenous. 7. There is a pervasive concern with the role and significance of power and of the conflict between both individuals and institutions in socioeconomic life. 8. Instead of an utilitarian framework that evaluates human and welfare in terms of individual utility or pleasure and separates considerations of means from those of ends, there is a focus on the identification of real human needs and on the design of institutions that can further assist their identification and clarification (Hodgson 1994: 69).

Taking these points together, one can conclude that modern economies are contexted by societies in which they are embedded. Practically, economies are never abstract but always concrete. The concern of time and its academic equivalent, which is history, and the concern for spatial dimensions and its variations match with the slogan that *culture matters* (Harrison and Huntington 2000). In general, institutionalist approaches have no other aim than highlighting that different social organizations and institutions (including religion, language, law, family structures and networks, systems of education, and industrial relations) make differences when trying to come up with statements regarding general principles of capitalist societies and economies. If culture makes differences (Jones 2006), capitalism does not exist in a vacuum but in a context with specific social regimes of living and producing. Trying to understand varieties of capitalism (Elsner and Hanappi 2008) is the ultimate acknowledgment that culture and institutional specifications matter, which finally means that academic domains of sociology matter.

Early institutionalist authors did historical studies highlighting religious systems as a crucial factor for the development of capitalism (among those Weber 1988). Recent business historians come back to the fact to acknowledge "cultural factors in economic growth" (Cochran 1960) and they postulate that the really fundamental problems of economic growth are non-economic" (Buchanan and Ellis 1955: 405). If "culture makes almost all the difference" (Landes 2000) the further conclusion must be that not only sociology but also history matters. The concrete historical changes provide the different colors of different variants of capitalism. As we know, capitalism in Singapore differs from capitalism in Zimbabwe, which differs from capitalism in Switzerland.

Accepting the idea that economies and societies are not filled by abstract but by real entities one has to refer to concrete coordinates of time and space (Ostrom 2005). If economics rediscovers history the recent history of economic thought does a break with recent mainstream and goes beyond *abstractivism*. Increasing (new) discussion about path-dependency (David 2007) wants to rediscover history. North is right when he says that the only empirical laboratory for social and economic change available for economists is the past (North 1997: 1). All these considerations meet fully with a program of evolutionary (nonequilibrium) economics, which goes back to Joseph A. Schumpeter ([1942] 1963).

It would require much more than a footnote to discuss what is new in recent developments, also what is new in *new* institutional economics (NIE) compared to an old one (OIE). A major conclusion is that we find a turn in economics that newly takes up elements of thought that belonged to nonmainstream or to heterodox economics. The question how the academic paths fit together is getting increasingly difficult. Where are borderlines and overlappings between heterodox and orthodox economics (Davis 2007)? The observation is that these camps are diffusing slightly. Heterodox economics will certainly not convert into neoclassical thought but established economists who are conventionally regarded as representatives of mainstream economics are partially crossing borders and take the liberty of doing interdisciplinary profits and advantages. This way, so-called orthodoxy seems to become more fragmented and splits up between a small share of innovative pioneers and traditionalists being still close to hard-core neoclassical thought.

Why Do Actors Do What They Do?

Among the many critiques of abstract and sterile economics one critique seems to be the loudest, the type of the human agent and his/her motivation. While *homo oeconomicus* is a figure that fits into all times and societies, having no sex, age, family, and no biographical history, real-world parameters show that there are differences. So, already Max Weber concluded that economics "argues with a non-realist human being, analogous a mathematical ideal figure" (Weber 1990: 30, transl. D.B.). Being distant to such a procedure as provided in theoretical economics, Weber distinguished between four ideal types of social action, which are the rationality of traditional action, of affective action, of value-orientation, and of purposive-rational utilitarian action (Weber 1972: part 1, ch. 1) of which only the last point of classification matches with the supposed rationality of *homo oeconomicus*.

Classical economics started with the conception of "self-interest" for reasons that can be reconstructed logically. Parsons did a sociology of economic thought and concluded that the abstraction was due to the "fact of finding a plausible formula for filling a logical gap in the closure of a system" (Parsons 1940: 188), which is characterized by Parsons as a *doctrine*. Thinking in terms that culture matters implies that people are guided by, at least, a *set of goals* that are implicit or explicit, conflicting or overlapping. Social psychology and phenomenology contributed much information about these spheres and a sociology of emotions is based upon the premise that people are not fully rationally controlled (Stets and Turner 2007). Although already famous economists like J. M. Keynes or J. A. Schumpeter referred to nonrational and psychological categories to integrate into their framework of thought (Bögenhold 2009), economic orthodoxy ignored those voices for a long time since an acknowledgment would imply that a clean model would get dirty.

In the last few decades an increasingly large number of Nobel laureates were awarded for behavioral works or they referred to more differentiated explanations as orthodoxy did (for a history of Nobel laureates and their programs, see Vane and Mulhearn 2005). Herbert Simon ([1955] 1962) coined the (famous) term of a *bounded rationality*. Later D. G. North added that economics treats the issue of motivation of human being like a black box: "Although I know of very few economists who really believe that the behavioral assumptions of economics accurately reflect human behavior, they do (mostly) believe that such assumptions are useful for building models of market behavior in economics and, though less useful, are still the best game in town for studying politics and the other social sciences. I believe that these traditional behavioral assumptions have prevented economists from coming to the grips with some very fundamental issues and that a modification of these assumptions is essential to further progress in the social sciences. The motivation of these actors is more complicated (and their preferences less stable) than assumed in received theory. More controversial (and less understood) among the behavioral assumptions, usually, is the implicit one that the actors possess cognitive systems that provide true models of the worlds about which they make choices . . ." (North 1990: 17). Reading North is like reading ultimate voices by heterodox economists. It has become difficult to discover the concrete rifts between heterodox economics and some sort of innovative economics when looking closer at the nature of contents rather than at the flags of camps and their associations.

In the meantime reverences to psychology have been practiced increasingly. Kahneman (2003) got highly recognized for his pioneering work in economic psychology. He received the Sveriges Riksbank Prize in Economic Science in memory of Alfred Nobel, also awarded to Akerlof. Akerlof (2007) in his function of an outgoing president of the *American Economic Association* recently did a plea to turn academic concentration towards issues of motivation and cognitive structures. Elsewhere, Akerlof and Kranton (2000) referred to dimensions like identity and social norms, which belong much more to sociological or psychological ground than on economic one. Akerlof and Shiller worked out in their study *Animal Spirits* (2009) that a functioning of the whole capitalist system is heavily based upon sociopsychological foundations. They (2009) take up several questions that were taken up by J. M. Keynes earlier. What sounds very convincing and very evident with everday life observations must sound revolutionary by those who practiced orthodox (neoclassical) economics during most of the 20th century. Here, innovative (mainstream) economics partially meets with heterodox economics. It is very important to acknowledge that nothing remains as it always has been, even not economics. The dichtotomy of heterodoxy versus orthodoxy seems to have got new puzzles, which have to be taken into account.

Observing recent trends correctly indicates that daily life of textbook teaching may remain what it has been for a long time but other fractions tend to converge due to the fact that new times produce new questions and provoke new combinations. Nearly 20 years ago Frey ([1992] 1999) realized: "In sociology and many parts of political science, but implicitly also in law, a model of human behaviour is generally assumed which differs strongly from the economic concept. . . . People's actions are taken to be influenced by moral and social factors. These social determinants of human behaviour are acquired by socialization and internationalisation processes" (Frey [1992] 1999: 9). Seemingly, the message has gained further recipients. In this respect a lot of recent offensives towards heterodox economics seems to have forgotten their own academic history. A sociology of the academic division and the related changes through the 20th century shall argue in favor of the increased necessity to reintegrate the social sciences (Mikl-Horke 1999). A broader history of economic and sociological thought may demonstrate that recent discussion has origins that go back for more than a century in the history of economic thought. Although sketchy and perhaps sometimes only between the lines, this article tries to highlight some continuities in discontinuities and vice versa: economics tends to have not completely lost the link to society but it is obviously in a position now to enter again the classic unit of economy and society and economics *and* sociology.

Where to Go and Where to Meet? Research Ground for Future Interdisciplinary Economics

Even the future of *academic* development is rather difficult to forecast, too complex is the interplay of different factors and of individual contributions by authors within quasi "open" developments. Scientific progress is often contingent and never rational in a sense that it follows arithmetic rules of combinations. The "market" for ideas is not perfectly an efficient or perfect market. Academic progress is also related to a series of mistakes by which intellectual resources are wasted, and as a consequence there are indeed intellectual gems laying unexploited waiting for someone to grasp (Boettke 2000).

What we have discussed so far is that the frontier of orthodox economics goes seemingly into a direction that tends to converge partially with some ideas of earlier heterodox critique. Newest economics takes up again academic perspectives that were provided by old institutional thought asking for concrete economies in concrete societies. Of course, many new thematic arenas have opened up during the last hundred years (among them game theory, transaction cost theory, principial agent theory, public choice theory, welfare economics, and many others) so that comparisons between up-to-date economics and earlier forms suffer seriously in many respects. However, reading the signs of current days correctly, tendencies towards an increasing level of abstractness and sterility seem to find an increasing number of opponents rather than supporters. Heterodox economics as a denominator serves to be almost defined negatively as being *not* mainstream economics. A narrower look shows that the term is a rather wide umbrella hiding specific camps of discussion that are sometimes contradictory and opponents among each other, for example, from Marxian economics to Austrian economics, or that are restricted just to individual authors and related discussion as, for example, on Veblen or Keynes.

The article will conclude by dropping two thematic fields that may provide reasonable ground where orthodox and heterodox economics should engage in order to draw chances to get established as common research fields that bridge the somehow sterile confrontation between orthodoxy. The areas to be mentioned are (i) to invest increasingly into history of economic thought, and (ii) to import network research in order to bridge the micro-macro gap and to arrive at a more adequate understanding of market processes.

History of Economic Thought: Looking Back to Gain Orientation for the Future

If students start to get into a new academic discipline as, for example, medicine, biology, or economics, they usually want to learn what is the *current* state of thought. A majority of people do not want to learn to know which discussion was on the agenda 50 or 100 years ago but what are predominant portraits of *recent* debate. What is uncontested terrain, which are competing theories, and where could be academic profit of future engagement? The difficult matter is that academic progress and its change must be conceptualized as a series of processes of shortcomings, which backwards appear as a never-ending story of failures or mistakes to express it starkly. Evolutionary economists take as their credo to look at the inner dynamics of change to arrive at an understanding of principles; theoretical economists should treat their subject similarly. One has to gain a careful understanding of the history of the own discipline to see the bigger and the smaller lines that have led to recent discussion and to the current state of the art. In such light, recent discussion gets much more colors and our current knowledge comes up in a historically transcendent way as a snapshot in a series of academic overcomes, being failures or innovations.

Economic theory evolves in specific *contexts* of social life and societal organization. In some way they mirror the times of their origins and serve as a diagnosis of related systems of thought. As Boettke (2000) puts it:

> The use of intellectual history instrumentally follows both from the idea that all that is important in the past is *not* necessarily contained in the present, and the idea that mining the past might offer concepts which point the way to more productive theory construction today. Following this path we may find dead-ends in current trends of thought which force us to reconsider the earlier moment of choice and then imagine the path that could have been followed instead. . . . But reading an old work in economics is not unlike watching a silent film or news clips of an old baseball game. . . . There are works in the past from which we can still learn important ideas which are useful for addressing the problems we find pressing today. Intellectual errors are made all the time, knowledge gained in one period can be lost due to the fads and fashion which govern the world of ideas There are works in the past from which we can still learn important ideas which are useful for addressing the problems we find pressing today. Intellectual errors are made all the time, knowledge gained in one period can be lost due to the fads and fashion which govern the world of ideas. (Boettke 2000)

These intellectual entrepreneurial profit opportunities have their sources in the awareness of a flux of different positions and paradigms, authors, and interests (Boulding 1971).

History of economic thought (HET) is often counted as being part of the plurality of heterodox enonomy (Lee 2010) but it is also taught in very classic mainstream departments although being currently in strong defense to keep positions. Heterodox economics is not only a part of the pluralism in economics but it is also very pluralist in itself. Sometimes we find cumulative histories of academic processes describing how knowledge in economics changed and accumulated, in other cases history of economics is mostly concerned with specific camps of thought (for example, OIE or Marxism) or with individual authors and their influence (Becker 2009). Since it should be an integral part of the identity of a profession (and a profession member) to be familiar with the tradition of the own discipline, further investment in the history of economic thought should be a unifying issue for future orthodox and heterodox thought in economics. Since we need to know the own intellectual history in order to find innovative academic concepts for the future, dealing with the history of economic thought is also a tool to undertake economics of the future.

Although plenty of excellent books in the area of history of economics are available (Backhouse 2002; Blaug 2006; Canterbery 2005; Heilbroner 2000), one of the major and basic books in this area is still J. A. Schumpeter's *History of Economic Analysis* (Schumpeter 1954). The preface of the book gives a thorough discussion why histories of science are necessary for systematic reasons, and this not only in economics but also in other academic fields. In his (substantial) introduction to his study, Schumpeter raises explicitly the question "why do we study the history of economics?" and he continues to add his own answer, which is concerned with the issue why we study the history of any science in general and with economics specifically.

According to Schumpeter there are four main reasons to study history. *First* of all, it would have pedagogical advantages. He argues that for the students it is very difficult to approach a field without knowing how it is related to the specific historical time. For a thorough understanding an historical background is required. One could affirm that the methods that are presently in use already embody what has been done in the past, and what is not part of it is not important anymore and is not worth taking into consideration. However, actually our present methods and their results are meaningful only with reference to the historical background. "Scientific analysis is not simply a logically consistent process that starts with some primitive notions and then adds to the stock in a straight-line fashion. It is not simply progressive discovery of an objective reality" (Schumpeter 1954: 4).

The *second* reason is that when reading "old" theories one could find other interpretations of them or new ideas; Schumpeter writes "our minds are apt to derive new inspirations from the study of the history of science" (Schumpeter 1954: 4–5). In his discussion Schumpeter adds an example: "The productivity of this experience may be illustrated by the fact that the fundamental ideas that eventually developed in the theory of (special) relativity occurred first in a book on the history of mechanics" (Schumpeter 1954: 5).

The *third* cause is that history can give us insights into the ways of the human mind. Particularly in the history of science various types of logic are used and scientific performances are self-revelatory by nature, that is, they reveal the mental processes that have been made in order to achieve a certain law or theory. "Scientific habits or rules of procedure are not merely to be judged by logical standards that exist independently of them; they contribute something to, and react back upon, the logical standards themselves" (Schumpeter 1954: 5). Finally, the *fourth* point deals especially with economics, which is described as a unique historical process. For Schumpeter, all his points noted before apply also for economics directly: Fundamentally this process does not differ from the analogous processes in other fields of knowledge but "much more than in, say, physics is it true in economics that modern problems, methods, and results cannot be fully understood without some knowledge of how economists have come to reason as they do. In addition, much more than in physics have been lost on the way or remained in abeyance for centuries" (Schumpeter 1954: 6).

Given these insightful instructions by Schumpeter as a plea for increased or, at least, continuous attempts to invest into a history of economics one has to consider Schumpeter's writing also as a good exemplification of what a history of economic writings can highlight, which is that brilliant ideas are often hidden and neglected for (too) long a time. If one wants to analyze a painting hanging on a wall, one must try to go a few steps backwards to see the painting as a whole in order to get a sense of the full composition. The same applies for dealing with science and economics specifically. History of economic thought is a neglected academic area of necessary *contextualizing* of knowledge in order to provide a more sufficient working compass.

Bridging Micro and Macro: Networks as Social Embeddedness

In the second chapter of the same introduction Schumpeter (1954) continued to discuss the division of academic areas in economics, which he coins "techniques of economic analysis." He writes that what distinguishes a *scientific* economist from a *simple* economist is a command of techniques that we classify in different fields, that is, economic history, statistics, economic sociology and theory, and applied fields. In this context the wording of *theory* is always written with quotation marks as so-called "theory" to underline that it is problematic to talk about theory so as if a commonly used understanding exists. In fact, there is no ultimately defined understanding of theory at all, different types of theory coexist (see, for recent contributions, Bunge 1996; Haller 2003: Ch. 1; Schülein 2009: 42–65) and the question when an academic statement receives the status of being theory remains still on the agenda. The simple missing of empirical data is not an ultimate indication that such a piece must be automatically qualified for being theoretical. For our discussion on convergencies, divergencies, and challenges of orthodox, heterodox, and future economics the suggestion is still very important to open up a perspective that economic history, economic sociology, and further applied sciences belong to the techniques of economic analysis. From today's point of observation, we find a proposal for—*interdisciplinary*—working to find appropriate academic answers when dealing with economic issues.

Economics is seen as a box of tools. The suggestion to acknowledge economic history is already treated earlier in our discussion. To address economics with the slogan "history matters" stands for the need to acknowledge *concrete* economies. Nobody will hope to understand the economic phenomena of any, including the present, epoch who has not an adequate command of historical *facts* and an adequate amount of historical *sense* or of what may be described as *historical experience*. The historical report cannot be purely economic but must try to evaluate how economic and noneconomic facts are related to one another. Schumpeter talks about institutional facts that are not purely economic ones (Schumpeter 1954: 12–13).

Finally, a further fundamental field of economic techniques is regarded within economic sociology, which shall be, among other topics, responsible for behavioral and institutional contributions. "Economic analysis deals with the questions how people behave at any time and what the economic effects are they produce by so behaving; economic sociology deals with the question how they came to behave as they do. If we define economic behavior widely enough so that it includes not only actions and motives and propensities but also the social institutions that are relevant to economic behavior such as government, property inheritance, contract, and so on, that phrase really tells us all we need" (Schumpeter 1954: 21).

Having economic sociology and economic history conceptualized as techniques of economic analysis we are very close to a (newly) modern understanding of a wide social science based on understanding how economy and society are linked together. Since they belong by nature ultimately together it is increasingly necessary to take attention of these facts by doing a science of economic life. Ideas by Schumpeter provide a manual how a reasonable division of academic works may look like. Being on that ground, one of the tools that has evolved during the last decades is social network analysis. Social network analysis goes back to Georg Simmel, who started reflecting on different social circles people have. This type of thought differs considerably from a view in economics at that time that conceptualized a type of man where information is shared equally. In a real world people have asymmetric information, which is, among other things, based upon different sets of resources about who to know and with whom to talk. Social network analysis interprets these circumstances as different individual webs of group affiliations. In his "Die Kreuzung sozialer Kreise" Simmel (1908) investigated the intersection of social circles, which were concentric in premodern societies and that are partially overlapping in modern ones. Later, anthropologists like Mauss or Levy Strauss treated these exchange networks in their own studies (Collins 1988). Different network designs provide different opportunities to communicate, to receive information and so they create different structures of cultural capital. In the meantime one has to distinguish between ego-centered network analysis and organizational network analysis, which host different discussion camps each. Network analysis asks for modes and contents of exchanges between people or organizations where symbols (concepts, values, norms), emotions (love, respect or hostility), or goods or services (especially financial subsidiaries and gifts) get transported (Turner 1998: Ch. 38).

Network research studies usually strengthen and highlight the inner dynamics of societies (for an overview, see Scott 2009; Carrington, Scott, Wasserman 2009; Wasserman and Faust 2009; Barr 2009; Marin and Wellman 2010) and the principal premise is that the presently existing, largely categorical description of social structure has no solid theoretical grounding; furthermore, network concepts may provide the only way to construct a theory of social structure (White,

Boorman, and Breiger 1976: 732). Network study research has become a cross-disciplinary evolving subject with applications in many diverse fields of social and economic life. Among them, research on market dynamics is one of the most challenging ones to shed light on a subject that is very often left as a black box by mainstream economists (Swedberg 2003). Markets function upon a basis of communication and social rules, which may be addressed by social network oriented research perspectives. At least two of the crucial research conclusions Fligstein (2001) drew in his *Architecture of Markets* are relevant for network research, which are: "What social rules must exist for markets to function, and what types of social structures are necessary to produce stable markets?" and "What is a 'social' view of what actors seek to do in markets, as opposed to an economic one?" (Fligstein, 2001: 11, 14). Markets are always in transition, they come up, they go down, they change. These markets are carried out by actors having sets of people they know and whom they trust while other people may be regarded as hostile competitors. However concrete markets may look, they always have very social traits, and economics would fall shortly not asking for those issues. Competition processes must also be analyzed and understood as ongoing social processes that are involved in social structures and that are permanently in processes of reorganization (White 1981, 1988; Burt 1995).

Orthodox and heterodox economics both could take advantage of these conceptual ideas in order to innovate their research program. Although only very sketchily discussed here, an idea of the strategic potential of social network analysis might have become transparent. In many respects, network analysis is an excellent exemplification of what the term of *social embeddedness* can deliver. Network analysis furnishes those popular formulations that have become "economic sociology's most celebrated metaphor" (Guillén et al. 2002: 4). Social embeddedness was introduced by Granovetter's (1985) article in which he discussed "social embeddedness of economic behaviour and institutions" (Granovetter 1985) without forgetting to hint at the fact that Karl Polanyi in his study *The Great Transformation* (Polanyi 1944) used the term much earlier by showing competing modes through which people are integrated into societies, market exchange, reciprocity, and mechanisms of redistrbution. All these systems that provide resources to human actors through different levels of inclusion function through principles of social networks. An economics that wants to arrive at an approriate understanding of the dynamics of economic affairs in societies and at a global level cannot afford to neglect those social dimensions (Bögenhold and Marschall 2008).

Conclusions

Orthodox economics and heterodox economics are abstractions. Orthodox economics is always in progress and gets permanently new colors losing old ones. Orthodox economics is best characterized as such economics that are on the agenda and that receive public legitimation. Heterodox economics wants to oppose mainstream economics by dealing with a series of forgotten or neglected matters that are also in defense since these topics often do not fall into the catalogue of defined topics valuable for public funding. In some way, one may portray this frontal system as two opposed camps that have better or worse financial funding because of being legitimate or illegitimate sciences. However, this portrait is a bit crude since orthodox economics is pluralist in some respects and heterodox economics as well (Colander 2010; Fine and Milonakis 2009). Heterodox economics can be defined best as being *not* mainstream but behind the denominator one finds a variety of different topics around quite divergent pieces of thought that may be completely exclusive of each other. Therefore heterodox economics, which started a hundred years ago, was identified with some very well known "heterodox" economists but heterodox economics has evolved by multiplying and getting pluralistic in the meantime.

The same may be stated for orthodox economics, which splits up into a few innovators and a majority of people working in routines doing a type of economics that has always been done before. But orthodox economics has also broadened the range of topics, specializations, and applications so that even here tendencies of fragmentation and heterogenity are visible. A careful analysis must ask if there is common ground between heterodoxy and orthodoxy or if common ways to future terrains exist that may be interesting for the creative elites of both camps to arrive at a state of future economics that is unified by throughly discussed serious research questions that try to go down to the ground of common subjects instead of just sharing around own flags of camps.

The argumentation in this article tried to discuss tendencies within mainstream economics that lead to the fact that some—by Sveriges Riks bank prizes publicly honored—economists tend to leave traditional ground by opening up for fields that belong to heterodox economics, history, psychology, and sociology. Noneconomic social sciences should observe and analyze these trends very carefully in order to react with strategies for this increased *social-scienciation* of economics. It may also be that orthodox economics breaks apart into further pieces of affiliation and schools of thought. In case that the discussed tendencies have a piece of evidence, heterodox economics, history, psychology, and sociology can come up with a charming offense of "welcome back," unifying at their terrain. Despite all logic of academic strategies, a few (of some) topics were discussed that provide a need for further investment such as into history of economic thought, which is almost in defense. Looking around at recently established departments of economics we find a trend that an increasing number of professors have never spent substantial time in reading about heroes of the own discipline but running computer programs in which models are calculated based on a few abstract axiomatic premises. No modern machine breakers are required but people who sensitively raise questions concerning the tools of analysis and the final rationale of knowledge to acquire. Serious scientists must be like captains at sea, always looking at the horizont and observing how weather and winds are changing instead of looking too narrowly at the waves around.

A point of further discussion was that up-to-date economics is increasingly willing to open up for topics of cognitive structures and motivation. Even raising these items explicitly is a revolt against ideas of the abstraction of *homo oeconomicus*. Economic sociology and economic psychology share many of these insights since they belong commonly to their academic identity but they should be curious as well as careful when meeting with those new wielders of economics. Cooperation is explicitly the philosophy of a program of interdisciplinarity, which was not only claimed by Schumpeter in his *History of*

Economic Analysis but for which he also argued for and reflected on. Many recent interesting pieces of discussion may be synthesized, one of them seems to be a tremendously evolving discussion in the area of network analysis, which promises to bridge the micro-macro gap and that potentially helps to make an appropriate understanding of economic and social structures more dynamic, especially research on markets or organizations may find challenges here.

Note

1. The article benefited from discussion and comments during the workshop "Assessing Heterodox Economics in a European Context," Bremen University, June 26–27, 2009, and the workshop "Future of Socioeconomics," University of Economics at Vienna, October 9, 2009. The author is grateful to Wolfram Elsner and Fred Lee and three anonymous reviewers for helpful comments and critique on an earlier version, which forced to some principal rewriting.

References

Akerlof, G. A. (2007). "The Missing Motivation in Macroeconomics." Presidential Address. Paper prepared for the Conference of the American Economic Association, Chicago.

Akerlof, G. A., and R. E. Kranton. (2000). "Economics and Identity." *Quarterly Journal of Economics* 115: 715–753.

Akerlof, G. A., and R. J. Shiller. (2009). *Animal Spirits: How Human Psychology Drives the Economy, and Why it Matters for Global Capitalism.* Princeton: Princeton University Press.

Backhouse, R. (2002). *The Ordinary Business of Life. A History of Economics from the Ancient World to the Twenty-First Century.* Princeton: Princeton University Press.

Barber, W. J. (1997). "Reconfigurations in American Academic Economics. A General Practitioner's Perspective." *Daedalus* 126: 87–103.

Barr, T. (2009). "With Friends Like These. Endogenous Labor Market Segregation with Homogenous, Nonprejudiced Agents." *American Journal of Economics and Sociology* 68(3): 703–746.

Becker, J. et al. (2009). *Heterodoxe Ökonomie.* Marburg: Metropolis.

Blaug, M. (2006). *Economic Theory in Retrospect.* Cambridge: Cambridge University Press.

Boettke, P. J. (2000). *Why Read the Classics in Economics?* George Mason University, Unpublished Paper.

Bögenhold, D. (1995). Mythenjäger im Konvoi. In *Soziale Welt und soziologische Praxis. Festschrift zum 65. Geburtstag von Heinz Hartmann.* Ed. D. Bögenhold et al. Göttingen: Vandenhoek & Ruprecht.

———. (2009). "Die Psychologie im Wirtschaftsleben. Keynes und Schumpeter als Pioniere." In *Der Mensch im Mittepunkt wirtschaftlichen Handelns.* Eds. G. Raab and A. Unger. Lengerich: Pabst Science Publishers.

Bögenhold, D., and J. Marschall. (2008). "Metapher, Methode, Theorie. Netzwerkforschung in der Wirtschaftssoziologie." In *Netzwerkanalyse und Netzwerktheorie. Ein neues Paradigma in den Sozialwissenschaften.* Ed. C. Stegbauer. Wiesbaden: VS-Publishers.

Boulding, K. (1971). "After Samuelson, Who Needs Adam Smith?" *History of Political Economy* 3(2): 225–237.

Buchanan, J. M. (1964). "What Should Economists Do?" *Southern Economic Journal* 30(3): 213–228.

Buchanan, N. S., and H. S. Ellis. (1955). *Approaches to Economic Development.* New York: Twentieth Century Fund.

Bunge, M. (1996). *Finding Philosophy in Social Science.* New Haven and London: Yale University Press.

Burt, R. S. (1995). *Structural Holes: The Social Structure of Competition.* Cambridge: Harvard University Press.

Canterbery, R. (2005). *A Brief History of Economics. Artful Approaches to the Dismal Science.* Singapore: World Scientific Publishing.

Carrington, P. J., J. Scott, and S. Wasserman. (2009). *Models and Methods in Social Network Analysis.* Cambridge: Cambridge University Press.

Cochran, Th. C. (1960). "Cultural Factors in Economic Growth." *Journal of Business History* 515–530.

Colander, D. (2010). "Moving Beyond the Rhetoric of Pluralism: Suggestions for an Inside-the-Mainstream Heterodoxy." In *Economic Pluralism.* Eds. R. Garner, E. K. Olsen, and M. Starr. London: Routledge.

Collins, R. (1988). *Theoretical Sociology.* San Diego: Hartcourt Brace Jovanovich.

———. (2002). *The Sociology of Philosophers.* Cambridge: Harvard University Press.

David, P. A. (2007). "Path Dependence: A Foundational Concept for Historical Social Science." *Cliometrica* 1: 91–114.

Davis, J. B. (2007). *The Turn in Recent Economics and Return of Orthodoxy.* Research Paper, University of Amsterdam.

Dorfman, J. (1946–1959). *The Economic Mind in American Civilization.* Vol. 5. New York: Viking Press.

———. (1955). "The Role of the German Historical School in American Thought." *American Economic Review.* Supplement 45: 17–28.

Elsner, W., and H. Hanappi (eds.). (2008). *Varieties of Capitalism and New Institutional Deals.* Cheltenham: Edward Elgar.

Fine, B., and D. Milonakis. (2009). *From Economics Imperialism to Freako-nomics.* London and New York: Routledge.

Fleck, L. (1980). *"Entstehung einer wissenschaftlichen Tatsache."* Frankfurt: Suhrkamp.

Fligstein, N. (2001). *The Architecture of Markets.* Princeton: Princeton University Press.

Freeman, A. (2009). *The Economists of Tomorrow,* Munich, MPRA Paper No. 15691.

Frey, B. ([1992] 1999). *Economics as a Science of Human Behaviour. Towards a New Social Science Paradigm.* Dordrecht: Kluwer.

Granovetter, M. S. (1985). "Economic Action and Social Structure: The Problem of Embeddedness." *The American Journal of Sociology* 91: 481–510.

Guillén, M. F., R. Collins, P. England, and M. Meyer. (2002). "The Revival of Economic Sociology." In *The New Economic Sociology: Developments in an Emerging Field.* Eds. M. F. Guillén, R. Collins, P. England, and M. Meyer. New York: Russell Sage.

Haller, M. (2003). *Soziologische Theorie im Systematisch-Kritischen Vergleich.* Stuttgart: UTB.

Harrison, L. E., and S. P. Huntington (eds.). (2000). *Culture Matters. How Values Shape Human Progress.* New York: Basic Books.

Heilbroner, R. L. (2000). *The Wordly Philosophers.* London: Penguin Books.

Hodgson, G. M. (1994). "The Return of Institutional Economics." In *The Handbook of Economic Sociology.* Eds. N. J. Smelser and Richard Swedberg. Princeton and New York: Princeton University Press and Russell Sage.

Jevons, W. S. (1871). *Theory of Political Economy.* London: McMillan.

Jones, E. L. (2006). *Cultures Merging. A Historical and Economic Critique of Culture.* Princeton: Princeton University Press.

Kahneman, D. (2003). "A Perspective on Judgment and Choice: Mapping Bounded Rationality." *American Psychologist* 58: 697–720.

Kuhn, Th. S. (1962). *The Structure of Scientific Revolutions.* Chicago: University of Chicago Press.

Landes, D. (2000). "Culture Makes Almost All the Difference." In *Culture Matters. How Values Shape Human Progress.* Eds. L. E. Harrison and S. P. Huntington. New York: Basic Books.

Lee, F. S. (2004). "To be a Heterodox Economist: The Contested Landscape of American Economics, 1960s and 1970s." *Journal of Economic Issues* 38(3): 747–763.

——. (2009). *A History of Heterodox Economics. Challenging the Mainstream in the Twentieth Century.* London: Routledge.

——. (2010). "Pluralism in Heterodox Economics." In *Economic Pluralism.* Eds. R. Garner, E. K. Olsen, and M. Starr. London: Routledge.

Lee, F. S., and S. Harley. (1998). "Peer Review. The Research Assessment Exercise and the Demise of Non-Mainstream Economics." *Capital and Class* 66: 23–53.

Marin, A., and B. Wellman. (2010). "Social Network Analysis: An Introduction." In *Handbook of Social Network Analysis.* Eds. P. Carrington and J. Scott. London: Sage.

Mikl-Horke, G. (1999). *Historische Soziologie der Wirtschaft.* Munich: Oldenbourg.

Nelson, R. H. (2001). *Economics as Religion: from Samuelson to Chicago and Beyond.* Pennsylvania: Pennsylvania State University Press.

North, D. C. (1990). *Institutions, Institutional Change and Economic Performance.* Cambridge: Cambridge University Press.

——. (1997). *Where Have We Been and Where Are We Going?* St. Louis, Manuscript.

Ostrom, E. (2005). *Understanding Institutional Diversity.* Princeton: Princeton University Press.

Parsons, T. (1940). "The Motivation of Economic Activities." *Canadian Journal of Economics and Political Sciences* 6: 187–203.

Parsons, T., and N. Smelser. (1956). *Economy and Society: A Study in the Integration of Economic and Social Theory.* Glencoe, IL.: Free Press.

Polanyi, C. (1944). *The Great Transformation: The Political and Economic Origins of our Time.* New York: Rinehart.

Schülein, J. A. (2009). "Soziologische Theorie und ihr Gegenstand." In *"Soziologie für das Wirtschaftsstudium."* Eds. J. A. Schülein, G. Mikl-Horke, and R. Simsa. Vienna: UTB.

Schumpeter, J. A. (1942). *Capitalism, Socialism and Democracy.* London: Allen & Unwin.

——. (1954). *History of Economic Analysis.* Oxford: Oxford University Press.

——. (1963). *The Theory of Economic Development.* New York and Oxford: Oxford University Press.

Scott, J. (2009). *Social Network Analysis.* London: Sage.

Simmel, G. (1908). "Die Kreuzung sozialer Kreise." In *Soziologie. Untersuchungen über die Formen der Vergesellschaftung.* Ed. G. Simmel. Berlin: Duncker & Humblot.

Simon, H. A. (1955). "A Behavioral Model of Rational Choice." *Quartely Journal of Economics* 69: 99–118.

——. (1962). "The Architecture of Complexity." *Proceedings of the American Philosophical Society* 106(6): 467–482.

Stets, J. E., and J. Turner (eds.). (2007). *Handbook of the Sociology of Emotions.* New York: Springer.

Swedberg, R. (2003). "Economic and Sociological Approaches to Markets." In *Richard: Principles of Economic Sociology.* Ed. R. Swedberg. Princeton: Princeton University Press.

Turner, J. H. (1998). *The Structure of Sociological Theory*. Belmont: Wadsworth Publishing.

Vane, H. R., and C. Mulhearn. (2005). *The Nobel Memorial Laureates in Economics. An Introduction to Their Careers and Main Published Works*. Cheltenham: Edward Elgar.

Walras, L. ([1874] 1954). *Elements of Pure Economics*. Homewood, IL.: Richard D. Irwin.

Wasserman, S., and K. Faust. (2009). *Social Network Analysis*. Cambridge: Cambridge University Press.

Weber, M. ([1921] 1972). "*Wirtschaft und Gesellschaft*." Tübringen: J. C. B. Mohr.

——. ([1904] 1988). "Die protestantische Ethik und der Geist des Kapitalismus." In "*Gesammelte Aufsätze zur Religionssoziologie*." Vol. 1. Ed. Max Weber. Tübingen: Mohr.

——. ([1898] 1990). "*Grundriß zu den Vorlesungen über Allgemeine (theoretische) Nationalökonomie*." Tübingen: J. C. B. Mohr.

White, H. C. (1981). "Where do Markets Come From?" *American Journal of Sociology* 87: 517–547.

——. (1988). "Varieties of Markets." In *Social Structures: A Network Approach*. Eds. B. Wellman and S. D. Berkowitz. Cambridge: Cambridge University Press.

White, H. C., S. A. Boorman, and R. L. Breiger. (1976). "Social Structures from Multiple Networks I: Blockmodells of Roles and Positions." *American Journal of Sociology* 81: 730–780.

The Economists of Tomorrow: The Case for Assertive Pluralism in Economics Education

By ALAN FREEMAN*

ABSTRACT. This article presents the case for "assertive pluralism" in economics education and proposes how to achieve it, illustrating the point with reference to the U.K. Subject Benchmark Statement in Economics (SBSE). It proposes a revision of the benchmark, prioritizing the role of *controversy* in the teaching of economics, combined with pluralistic principles that uphold and guarantee critical and independent thinking. This reform is a necessary response to what Colander et al. (2009) term the "systemic failure" of economics—the inability of the profession, taken as a whole, to anticipate and understand the financial crash and recession of 2008. Failure on this scale testifies to a more deep-seated weakness in economics than commonly recognized. It arises from what Turner (Tett 2009) terms the regulatory capture of the economics profession by narrow financial interests. The public, and the economics profession, require specific protection against the pressures that have produced this systemic failure. This requires a rethink of the relation of economics to society, founded on a rejection of the idea that the function of economics is to provide a single, unequivocal solution to every problem of policy. Instead, the article explains, good economics should be constrained to evaluate the full range of relevant solutions to any given policy issue, leaving the decisionmakers accountable for the decisions they make on which solution to adopt.

Introduction

This article is a proposal to change the way economists are educated by applying the principle of "assertive pluralism" to the definition and concept of economics.

This will equip the public to recognize bad economics, which I define as economics that takes no precautions against the possibility

*Association for Heterodox Economics.

American Journal of Economics and Sociology, Vol. 69, No. 5 (November, 2010).
© 2010 American Journal of Economics and Sociology, Inc.

of error. It offers a remedy for what Colander et al. (2009) describe as a "systemic failure" of economics, prior to the crash of 2008. And it offers the profession a defense against the cause of this failure, which, following Turner (Tett 2009), I describe as its regulatory capture by financial interests.

The objectives are intimately linked: a definition of good economics equips the public to demand good economists. By embedding this definition in the requirements placed on economics education providers, a supply of good economists will be created. Both will conspire to produce a generation of economists who can react, and prepare for, those changes in the world that their predecessors were so poorly placed to foresee or react to.

The U.K. Context

The methodology proposed—assertive pluralism—has wider implications for the reform of economics. It is a general principle, applicable equally inside and outside the United Kingdom and in all spheres of economic practice and theory including research, publication, selection, and promotion, the procurement of policy advice, and, not least, funding. I focus however on U.K. higher education. For the information of readers unfamiliar with the way this has evolved, at this point some context may be helpful.

The article outlines the rationale for, and principles behind, a pluralist Subject Benchmark Statement for Economics (SBSE). It is an offshoot of a consultation (Freeman 2007) undertaken by the Association for Heterodox Economics (AHE) to provide input for a consultative review of the SBSE undertaken by the U.K. Quality Assurance Agency (QAA) in 2007. This led to an AHE-sponsored paper (Freeman 2009) in a special edition of the *International Review of Economics Education* (Denis 2009), a journal published by the Economics Network, the main practitioner body for developing economics teaching in the UK.

The discussion it reflects is thus quite well advanced in the United Kingdom. In 2009 the AHE was asked to address the U.K. Committee of Heads of University Departments of Education (CHUDE), which is formally charged with establishing the SBSE. With CHUDE's support the AHE proposed a panel on pluralism in economics education to the 2010 conference of the Royal Economic Society (RES), effectively the profession's highest U.K. body.

The RES however declined to accept. Such refusal, two years into the present crisis, to even consider a discussion on curriculum change, adds weight to the conclusions of this article that significant structural and institutional reforms are required in economics.

Subject benchmarks were themselves introduced by the QAA, itself established following a review of higher education conducted at the request of the U.K. Labour government in 1997, headed by Ron Dearing.[1]

The QAA, continuing the practice of "audits," which began in 1990, initially concentrated on the teaching and learning process as such, rather than content. However Dearing had recommended that "standards should be developed by the academic community itself, through formal groupings for the main areas of study." Accordingly in 1999, the first three subject benchmarks were released for consultation and a further 19 in 2000. By the middle of the last decade, benchmarks existed to cover almost all subjects. In consequence, imperceptibly but relentlessly, the content of teaching entered into the definition of "quality" of teaching in the United Kingdom.

A latent conflict between standards and diversity was recognized from the outset. As Dearing (1997: 10.3) noted:

> Uniformity of programmes and national curricula, one possible approach to the development of national standards, would deny higher education the vitality, excitement and challenge that comes from institutions consciously pursuing distinctive purposes, with academics having scope to pursue their own scholarship and enthusiasms in their teaching. The task facing higher education is to reconcile that desirable diversity with achievement of reasonable consistency in standards of awards.

Most subjects took special measures (see Freeman 2007) to safeguard their subject against uniformity. They specified the range of views with which students should be acquainted, and clarified that students should be knowledgeable about the controversies in their subjects.

Economics alone sought a prescriptive approach, making little or no explicit provision for pluralism. This highlights a problem we will return to. Subject benchmarks, by virtue of the way the U.K. process evolved, were self-defined. The SBSE thus expressed the subject's view of itself, not any external imposition. The fact is that economists in the United Kingdom, given the chance to conceptualize their subject, of their own free will described it as closed deductive system with a single synthetic view.

Noting how anomalous this stance was, a point that appears to have escaped both economists and the wider HE community, the AHE opted to propose a reform of the benchmark by using "assertive pluralist benchmarking" to create explicit safeguards for pluralism, and by implication, heterodoxy.

What Is Assertive Pluralism?

Pluralism has a specific meaning that this article will clarify. It is "assertive":[2] the pluralist economist is not merely allowed, but required, to consider a variety of approaches to problems in the real world. It is "critical": the pluralist economist makes explicit the alternative theoretical approaches considered, the different solutions and policies that arise, and the basis for choosing between them.

Whenever, in history, economic theory has positively and usefully informed policy and particularly changes in policy, it has done so by questioning accepted precepts, reexamining fundamental principles without prejudice, and above all engaging in and promoting controversy. The central argument of this article is the next generation of economists should be steeped in this principle, if they are to avoid repeating the mistakes of the economists of yesterday.

This is a radical idea. It calls into question the entire idea of a general consensus to which all economists can sign up—and with it, the entire idea of "synthesis" that has driven the subject's postwar development. Pluralism implies that a subject is better defined by its actual controversies than its alleged agreements.

Pluralism also redefines the "social compact" between economists and society. It redefines the product of economics. It reconsiders the idea that the job of economics is to offer a single unqualified answer to any question of economic policy. If consistently implemented, it would mean that decisionmakers should neither accept, nor even ask for, a single answer to any question of economic policy. They should instead be informed of the *range* of possible policies that might be applied, and should then take responsibility for choosing between these options.

The need for such a fundamental shift of perspective is illustrated by Anatole Kaletsky's complaint that "[i]n the search for the 'guilty men' responsible for the near-collapse of the global economy, one obvious group of scapegoats has escaped blame: the economists." By this he means "the academic theorists who win Nobel prizes, or dream of winning them."

> To see why these seemingly obscure academics deserve to be hauled out of their ivory towers and put in the dock of public opinion, consider why the bankers, politicians, accountants and regulators behaved in the egregious ways that they have . . . The answer was beautifully expressed two generations ago by John Maynard Keynes: "Practical men, who believe themselves to be quite exempt from any intellectual influence, are usually the slaves of some defunct economist. Madmen in authority, who hear voices in the air, are distilling their frenzy from some academic scribbler of a few years back."

The problem with this judgment—which though vituperative, gives vent to feelings of public outrage that it would be perilous to ignore—is that it fails to explain why our bankers, politicians, accountants, and regulators chose to let themselves be deluded by such scoundrels.

Economics, as delivered to the public, is the outcome of the procurement system—the mechanisms that lead to its production. These same bankers, politicians, accountants, and regulators also hired economists to furnish them with the rationale for their egregiousness. They got what they paid for. When decisionmakers wish to absolve themselves from the awkward job of making decisions, "the economists tell us so" provides an all-too-convenient excuse.

By hiring economists to tell them a single, unique answer—usually, as we shall see, the answer they wished in any case to give—they themselves created the supply of the product that they now no longer demand. Pluralism, properly implemented, will deprive the decisionmakers of the opportunity to delegate to the economists the work that is rightfully theirs.

The Systemic Failure of Economics

Recent criticism of economics is unprecedented in living memory. It extends to the authoritative heights of the profession and questions its most cherished beliefs. Ideologically its sources range from Stiglitz (2008) to the pro-market Buiter (2009). Space prevents us from reproducing this criticism in the detail that may be found on our reference website www.emperorstailors.com;[3] yet whatever one may think of its validity, to deny its existence defies the laws of evidence. Colander et al. (2009) summarize what may reasonably be termed a critical consensus:

> If one browses through the academic macroeconomics and finance litera-
> ture, "systemic crisis" appears like an otherworldly event that is absent
> from economic models. Most models, by design, offer no immediate
> handle on how to think about or deal with this recurring phenomenon. In
> our hour of greatest need, societies around the world are left to grope in
> the dark without a theory. That, to us, is a systemic failure of the economics
> profession.

Gillian Tett reports yet stronger charges from Adair Turner, chair of the U.K. Financial Services Authority (FSA):

> In recent years, he argues, "the whole efficient market theory, Washington
> consensus, free market deregulation system" was so dominant that it was
> somewhat like a "religion". This gave rise to "*regulatory capture* through
> the intellectual zeitgeist." (Tett 2009, our emphasis)

Buiter (2009) highlights the core of this critical consensus.

> In both the New Classical and New Keynesian approaches to monetary
> theory (and to aggregative macroeconomics in general), the strongest
> version of the efficient markets hypothesis (EMH) was maintained. This is
> the hypothesis that asset prices aggregate and fully reflect all relevant
> fundamental information, and thus provide the proper signals for resource
> allocation. Even during the seventies, eighties, nineties and noughties
> before 2007, the manifest failure of the EMH in many key asset markets
> was obvious to virtually all those whose cognitive abilities had not been
> warped by a modern Anglo-American Ph.D. education. But most of the
> profession continued to swallow the EMH hook, line and sinker, although
> there were influential advocates of reason throughout, including James
> Tobin, Robert Shiller, George Akerlof, Hyman Minsky, Joseph Stiglitz and
> behaviourist approaches to finance. The influence of the heterodox
> approaches . . . was, however, strictly limited.

These all rebut the ill-considered claim that, since economics has produced heterodox writers, it is already pluralist, a hypothesis akin to crediting Mary Tudor with the rise of Protestantism. The issue is not whether dissent exists, but what happens to it. The critics' complaint is that the *system*, as a whole, delivered wrong results: that the considered advice given to decisionmakers was grounded in erroneous theory. The touchstone is not whether dissent existed, but how it affected the advice normally given, the theories normally used, and the qualifications normally awarded. We now therefore turn to a closer study of the system that produced this normal advice.

Economics and the Treatment of Dissent

The distinguishing feature of Buiter's list of dissenters is that, had they been considered, different economic judgments would have been offered to decisionmakers. This "select club of the seers who saw it all coming" as the *Times* describes it (Thornton 2009) extends to Roubini (Mihm 2008), Brenner (2002), Shiller (2006), Turner (2008), Pettifor (2006), Stiglitz (2008), and Wade (2008).

The profession's approach, I will argue, is not that such dissenting views are wrong, but that it does not need to consider them. The point is clearly, if unintentionally, made by Portes (2008), outgoing General Secretary of the Royal Economics Society. Questioning

> [a]dministrators, who may not have deep disciplinary backgrounds, [who] nevertheless impose their own views rather than deferring to professional standards,

he singles out for derision a referee who rejects a funding proposal with the words

> "despite the excellence of the partners' record within mainly economic science, they fail to include alternative, complementary or even competing approaches."

Portes laments that "Referees like these have regrettably been taken seriously."

Consider this text carefully. Actually, the administrators, from Portes's own testimony, did not "impose their own views." They asked the researcher to include *views other than his own*. Portes's inadvertent but revealing definition of "professional standards" is that research based on a single idea is superior and it is positively wrong to consider anything else.

As early as 1992 this tendency was sufficiently threatening to move 44 economists, including four Sveriges Riksbank Prize Laureates, to sign a declaration in the *American Economic Review* (Hodgson et al. 1992) in defense of pluralism. It brought no discernible improvement. There is countless further testimony that the standard view of an economist's job is to acquire, from his peers, a *single* theory around which consensus exists, and apply it.

The Institutional Origin of Systemic Failure

Reduced to essentials, the behavior of a regulated system depends on the interaction between behavioral rules and institutional practice. I have identified the informal, but effective rules, under which economics operates. How does this impact its practice? They lead, I will show, to *selection for conformity*. Its practitioners are dominated by a compulsion to agree. I will now show that this introduces two risks: adverse theoretical selection, and—as Adair Turner (Tett, *op. cit)* notes, regulatory capture.

The risk of adverse theoretical selection arises not from the way theories are applied, but from the process that verifies them. If a theory can be verified external to a profession, conformity might ensure that this correct theory is applied. But conformity as such is no more likely to enforce valid theory than wrong theory.

The problem is precisely the lack of any tested mechanism to verify economic theories externally. Economics bows to no authority. It has no regulatory structure worth speaking of, nor a code of conduct, nor a code of ethics.[4] And it does not merely enforce theories: it produces them. If it creates a wrong theory, the only safeguard against enforcing error as assiduously as truth, it would appear, is peer review.

But peer review is not a safeguard against wrong theory. Peer endorsement, it is well known, is an indicator of approval, not merit. Ample research demonstrates that in the absence of explicit safeguards, assessors confuse dissent with poor quality, assigning lower ratings when they simply disagree with what is said.[5]

The process that passes judgment also selects the judges. If those who share a certain viewpoint assign higher quality ratings to those they agree with, these will secure higher status. They will then themselves be disproportionately entrusted with the function of judgment. Those who dissent—the "heterodox"—will attain lower rankings and will be less likely to become judges. A positive feedback loop will be established, selecting on no other basis than approval by the representatives of orthodoxy.

Such a process eliminates over time, in the names of both efficiency and quality, the intellectual capacity to generate correct theory; at the same time it suppresses the mechanisms for eliminating error. It breeds out the stock of innovative or creative thinking. This, the evidence suggests, is what has happened. The residual capacity of economics to generate new ideas, as we have already pointed out, arises almost exclusively from the ranks of those who have so far contrived to resist or evade the mechanism's consequences.

Keynesian Once Again: How Economists Change Their Minds

Lee and Harley (1998: 41) studied the relation between rating, university status, and the hiring of heterodox economists arising from the first Research Assessment Exercise (RAE) in 1992. They found a more or less inverse correlation between rating and the hiring of heterodox economists. The RAE itself was making it difficult, if not impossible, for dissenting economists to be hired in high-performing, high-funding, research-oriented economics departments.

In the lowest ranked departments (RAE 2) 14 out of 63—26 percent—of hirings were heterodox. In departments ranked 3, the proportion was 9.7 percent; in those ranked 5 or 4, one economist hired in every 70 (1.4 percent) was heterodox.

Lee's research (Lee 2007) demonstrates that the review system goes beyond merely securing "favor" for a particular idea: it eliminates the capacity to generate alternatives. This is the logical outcome of an outlook that identifies dissent with poor quality. If there is only one correct view, it is self-evidently wasteful to invest in producing any other. Contrarian research is not funded, dissident work is notpublished, heterodox lecturers are not hired, and survivors are not promoted.

Conformity necrotizes the capacity for change. If Wolf (2008) is to be believed we are now all duty bound to become Keynesians yet again—yet it takes years to become an accomplished Keynesian macroeconomist. A specialism is an expertise, not a fashion item. From whom should future economists learn ideas that *differ* from those of their teachers? How can we nurture the dissidents that will be needed in the next crisis?

Who Regulates Economics?

We have noted that, *were* there an external standard of quality, the risk of adverse theoretical selection by even a narrowly-based system might be reduced. What actual external conditions govern the theories selected by the system we have analyzed?

When all is said and done, the only real external constraint on economists is money. Those who judge its policies, and those who benefit, also pay for them. Why should this matter? Because as Freeman and Kliman (2008) note, economics is uniquely close to policy—notably, policy on which large fortunes depend.

Economics is itself a regulatory system. True, it does not directly intervene in decision-making process, or infrequently so. However, it provides the *language* of decisions, the bulk of which are allocative and monetary. It provides the criteria used to judge whether decisions were right. To take just two examples, it furnished the rationale for dismantling postwar regulatory constraints on financial institutions, and for the structural adjustment programs the IMF and World Bank have demanded of debtor countries for the past 30 years.

Such decisions have enormous material consequences. It makes a real difference when economic theory comes down on one side or the other of any dispute in fiscal policy, bank regulation, trade policy, or wage and labor relations. Huge social conflicts testify to the seriousness that the protagonists attach to economic judgments.

The principle of *cui bono* is relevant. Whose fortunes depend on whether hypotheses like EMH are adopted in the policy sphere? Clearly, those to whom the decisions are applied—not least governments and most of all, financial institutions.

But these same institutions finance the economics profession. Governments and financial bodies directly employ most professional economists, and are heavily involved in processes that influence the selection of economic theories. They award prizes, fund departments, hand out grants and consultancies, and, in the case of international monetary authorities, directly intervene in selecting personnel. The risk attached—raised in Freeman (2009)—is well-known to public choice theory and, as noted, has been made explicit by Adair Turner, who as chair of the FSA ought to know something about it. Regulatory capture occurs when private interests intervene in the regulatory system to ensure it decides in their favor.[6]

Indeed, it is astonishing that this risk remains unrecognized by the profession, which is quick enough to point to dangers affecting others. The same Richard Portes who, as RES secretary inveighed against heterodox economics in 2008, received £58,000 in 2007 for a report commissioned by the Icelandic Chamber of Commerce giving the Icelandic banking system a clean bill of health (Portes 2007). No committee of ethics considered the propriety of this payment, and the RES does not even have any procedures to consider whether there might be some conflict between such activity and Portes's status as its General Secretary. One only has to imagine the consequences if, for example, the Chief Executive of the British Medical Association were to receive a direct payment for writing an unsubstantiated endorsement of a controversial and potentially lethal drug, to grasp the astonishing laxity of our profession.[7]

With the possible exception of health, no field of human knowledge benefits from such large quantities of goal-directed funding from organizations whose interests directly depend on the conclusions arrived at.[8] What defense can be offered to the public against the risks that may arise? The corrective, I argue, begins with the economists of tomorrow: namely, the students of today.

The Case for Assertive Pluralism

We have already referred to the strong adverse effect of benchmarking and research assessment on academic economics. Is the remedy to do away with these or the peer-review method they apply? Perhaps, but this does not get to the root of the matter. The problem is that the drive for conformity and the process of adverse selection operate within economics regardless of the institutional context, for example, in countries without benchmarking or an RAE. And we have already noted that the U.K. benchmark was drawn up by the profession itself, of its own free will. The problems, I conclude, arise from within the economics profession itself, and its unique relation to society. What must change is the conduct of that profession, and this in turn must express a rethink of the relation between the economist and society.

The problem is not just that economics has produced a bad consensus seriously misinforming policymakers in the run-up to a crisis, but the very fact that it strives to produce a consensus at all: that it treats dissent and controversy as a failing instead of a virtue

A good economist should constantly expect to be surprised. Any thinking person should be skeptical that a single, summative canon of knowledge will ever suffice to grapple with real economic processes. The entire project of a definitive body of economic knowledge, the AHE contends, is misconceived.

The solution is to embed the principle of controversy in the definition of economic theory. The defining characteristic of the economist of tomorrow should be the capacity to handle *disagreement*: to identify, select, adapt, and critically interrogate the *range* of theories relevant to each concrete problem. In particular, for any given thesis considered, she or he should be capable of "testing to destruction" the thesis by confronting it with the most damaging evidence against it.[9] Only thus can she or he hope to confront each juncture with the fresh mind required to understand it. This is the rational basis for pluralism.

The Case for Critical Pluralism

The best way to define pluralism more precisely is to address the most common misconceptions about it. This is the subject of the next two sections.

The first of these entertained by not a few heterodox economists—is that pluralism is a means to replace one orthodoxy by another. Actually, the objective of critical pluralist economics is an end to orthodoxy. Instead it seeks real understanding of variety. It aims to equip practitioners to select, from all appropriate theories, that which best fits the evidence. To achieve this, students first need to understand, not where economists concur, but why they disagree.

Pluralism goes hand in hand with critical thinking. Beyond the different predictions of conflicting theories, the student needs to grasp the premises on which each rests. Consider, for example, the EMH itself. As Buiter notes, it has become an implicit assumption in financial theory. Yet it is an assumption, not a proven theory. The possibility that circumstances might arise in which it was not valid must always be considered, even if only to identify when it might be valid. To be competent to undertake such questioning, researchers are needed who, firstly, understand it is not an established fact, and who, second, understand at least some approaches that do not presume it holds.

A shortlist of such alternatives would include the Austrians, whose core proposition is not the Walrasian assumption that the market functions free from disruption, but that no superior mechanism exists; Keynes's vigorous critique of Say's Law, Marx's startlingly relevant account of capitalist crisis, Schumpeter's notion of creative destruction, and behavioral accounts such as Shiller's.

Pluralistic education would have equipped today's economists with an understanding of such theories *even* if EMH-based models furnished their method of choice. They would then, as the crisis approached, have supplied early warnings of the relevance of Keynes's theory of liquidity preference, the importance of flow-of-funds accounting, and the business-cycle disputes of the 1920s that gave us both the NBER and Hayek's theory of the trade cycle. Acquaintance with Schumpeter would have sensitized them to the importance of underlying long trends, and they would have been attuned to behavioralist and institutionalist critiques.

They would also have understood historical context. Having absorbed the lessons of a past stage of history, they could have dusted off their economic history and history of thought textbooks to study the relation between 2009 and 1929. They would have recollected the warnings of Galbraith and Minsky, and realized that received opinions on the role of the banks and the state should be set aside once their presupposed conditions no longer applied.

Three outstanding benefits of pluralism can now be summarized: it equips the economist to respond to *new or unanticipated phenomena*. It equips the economist to check, critically and regularly, the *nonevidenced assumptions* that inform any judgment, and refrain from employing them in the absence of solid evidence. And it constrains the economist to react creatively to *unsolved* problems, pushing forward the frontiers of knowledge without falling back on a formulaic catechism.

Pluralism as a Standard of Attainment

A second misconception is that pluralism is excuse for laxity. Pluralism is not a substitute for a standard: it *is* a standard.

Pluralism does not claim there is no such thing as truth or falsehood. It does state that the ultimate test of theory is evidence. The purpose of research is to judge what is true, and the purpose of education is to equip students to make judgments. These may not be made in *advance* of conducting empirical tests. We do not yet know whether the present crisis is best understood using the approach of Buiter, Shiller, Krugman, Hayek, Friedman, Keynes, Schumpeter, or Marx. Therefore, without prior prejudice, we must confront each approach, excluding none, with the evidence as it emerges—and *then* judge between them.

Pluralism is not a method contrary to that of the sciences but the method *of* the sciences, as Fullbrook (2001, 2008) has accurately shown, drawing on a wealth of work in the philosophy of science. No evidence supports Portes's view that pluralism constitutes a relaxation of professional standards. To the contrary it is far more *difficult*—but also far more necessary—to understand, and represent fairly, a point of view with which one disagrees, than simply to repeat one's own beliefs, or worse still the beliefs of one's superiors. Moreover, it is greatly more probable that a student who understands the arguments against any theory will truly grasp what that theory actually says.

Pluralism is not relativism. It does not give researchers or students license to assume whatever they feel happy with. To the contrary, it requires competent economists to be conversant with theories they may be singularly unhappy with.

Pluralism also, importantly, does not reduce to the idea that no theory can be discounted and every idea, no matter how bizarre, must be entertained. Some critics of my 2009 article have argued, for example, that pluralism implies creationism should be mandatory. Not so: creationism is not a theory supported by evidence, and this is an important difference. The case for creationist teaching in biology in the United States, for example, is stated in terms of the *flaws* in evolutionary theory. But every science possesses flaws and contradictions, and this is what moves scientific theory forward. This does not compel us to travel backward, by treating as "legitimate theory" theses for which there is no evidence.

The profound flaw in economics' claim to function as a science is that it rules out perfectly viable theories that are strongly supported by evidence—such as Marx's account of the tendency of the rate of profit to fall, or Keynes's (hastily rediscovered of late) account of liquidity preference. It does so on no basis other than that these ideas do not conform to current thinking. But this is the precise reason for considering them: How can we make a judgment on any theory, if we are not allowed to consider the alternatives? Comparing economics again to the medical profession, scarcely a member of the public has not heard of the right to a second opinion. Why should this not apply to economists, whose diagnoses affect not just one life at a time, but millions?

Ginger Rogers once remarked she had to do everything Fred Astaire did, but backwards and in high heels. Pluralist economists not only pursue their own preferred line of thought, but that of their own main opponents. The commonest objection during our consultation process was that pluralism was *difficult* for students, who did not like having to understand so many theories. This is true, but it cannot simultaneously be claimed that pluralism is difficult, and that it will lead to lax standards.

Things Fall Apart: The Myth of Synthesis

I now come to the heart of the issue, again arising from a misinformed objection. The most common defense of the existing SBSE is that, since it was drawn up by economists of all views, it includes the whole range of economic ideas.

This is demonstrably false. One searches the benchmark in vain for Austrian economics, behavioralism, evolutionary economics, feminism, Keynesianism, Marxism, or any identifiable body of theory. One need only compare the SBSE with the politics benchmark (Freeman 2008) to illustrate this point:

> The scope of politics and international relations is broad, the boundaries often being contested or in movement. Perhaps in no other academic discipline are the subject matter and approaches so much in contention and in flux . . . International political theory could be taught as contending approaches such as realism, neo-realism, neo-liberalism, institutionalist theory, feminism, pluralism, Marxism or critical theory; it could also be taught as normative theory.

The point is that pluralism is not an amalgam of isolated fragments from views that utterly conflict with each other. It is the systematic deployment of controversy as the founding principle of understanding and action. Beneath these two opposed specifications lies a conceptual and paradigmatic abyss.

Thus, the SBSE asserts that "analysis is both static . . . and dynamic." Nice try, but plain wrong. It is not possible to be static *and* dynamic any more than to stand up whilst falling down: one may be static *or* dynamic. The SBSE should have specified "analysis begins from the irreconcilability of static and dynamic approaches." The non-equilibrium approaches associated with Keynes, Marx, and the Austrians, and the comparative static approach of Walras and his successors, span a century of dispute; this is a *choice*, not a bygone family spat. Difference between approaches, not their similarity, is the defining characteristic of any important area of human knowledge.

Behind this lies a basic question mark, hanging over the "compact between economics education and society" that has reigned since the idea of *synthesis* entered the vocabulary of economics. To present irreconcilable theories as a "balanced mix" is a sin against logic.

The urge to do so expresses an almost Ibsenesque urge to conceal unresolved differences. The end effect is as suppressive as it is repressive.

The SBSE, in all innocence, defines economics as the "study of the factors that influence income, wealth and well-being," aiming at the "allocation, distribution and utilization of scarce resources." The intention is welcome, but unfortunately this is not a synthesis. It is a single, deeply contested view, presented as a common denominator. An institution that assents to it signs away the right to present to its students any economic idea arising from a different standpoint—for example, that scarcity is socially produced. To begin with, it disqualifies most theories of ecological, Marxist, or feminist inspiration.

This suppression is self-inflicted: a prescriptive definition is *unnecessary*; no other social science has done it, the QAA counsels against it, and it is perfectly legitimate to define a subject by its differences.

Behind this lies a deeper lesson: the age of economic synthesis, I contend, has run its course. Making policy is the job of policymakers. A useful economic advisor does not write scripts for decisionmakers, but obliges them to take decisions. The most outstanding contributions to economics historically are honored, not for the answers they delivered, but for the profundity of the questions they asked; for all these reasons, the greatest gift we can bequeath our future students is a firm understanding of their own limitations.

Pluralist Benchmarking—A Declaration of Intent

What might be the function of a pluralist benchmark? Benchmarks as defined by the QAA are not curricula (although the SBSE, mistakenly, reads like one) but instruments for getting an answer to the question "are our institutions fit for purpose?" A good economics benchmark would therefore define criteria by which the *public* may judge if an institution can provide students with the skills and competence to deliver good economics.

Tracing the chain of logical links backward from this desired output competence requires us to begin at the beginning—assessment.

A pluralism benchmark would assess students' capacity for critical and pluralistic reasoning. It would define excellence not as the ability to reproduce or conform to a canon, but as the capacity to think outside it. It would test not just knowledge of what the experts and their teachers have to say, but their understanding of what their opponents also say.

Competence in economics is, in short, the capacity to think originally and independently. This requires students to be cognizant of, and indeed familiar with, the variety of theories relevant to any chosen field of empirical study. They need to understand what these theories presuppose, and subject these presuppositions—not just their immediate predictions—to the empirical test of evidence. Finally, they must demonstrate the capacity to make independent judgments between theories on this basis.

Following this logic, outcome provides the key to assessment, and assessment provides the key to instruction. Teaching would introduce students, from day one, to the idea of controversy and debate. To take one example, consider the standard microeconomic theory of supply and demand. Objections and alternatives to that theory come from many quarters: from all critics of Say's Law such as Marx and Keynes; from Chamberlin's conception of "monopolistic competition"; from studies of particular markets that do not comply with the theory of perfect competition, such as labor markets as analyzed by Card, Krueger, and Manning;[10] from Kaleckian theories of price formation; from feminist economics; from the literature on imperfect information and bounded rationality; and not least, from the growing if belated recognition that financial markets simply do not behave like commodity markets.

These specialist fields are all the subject of vigorous dispute. In studying any one of them, the mark of competence should no longer be exclusive mastery of any one approach, but the ability to offer the decisionmaker a reasoned choice between them.

Take a second example: pluralist practitioners should not just know of Ricardo's theory of comparative advantage. They should understand its theoretical challengers: mercantilism, the Listian corpus including modern-day developmental nationalism, developmentalist critics from Arthur Lewis to Prebisch and Singer, the Dependency School, and in modern times anti-globalization theory and the New Trade Theory of Fujita, Krugman, and Venables.[11] They should understand why Ricardian theory has been so rarely applied, and why the alternative tradition, which Reinert (2004) terms the "other canon," held so much sway.

Students schooled in this outlook would neither automatically support nor dismiss orthodox trade theory. They would not be clones of any "defunct economist." They would, in a word, make up their own minds.

Such students would understand Ricardo's theory far better than those trained simply to reproduce its mathematical basis, logically beautiful though this is, because they would understand not merely what Ricardo was arguing in favor of, but what he was arguing against; and they would understand in turn the assaults on Ricardo made since that time, and the responses of his defenders.

Conclusion: Resourcing Pluralist Institutions

Once we understand the kind of students required, and the kind of courses that can produce such students, the kind of educational institution required becomes clear. I have shown that this calls for a radical inversion of the criterion of quality, such that the excellence becomes once again synonymous with range of intellect in place of exclusivity of technique. Who, then, can teach pluralist courses, and who can turn out pluralist students?

The answer should be: the institution that can deliver a pluralist benchmark. Does it recruit, and offer, a range of educators, a range of courses and ideas, and a range of teaching materials, providing students access to the variety of theories they need to reach good judgments? Does it demonstrate controversy in research? Do its staff, including those of a mainstream persuasion, possess expertise, as revealed by their publication record, of heterodox theories, of methodology, of the history of thought?

Merely to pose the question in this way is to highlight the difficulties. According to such a criterion, it would be a bold head who would offer her or his department as a flagship. Yet it is for precisely this reason that "assertive pluralism" holds the key to reform.

To be effective, as regulatory and behavioral theory tells us, the response will depend on the rewards. The evolutionary mechanisms of past decades were driven by a mechanism that rewarded conformity. A economics benchmark for the 21st century should consciously and explicitly reward diversity. Economic pluralism should in turn be a requirement of funding. Given such an explicit linkage—and only given this linkage—the possibility exists to train a generation of economists capable of avoiding the mistakes of their teachers. Given moral courage, political will, and academic integrity, this is an achievable outcome.

Notes

1. Huckle (2002) gives a readable account of the history of subject benchmarking in the United Kingdom that those new to the issue may find helpful.

2. I thank Andy Denis for this term. In Elsner (2009) "active pluralism" means something very similar.

3. The succession of letters to the queen when she famously asked the LSE why "nobody saw it coming" (Pierce 2008) is worthy of special note. Early contributors included Nick MacPherson, permanent secretary at the Treasury, and Goldman Sachs chief economist Jim O'Neill who jointly and severally apologized for "a failure of the collective imagination." See also Hodgson (2009).

4. De Martino (2005) proposes an economists' oath based on the Hippocratic Principle "First do no harm." Many Harvard MBA students (http://mbaoath.org/) now swear an informal oath; Garvin claims to be the first management school (http://www.highbeam.com/doc/1G1-151558443.html), with a formal oath of honor.

5. Gans and Shepherd's (1994) collection of peer-rejected classics is justly celebrated. Chubin and Hackett (1990:12) record widespread skepticism that peer review selects for merit in the natural sciences. See also Ietto-Gillies (2008).

6. Thus Briody and Prenzler (1998) directly apply the term "systemic capture" to account for regulatory capture, which they define as the "procuration of an entire regulatory system by the regulated industry."

7. Portes himself saw fit, however, when questioned in 2008 about the weakness of his testimony by a leading London hedge fund, to accuse his interlocutor of spreading false rumors in order to bring turmoil from which the fund might profit, and to denounce it to the British and Icelandic supervisory authorities.

8. See, for example, Desai (1994) for a detailed analysis of the conduct of the think tanks on which the Thatcher government drew in motivating its economic policies.

9. Freud, in *The Psychopathology of Everyday Life*, notes that Darwin evolved the habit of carrying around with him a notebook in which he immediately recorded anything he observed that contradicted his views. He did so, Freud approvingly notes, because he realized that the pressure to

forget what is inconvenient is particularly strong, and so particular measures need to be taken to counter it.

    10. See Card and Krueger (1995) and Manning (2003).

    11. See Fujita et al. (1999).

References

Brenner, R. (2002). *The Boom and the Bubble: The US in the World Economy.* Verso.

Briody, M., and T. Prenzler. (1998). "The Enforcement of Environmental Protection Laws in Queensland: A Case of Regulatory Capture." *Environmental and Planning Law Journal* 15(1).

Buiter, W. (2009). "The Unfortunate Uselessness of Most 'State of the Art' Academic Monetary Economics." *Financial Times*, March 3.

Card, D., and A. Kruger. (1995). *Myth and Measurement.* Princeton, NJ: Princeton University Press.

Chubin, D., and E. Hackett. (1990) *Peerless Science: Peer Review and U.S. Science Policy.* Albany: State University of New York Press.

Colander, D., H. Foellmer, A. Haas, et al. (2009). "The Financial Crisis and the Systemic Failure of Academic Economics," Kiel Institute for the World Economy.

Dearing (1997). *National Committee of Inquiry into Higher Education (Dearing) Report of 1997.* London: HMSO.

Denis, A. (Ed.) (2009). *International Review of Economics Education Volume 8, Issue 2,* special issue on Pluralism in Economics Education [http://www.economicsnetwork.ac.uk/iree/v8n2/ accessed 24 May 2010].

Desai, R. (1994). "Second-Hand Dealers in Ideas: Think-Tanks and Thatcherite Hegemony." *New Left Review* I(203) (February).

Elsner, W. (2009). Report to the Bremen Conference on Peer Review in Economics. Manuscript.

Freeman, A. (2007). "Catechism Versus Pluralism: The Heterodox Response to the National Undergraduate Curriculum Proposed by the UK Quality Assurance Authority." Presented at the annual conference of ICAPE, Utah, June 1–3 [http://mpra.ub.uni-muenchen.de/6832/1/MPRA_paper_6832.pdf, accessed May 24, 2010].

——. (2008). "Submission from the AHE to the International Benchmarking Review on Research Assessment." *On the Horizon* 16(4): 279–285.

——. (2009). "The Economists of Tomorrow." [http://ideas.repec.org/p/pra/mprapa/15691.html].

Freeman, A., and A. Kliman. (2008). "Beyond Talking the Talk." In E. Fullbrook (Ed.), *Pluralist Economics.* Zed Books.

Fujita, M., P. Krugman, and T. Venables. (1999). *The Spatial Economy: Cities, Regions, and International Trade.* Boston: MIT Press.

Fullbrook, E. (2001). *Real Science is Pluralist; An Argument for Pluralism in Economics.* Post-Autistics Economics Network.

———. (2008). *Pluralist Economics.* Zed Books Ltd.

Gans, J., and G. Shepherd. (1994). "How the Mighty Have Fallen: Rejected Classic Articles by Leading Economists." *Journal of Economic Perspectives* 8: 165–79.

Hodgson, G. (2009) (originator). *Letter from Ten UK Economists* [http://www.feed-charity.org/user/image/queen2009b.pdf].

Hodgson, G., U. Mäki, and D. McCloskey. (1992) (originators). "A Plea for a Pluralistic and Rigorous Economics." *American Economic Review* 82(2).

Huckle, M. (2002) "Driving Change in the Profession: Subject Benchmarking in UK Library and Information Management." *Libri* 52: 209–213

Ietto-Gillies, G. (2008). "A XXI-Century Alternative to XX-Century Peer Review." *Real-World Economics Review* (45).

Lee, F. (2007). "The Research Assessment Exercise, the State and the Dominance of Mainstream Economics in British Universities." *Cambridge Journal of Economics* 31(2): 309–325.

Lee, F., and S. Harley. (1998). "Peer Review, The Research Assessment Exercise and the Demise of Non-Mainstream Economics." *Capital and Class* (66): 23–53.

Manning, A. (2003). *Monopsony in Motion.* Princeton University Press.

Martino, G. (2005). "The Economists' Oath." *Challenge* July–August.

Mihm, S. (2008). "Dr. Doom." *New York Times* August 15.

Pettifor, A. (2006). *The Coming First World Debt Crisis.* Palgrave.

Pierce, A. (2008). "The Queen Asks Why No One Saw the Credit Crunch Coming." *Daily Telegraph* November 5.

Portes, R. (2008). *Royal Economic Society Valedictory.* Royal Economic Society Bulletin No. 141.

———. (2007). [http://www.iceland.org/media/NewsletterUK/Newsletter_-_November_2007.pdf].

Reinert, E. (2004). *Globalisation, Economic Development and Inequality: An Alternative Perspective.* Cheltenham: Elgar.

QAA (2004). *Recognition Scheme for Subject Benchmark Statements.* Gloucester: QAA.

Shiller, R. (2006). *Irrational Exuberance* (2nd ed.). Broadway Business.

Stiglitz, J. (2008). "The Triumphant Return of John Maynard Keynes." *Project Syndicate* December 1.

Tett, G. (2009). "Could 'Tobin Tax' Reshape Financial Sector DNA?" *Financial Times* August 27.

Thornton, P. (2009). "Worst of Slump Yet to Come, Says Economist." *Financial Times* July 2.

Turner, A. (2009). "The Financial Crisis and the Future of Financial Regulation." *Economist's Inaugural City Lecture*, London: FSA.

Turner, G. (2008). *The Credit Crunch: Housing Bubbles, Globalisation and the Worldwide Economic Crisis.* Pluto Press (UK).

Wade, R. H. (2008). "Iceland Pays the Price for Financial Excess." *Financial Times* July 2.

———. (2010). "Iceland Needs an Independent Center of Economic Analysis." *Flettabladid* April 28.

Wolf, M (2008). "Keynes Offers Us the Best Way to Think About the Crisis." *Financial Times* December 24.

Heterodox Economics and the Scientist's Role in Society

By Marco Novarese[†*] and Andrea Pozzali[‡]

ABSTRACT. The present work starts from a simple question: Why should a state pay the salary for an academic researcher in economics? Generally speaking, research should be financed because it is useful for socioeconomic development; knowledge represents a productive input and it increases social welfare. How much does this argument hold for economic knowledge? Is economics helping in improving wealth and well-being? This article will show how the incentive structure and the internal organization of the discipline prevent a positive answer to such questions. In fact these institutions do not necessarily stimulate researchers to understand economies, and economics completely neglects its role in shaping values because of its pretense of objectivity. Two solutions are proposed: more pluralism and a wider capacity to discuss with the whole society.

Introduction

The present work starts from a simple question: Why should a state pay the salary for an academic researcher in economics? As futile as it might seem, this question raises some important points that need to be discussed carefully. Generally speaking, research should be financed because it is useful for socioeconomic development: knowledge represents a productive input and it increases social welfare. Knowledge

We thank two anonymous referees for their comments. This research has been carried on also thanks to the support of the Regione Piemonte—"Bando per le Scienze Umane e Sociali," which financed the project "Istituzioni, comportamento e mercati in contesti locali e globali."

*Direct correspondence to: Marco Novarese, Dipartimento di Scienze Giuridiche ed Economiche, Università Amedeo Avogadro, 15100, Alessandria, Italy, marco@novarese.org

†University Amedeo Avogadro; marco@novarese.com
‡European University of Rome; andrea.pozzali@gmail.com

American Journal of Economics and Sociology, Vol. 69, No. 5 (November, 2010).
© 2010 American Journal of Economics and Sociology, Inc.

drives progress and carries with it positive effects, both on a material and on an immaterial level. As for the first, the role knowledge has played in technological, economical, and social progress was reconstructed in many different analyses, both on a theoretical and on an empirical level (Mokyr 2002; Kuznets 1965). As for the second, human beings like to develop a more complete understanding of the world they live in, even in cases where their increased knowledge does not have an immediate application: this "insatiable curiosity" (Nowotny 2008) is what drives human endeavors in science, culture, and innovation.

How much does this argument indeed hold for economic knowledge, at least in the present situation? In other words: Are we sure that economics is helping us to gain a better understanding of how economic systems really work? Also, is economics helping improve wealth and well-being? Is economic knowledge useful for society, and to what extent? The point is worth considering as more and more researchers, even within the economics community, are questioning the effective role and social usefulness of the discipline. Indeed, a sort of paradox seems to arise: a discipline that is so involved with the attribution of "value" has been at the same time so little concerned in self-evaluating its own contribution to the social progress. Indeed, clear empirical reconstructions of the usefulness of economics for society seem to be almost completely lacking in the literature.

Many contributions to the subject are based on mere assertions, speculations, and wishful thinking. Empirical "evidence" often takes the form of selected, nonrepresentative events that, moreover, are often presented in anecdotal form. Convincing empirical evidence on the effect on the economy and society of economics is missing (Frey 2000: 17). The limits of economics, and its difficulties in producing a knowledge that can actually be useful for society, have been dramatically emphasized by the present financial crisis. Economists were not able to warn against what was going to happen. Some even wonder if their recipes, and their blind faith in the market, might have been among the factors responsible for the crisis. An extensive list of all the criticisms that have been raised in this sense by other social scientists, journalists, politicians, and even laypeople is beyond the task of this contribution, but a few examples are worth mentioning.[1]

The complete incapacity of economists to forecast the crisis and their lack of humility have been fiercely attacked by Giovanni Sartori (2008), a well known political scientist, in an editorial published in the top Italian newspaper. Luca Ricolfi (2009), sociologist and editorialist, noted that the only scholars capable to anticipate the crisis were noneconomists, such as Mandelbrot (2004) or Gilpin (2000). Nassim Taleb (2009), in his bestseller *The Black Swan*, blames the "scandal of prediction," that is, the arrogance of economists and their failure to recognize what they do not know, notwithstanding the systematic bias of their expectations. During an academic briefing on the turmoil of the international markets held at the London School of Economics, Queen Elizabeth asked why nobody had been able to notice what was going on. The "Festival of the Economy," held in Trento, represents one of the most popular events for public discussion of economics in Italy involving many scholars, workshops, and consistent media coverage. One of the main themes of the 2009 edition was "The Trial of Economists," in which some of the same arguments discussed here were debated on a public base.

These are just a few examples and many others may be available. The failure in forecasting the crisis has likely eroded the public consensus surrounding economics. The different criticisms posed to economics can be summarized in two main arguments: 1) economics is far from the real world and 2) it is (as a consequence) incapable of properly and fairly orienting public debate. Two different yet complementary reasons can help to explain these problems. The first requires taking into account the epistemological nature of economics, while the other has to do with the present configuration of the community of research in economics, the way that financial and symbolic rewards are distributed, and the resulting structure of incentives economists have to confront as a result.

From the epistemic and methodological points of view, economics is more and more based on complex mathematical tools, and its models are more and more focused on the formal side instead of the substantial one (models need to be mathematically tractable: for the sake of preserving the computability of the final solution, economists may easily choose to introduce hypotheses that are far from reality). The procedures for selecting new researchers and for funding research projects enforce this situation, creating a structure of incentives that is strongly biased toward the preservation of the status quo. The following sections will analyze these two points separately and will propose some solutions for overcoming the problem.

The Epistemic and Methodological Limits of Economics

Science always has a paradigmatic nature, as it is based on models that select problems and variables in order to frame empirical experience in a specific way. This is quite an obvious statement, one we are fully accustomed to; however, the mere force of habit can make it hard for us to recognize, in full, its profound implications. In particular, we might never forget the fact that our ideas are only an approximation of reality: they do not have a value on their own, but only inasmuch as they give us a good representation of the real world. We are at risk of hypostatizing our models, if we do not keep alive this implicit link between the models and the underlying reality.

Unfortunately, when it comes to economic knowledge, this link between models and reality has, to a great extent, been lost. Economics seems to be closed in a self-referent dimension, impervious to any influence by reality. The capacity to interact with the real world no longer matters. Economists are asked to manage a series of formal tools and analytical abstract ideas, necessary for being accepted by their peers:

> Economics has increasingly become the analysis of formal and self-defined problems within a closed academic field. Economics tends not to be used in order to meet the challenges posed by reality, but to engage in an academic discourse following accepted intellectual standards. No contribution to economic policy is intended. (Frey 2000: 17)

So the discipline is obsessed with formalism, which makes its development far from reality:

> For many orthodox economists, the scope of mathematical expression is taken to be so great that arguments which cannot be backed up, however loosely, by mathematical argument are seen either to be poorly expressed or not economics at all. Such a position legitimizes the tendency for orthodox economists to ignore those elements of heterodox economics that are not expressed mathematically. (Dow 2000: 160)

Objections and alternative points of view can thus be fully ignored on a purely formal level, notwithstanding their potential interest on a substantial ground. This lack of pluralism and of internal debate can carry with it dire consequences, as it gives birth to a partial and limited knowledge.[2] Under a purely epistemological point of view, it is well known, at least since the contribution of Popper (2002), that the essential trait of a research community should be the possibility of maintaining a climate of open discussion in which ideas are unceasingly exposed to public scrutiny and there are no a prioristic accepted truths. Conflict represents one of the basic attributes of the intellectual world: the clash between different point of views, perspectives, and methods is the main force that can sustain the development of new, innovative ideas (Collins 2002). The value of pluralism then, lies in a kind of ethical imperative, but also in its epistemological superiority: it is the only structuring principle that can guarantee that our knowledge can develop in a useful way.[3]

This need for more pluralism in economics has two dimensions. On one side, it must be intended as a competition between ideas and models, necessary for a better understanding of the real world. Different perspectives allow us to see different problems and compare many solutions.[4] On the other side, it should be, in fact, seen as the only guarantee to have an economic knowledge that can actually contribute to orienting public decision and policy making. As stated by Boulding (1969), sciences (especially social sciences), in fact, do not simply describe the world. Sciences also modify the observed world. Economics determines mental categories, ideas, politics, variables to be considered, and data to be gathered. As an example, inflation and income are cultural constructs with profound implications on public life. Economics can influence human behavior and modify the same environment it tries to describe. Saying that, as an example, people are motivated just by materialistic gains or losses can influence how people perceive political decisions and the same reality, also creating expectations and desires. It is known, for example, that economics students show more egoism in experiments (Frank et al. 1993).[5] A partial view of economics and a myopic representation of rationality, then, is not only inadequate on an epistemological ground: it can also affect reality in a nondemocratic way.

The Role of Economics and the Need for Pluralism

In a social division of labor, economists should have the role of suggesting how the world can be represented and seen. This carries many implications in terms of the practical, but also cultural, usefulness economics should have. Economics should contribute to the social and political debate, orienting it, or at least trying to. Competition among different views should be normal, public, and accessible to any interested person. The present organization of academic research denies both these simple needs. The debate is, at most, possible in the form of a competition between disciplines. Economics competes, in some way, with sociology, for example, but the real interaction is almost null. The mainstream approach in economics, indeed, denies any need for interaction with other scientists.

Given the present situation, it should come as no surprise that calls for a different approach to economics and for pluralism have been launched on several occasions (Sent 2006): we can here recall the "Plea for a Pluralistic and Rigorous Economics," issued in 1992 as an advertisement in the *American Economic Review* and signed by 44 economists, including Nobel laureates Franco Modigliani, Paul Samuelson, Herbert Simon, and Jan Tinbergen. The following year, in 1993, a consortium of over 30 groups in economics founded the International Confederation of Associations for Pluralism in Economics (ICAPE), whose statement of purpose suggests that "pluralism and intellectual progress are complements" (http://www.icape.org). In 2000 it was the turn of a group of economics students in France, who published a petition on the web in favor of a pluralistic approach to economics, under the banner "autisme-économie" (http://www.autisme.economie.org). In 2001, 27 economics Ph.D. students at Cambridge University in England issued a petition entitled "Opening Up Economics" ending their proposal as follows: "we are not arguing against mainstream methods, but believe in a pluralism of methods and approaches justified by debate. Pluralism as a default implies that alternative economic work is not simply tolerated, but that the material and social conditions for its flourishing are met, to the same extent as is currently the case for mainstream economics. That is what we mean when we refer to an 'opening up' of economics" (http://www.paecon.net/PAEtexts/Cambridge27.htm).

It is hard to evaluate if the above mentioned calls have caused a real effect in "opening up" economics. The attention to heterodox approaches is probably growing. The Internet helps to build and maintain new communities, by spreading information about papers (see Novarese and Zimmerman 2008) and conferences. However, it does not seem that all of this has had any relevant practical consequence on the way that the community of research in economics is structured. Mainstream economists have been particularly able to ignore any potential criticism or plea for pluralism. This has been done also by simply considering this type of argument as something that should not be considered as part of the "economic community," as it is the result of other type of "sociological," "esoteric," or "not representative" school of thought (Dobusch and Kapeller 2009).[6]

This strategy of denying any intellectual value to arguments that do not strictly adhere to the mainstream arguments is not something new in the intellectual world: it is one of the most diffused ways in which intellectual fortresses can be created and maintained over time (Collins 2002). As perfectly rational as they may seem, if considered from the point of view of the insiders who try to protect their position of acquired intellectual prestige, these arguments erroneously blur the distinction between facts and values, and between normative and positive analysis. As Commons (1990) states, social sciences (including economics) are guided by values. We cannot thus posit the existence of purely objective standards for the evaluation of science, as any comparison between different approaches and methodologies involve a dispute between conflicting values. This kind of disputes must be resolved through a cumulative decision-making process, in which the final aim is the definition of a "reasonable value," that always represents a compromise, and a temporary, solution (Bazzoli 2000). Mainstream economists a prioristically refuse to consider arguments that do not fit into their narrow, self-defined standards. Any conflict is denied and thus prevents any social process of negotiation and redefining of values to take place. Thinking that economics is free of values *de facto* leads to the imposition of partial values.

In Commons's (1990) view institutions arise from the bottom, but are selected at the top, where conflicts need to be mediated and solved considering all points of view. Economics can be seen as an institution among others, and therefore, it needs to be treated and studied as any other institution. Common's concern on the need to mediate among different interests should be taken into account also in respect to the conflict within this discipline. Pluralism should be allowed and enforced by the state: it's the only way in which we can guarantee that, in the process of defining the "reasonable social value," all different points of view can be openly discussed and confronted.

The Structure of Incentives, or How to Become a Good Economist

Considering the above reflections on the limits of economics in developing realistic models and ideas that can represent a sort of "useful knowledge" for society, one could wonder why it is so difficult to change things. From a social perspective, economists should develop ideas and useful solutions for the society. This social role is the rationale for having the state financing the work of economists. The problem is that the real incentive in economics is not for useful ideas. Indeed, apart from the social dimension, our work as researchers has another dimension: the legal one. This dimension has not so much to do with what an economist ought to do for society as a whole, but rather with the specific requirements imposed by the particular labor market he/she has to cope with. To be recognized as an economist in the "academic marketplace" (Caplow and McGee 2001) you need to be able to know and teach some given issues (otherwise you will not be selected); you need to be able to apply a well defined (and quite limited) set of tools and approaches. As seen, these tools are not only quite specific, but for the most part, they do not admit different points of view and do not even allow for an easy diffusion of economics results. Moreover, even the selection of research themes is highly constrained: some topics that are not considered to be relevant by mainstream economics are at risk of being completely neglected, notwithstanding their potential interest for society as a whole.

So to prove to be capable of being economists, researchers are forced to become specialists, approved by their own peers and not interested in dialoguing with society, neglecting their social role. The career depends on the success within the profession, and not on the real problems solved or in the skills of highlighting new issues. As Colander (1989: 34) puts in a short and very effective way: "The incentives in the economics profession are for articles, not ideas" (see also Frey 2000, 2003). The main criterion for the selection and evaluation of economists is represented by the publication record, and in particular, by the number of papers published in a limited set of so-called A-journals (Frey 2009). Even if this might be considered as a reasonable mechanism, it can lead to paradoxical consequences. In order to publish, economists need to conform to the academic style and logic. Choi (2002) proposes in clear terms a series of rules that young economists need to learn fast. Among many others, they need to be careful not to "put two good ideas in one paper." This last rule is quite astonishing in a job were ideas should be welcome, yet papers should focus on just one topic and follow specific rules.

Given the uncertainty in evaluating a researcher's work and capacities, proxy variables have to be used. These proxies are not necessarily perfect indicators. Yet as they can be easily measured, they tend to become the only goal (Simon 1991). Publication in a prestigious journal is a proxy that can give us hints concerning the effort a researcher has put in her work, and the significance of the results he or she has achieved, but it is not a perfect indicator of the quality of one's work and surely is not a reliable indicator of the effort. Instead of spending time understanding how economic systems work, economists have to use their time trying to have their paper published, regardless of its substantial content.

Peer Review and Freedom of Research

The incentive system, therefore, tends to reduce the room for different points of view, and to develop a sterile debate, with an inner language not understandable to the general public. Even worse, it also ends up reducing the effective researchers' freedom to pursue their own path of inquiry. In all developed countries, freedom of research represents a fundamental value (one that is even stated in some constitutions, for example, the Italian one). What does this mean? This kind of statement aims at protecting research from the possible interference from the state. Yet state intervention is not the only threat that can constrain researchers' work. Apart from the freedom of research against external interference, there should also be the need for a certain degree of freedom for researchers (to pursue their own preferred line of inquiry).

The justification of freedom of research should lie in the impossibility of knowing in advance which ideas are most useful, stimulating, and interesting for social development. The same ideas used by Hayek to explain the necessity of economic freedom hold here. Also, when dealing with research, freedom is a matter of comparison and competition between different approaches. When the possibility for this comparison and competition is limited by the presence of mechanisms that breed conformity and do not allow for dissent to be expressed, freedom itself can be at risk. The "logic of liberty" (Polanyi 1951) indeed requires a certain kind of tension between authority and heterodoxy, control and innovation, conformism and dissent: the balance between these two opposite forces should be maintained, not allowing for one of them to become the prevalent driver.

Both the legal dimension of research and the cognitive characteristics of human beings constrains this freedom. Peer reviews result in an insidious pressure on researchers to choose certain specific topics, tools, and methods.[7] As Frey (2003) pointed out, the tendency toward conformity could be particularly higher for young researchers, and this is highly detrimental for the development of new lines of thought and for the birth of new ideas and approaches. To be considered part of the community, researchers need to conform to the uses and approaches accepted by the mainstream: this need is stronger at the beginning of the career, when researchers are weaker. If a researcher starts his/her research from a mainstream point of view, and later tries to develop new ideas, it could be a good path, but literature on cognition and learning suggests that rules developed in the first part of the career tend to be reinforced and become stable. The path dependence evolution of the discipline (Dobusch and Kapeller 2009) can have an individual counterpart in single careers. After a researcher begins a career working on mainstream ideas, he/she can hardly switch to a different approach. As pointed out by Simon (1957), in fact, the value systems and the set of shared norms and behaviors that characterize a given institution can push individuals toward the preferential adoption of certain styles of thinking and reasoning, which in turn, produces a certain path of behavior.

We are not stating that the legal dimension is not at all legitimate. Mechanisms of evaluation are needed to avoid completely arbitrary research, and to prevent incapable scholars from entering the community. External control would be detrimental for the freedom of research (history gives us many important warnings in this regard), yet we believe there is a sort of tradeoff between the freedom for researchers (and its beneficial effects) and the legal dimension of the economics profession, as it is conceived these days. We even think that it is so biased against the possibility of dissent that it can end up severely limiting the same right to express freedom of thought. This is particularly relevant, as far as we are ready to recognize that science creates the world, as well as reflects it.

The Limits of Ethics

Given the above mentioned problems, what solutions can be envisaged at present? Can the whole matter be settled by simply referring to a kind of individual "ethics for economists" (granting, for the sake of the argument, that such ethics actually exist)? Or could we also refer more generally to a global "ethics for economics as a science?" Or should we take a step further, and say that ethics by itself is not enough?

Even if intellectual honesty, and open mindedness, should be the basic endowment of every good researcher, it rarely is in reality. We can surely try to teach these values, but individual ethics alone would hardly be able to solve the problem, as human decisions are deeply influenced by cognitive and motivational variables; besides, how many degrees in economics require a basic course of ethics?[8]

First of all, as recognized by Scitovsky (1976), among others, people are usually able to understand and appreciate an object only if it shows some aspects of redundancy, for example, similarities with their previous experiences. New issues need to be connected with something that is already known; people can rarely appreciate an entirely new kind of artistic expression, almost nobody is interested in news that does not connect to something already experienced. Following this idea, mainstream economists could hardly understand and appreciate alternative approaches, as these do not fit into their acquired mental schemas and do not resonate with other known experiences.[9] The basic training young economists receive has a clear impact on the specific path they will choose: even if this linkage should not be interpreted in a deterministic way (as already said, there is always the possibility of changing one's mind[10]), as long as heterodox approaches do not receive enough room in economics curriculum, the problem will not be solved.

Cognitive psychology has also shown that on average, people are not very good at judging their own ideas, and this holds in particular when people are called to evaluate if their behavior is more or less "ethical" (Epley and Caruso 2004; Epley and Dunning 2000; Messick and Bazerman 1996). As far as research in economics is concerned, we cannot rely on individual intellectual honesty because researchers are not able to accurately evaluate their own activity, and their related social utility. In the absence of a different selection mechanism, even an "ethical economist" should need to find an external justification, and if the only way in which he/she can find it is by making reference to the judgment of his or her peers, the ethical dimension could in the end have no practical consequences on his/her decisions.[11]

The fact that a researcher considers his/her approach to represent the best that is possible is not only almost inevitable, but it is also justifiable, at least according to the moral division of labor that goes hand in hand with the technical one. Jacobs (2005: 146–147) gives us a precise account of how this moral division of labor works, starting with an example of an everyday situation: a terrible childish row. In cases like these, parents should not just ask their children what has happened; they should also look for an impartial point of view by asking an uninvolved judge:

> It is worthwhile to look at the circumstances that made me call upon an arbitrator, because a generalization of these circumstances forms the

background of the judicial system, which is underpinned by a clear moral division of labor. I accepted beforehand the possibility that my children had done wrong. I was, however, suspicious about my ability to judge both sides of the quarrel, knowing that as a parent I naturally support my children. This gave me the idea of an arbitrator.

The same reasons are at the basis of the need for a legal system. Jacobs quotes Locke:

> For every one in that state [of Nature] being both Judge and Executioner of the Law of Nature, Men being partial to themselves, Passion and Revenge is very apt to carry them too far, and with too much heat, in their own Cases; as well as negligence, and unconcernedness, to make them too remiss, in other Mens. (1970: 369)

The moral division of labor also helps in simplifying decisions that otherwise would be too complex. One does not need to consider and evaluate the many aspects involved in a problem. It is possible to focus only on one side. So, speaking of the law, Jacobs also refers to lawyers:

> The moral division of labour even allows them [lawyers] a kind of moral refuge, in which some normal moral rules are suspended. They are free to do whatever they deem necessary for the defence of their client, as long as they remain within the limits of the law. It is, for instance, not forbidden for a lawyer to ask insinuating questions about the promiscuous conduct of a woman who has shed one of her lovers and now has filed charges of rape against him, while in normal life morality often asks us to shut up.

The problem of the moral division of labor arises each time an activity cannot be evaluated by means of an impartial and objective assessment or mechanism (like the one that is provided, under some specific circumstances, by consumer's choice in a free and competitive market); therefore, those who practice it cannot have a global evaluation of their work, but can and must rely only on a partial point of view. This is a problem that concerns many forms of specialization: moreover, the more the system of evaluation is partial, the more nonexperts are excluded from the full understanding of what is going on. For this reason, performances cannot be evaluated by nonexperts and therefore there is the need to certify *a priori* the skill of specialists.[12]

In the case we are considering, the partiality of researchers for example, the fact that they are chasing their career and not a hypothetical public interest is thus acceptable insofar as it forms part of a larger system that protects social welfare in other ways. This is possible if the system of incentives allows for real individual freedom (what we called "researchers' freedom"), which in turn represents the essential requisite for a free competition of different ideas and points of view. If this competition is not possible, the one dominant approach represents the only parameter of judgment, and the problems linked to the moral division of labor arise. Those who control and those who are controlled are part of the same (micro) system, and their detachment from the general society will go on further. This brings us back to the fact that ethics alone is not enough.

To sum it all up, the specific features of the present system of peer reviewing are inadequate to improve our understanding of economies and social systems. The system breeds conformism and strongly limits the possibility for competition and alternative points of view. Some of the main biases are known, and solutions have been proposed in the literature. Frey (2003) focuses on the specific procedure for reviewing contributions to scientific journals and argues that little changes (such as giving more power and more responsibilities to editors than to anonymous referees) could at least mitigate adverse effects. More specific corrections can also be envisaged, for example, by developing criteria that allow for a more balanced evaluation of alternative approaches (Lee 2008). In general, the different specific amendments to the present system seem to be based on two general principles: 1) allowing for an equal evaluation of different and heterodox approaches, and 2) letting other indicators enter the evaluation process, in addition to the mere adequacy to formal requirements.

A New "Social Contract" Between Economics and Society?

Apart from the specific and technical solutions that can be devised in order to produce a more balanced incentives structure, a first general consideration can be made, which is linked to the argument we raised at the beginning of this article, and is connected with the role of economics in society. As a matter of fact, it seems that economics has been following the model provided by other "hard" sciences, such as physics or medicine. Among other things, economics has embraced what we can consider to be a general tendency on the side of science: to consider itself as a separate realm that can operate in isolation from the laws and rules of the overall society. The presence of a sort of clear cut separation between science and society has been recognized since the first sociological accounts of the community of research, and was reflected also in philosophy of science (where scientific knowledge was given a separate status) and in the public perception of science (Merton 1973; Mulkay 1979). The implicit social contract that was stipulated between science and society was based on the fact that the first was recognized to have a substantial degree of autonomy, provided that it would in this way produce knowledge that was valuable for society.

During the course of the 20th century, this separation between science and society was progressively eroded, and it was replaced by a more profound understanding of the inevitable linkages between the mechanisms for the production of knowledge and the social context (Gibbons 1998). Science can no more pretend to operate in isolation from societal needs and demands: this is true in general, but it is even more so given that we live in complex societies, where the role and relevance of knowledge is continuously on the rise. As scientific knowledge is more and more likely to produce important effects on society as a whole, scientists need to be constantly aware that they do not operate in an ideal world, where the only concerns are linked to the need of finding the most refined and elegant solutions to abstract and theoretical problems. Moreover, science and scientists also have a responsibility in diffusing their knowledge to a wider audience because spreading knowledge among the public is part of a researcher's job. As economics is not value free, seeing that it imposes values on the external world, a continuous dialogue is necessary to spread and gather ideas.

Social values are social and political constructions. Economics should contribute to building knowledge and consciousness. So pluralism has to be seen in a very wide meaning: it should include contributions coming from outside academia too. A discussion between different academic approaches could not be sufficient. In describing the hypothetical dilemma of Jean, a scientist involved in genomic research, Philip Kitcher (2001: 195–196) touches some important points for the functioning of scientific research in a democracy:

> if Jean believes that the ground needs to be prepared for an open discussion that will avoid the tyranny of the ignorant, then she has the obligation to do some of the digging. In particular, she should use what skills she has to advance public understanding of the questions with which she [is] concerned and to encourage people outside science to appreciate the point of the inquiries she and her colleagues undertake. One aspect of this responsibility is supporting those in her community who attempt to articulate scientific ideas in popular settings (provided, of course, that they do so accurately); another is to think creatively about forms of education in science that would aim to give students a broad understanding of how particular fields hang together rather than serving as the early phases of an initiation into research science. Furthermore, insofar as the benefits of the projected investigation are epistemic, they deserve to be appreciated more broadly, and the task of improving public understanding of the sciences can be expected to stimulate and satisfy the curiosity of many people who are not involved with the fine details.

What holds for Jean, the hypothetical biologist, holds also in general for economists. Economics and society can no longer be considered as two separate spheres: it is necessary for the economic science to learn (as other sciences have done or are doing) to "come to terms" with social question and needs.

It is indeed quite hard to imagine that this kind of evolution could be the result of an inner push that originates within the economics community; however, we may think that the present situation, in which the empirical limit of the mainstream approach has been so clearly highlighted, could represent a good occasion for society to start inquiring more in depth into the ways in which economic knowledge is produced. This should not be done by imposing some sort of internal hierarchic control, as we have already said. Rather, what should be done is simple: researchers should be required to become more open to public debate.[13] As an immediate consequence, we may think, for example, that an economist should not only be assessed on the basis of his/her scientific output, but also on the basis of his/her teaching, ability to transform knowledge into active policy measures, and also the ability to disseminate his/her knowledge. This dimension in particular is too often overlooked, but it is also essential because it can have direct effects on the economy itself: a world in which people are able to understand the foundations of economic science and its paradigmatic nature may be completely different from a world in which such knowledge is limited. Divulgation activities such as writing in newspapers are currently not included in evaluation systems, even if they may be instrumental in giving birth to debates and collective discussions that could be, paradoxically, more "valuable" for society as a whole than an article in an "A-journal." Just like other scientists in general, economists, too, should be required to more actively communicate their knowledge to the public.[14] This should be done also to avoid a deep gap arising between the "economy of the street" and the "economy of the academy." The economic reality to which these two separate streams refer is unique:

> there is a strong trend to an "everyday economics" used by journalists, politicians, public administrators and persons managing the media. The respective books quite often result in best-sellers read by millions of persons. This kind of economics is far from the discourse dominating our field today: the formally oriented scholars with the highest reputation within the field are often virtually speechless. This, in turn, strengthens views which are far from the teaching and research of academic economics. (Frey 2000: 19)

Another way to reduce the self-referential isolation of the discipline, one that could also help to include dissemination activities into the evaluation process, might pass through a substantial reform of the peer-review process itself. Noneconomists, like civil servants, could be included in the evaluation juries. This is quite an extreme idea, given the present situation. Most of economics would probably consider this as a provocation. Yet, a hypothesis that may sound less strange is to start thinking at a wider composition, at least for those commissions that have to evaluate research projects. After all, money should be a powerful motivator for economists.

Notes

1. For other examples, see the contribution by Alan Freeman in this issue.
2. See also Freeman (this issue).
3. One could also provocatively argue that the epistemological primacy of pluralism is due to the fact that it enables a "perfect competition" between different alternative hypotheses. It is then quite paradoxical that the same

enthusiastic apologists of the free market for goods refuse the possibility of an open competition between alternative points of view in the "market for ideas," and have ended up building *de facto* a situation of monopolistic control on the discipline.

4. It is precisely the incapability of taking into consideration alternative hypotheses that many consider to be at the basis of the failure of economics in forecasting and in managing the financial crisis. Indeed, conceptual tools developed in mainstream economics are built on the presumption that markets operate, or tend to operate, in a situation of equilibrium, and are thus completely useless in situations of crises. Unfortunately, these are precisely the times when economics should be more helpful for society, and when a detailed understanding of the real functioning of economic systems would be more required and useful: "The majority of economists . . . failed to warn policy makers about the threatening system crisis and ignored the work of those who did. Ironically, as the crisis has unfolded, economists have had no choice but to abandon their standard models and to produce hand-waving common-sense remedies. Common-sense advice, although useful, is a poor substitute for an underlying model that can provide much-needed guidance for developing policy and regulation. It is not enough to put the existing model to one side, observing that one needs, 'exceptional measures for exceptional times'. What we need are models capable of envisaging such 'exceptional times' " (Colander et al. 2009: 3). The development of such models requires a completely different approach, based on the possibility that the market could operate in a situation of disequilibrium. It should come as no surprise, then, that the only economists able to warn against the danger of the crisis have been heterodox economists (see also Freeman this issue).

5. Recently, the sociology of scientific knowledge has started to analyze how economic models can contribute to alter the same reality they study (Knorr Cetina, and Preda 2005). It can be shown on an empirical ground, for example, how finance theory played an active, "performative" role in the stock market crash of 1987 and in the collapse of the hedge fund long-term capital management: "Financial economics . . . did more than analyze markets; it altered them. It was an 'engine' in a sense not intended by Friedman: an active force transforming its environment, not a camera passively recording it" (MacKenzie 2006: 12, where the author makes an explicit reference to Friedman's idea that economics should be intended as an "engine" to understand the world and not as an exact photographical reproduction of reality). By the way, this kind of research may be seen as a direct empirical proof of Keynes's well-known statement: "The ideas of economists and political philosophers, both when they are right and when they are wrong, are more powerful than is commonly understood. Indeed the world is ruled by little else. Practical men, who believe themselves to be quite exempt

from any intellectual influence, are usually the slaves of some defunct economist."

6. This is how, for example, Solow (2001) replied to the petition for a "post-autistic" economics by accusing the students who launched this petition of being bad mathematicians.

7. Here again we can find another pernicious effect of the lack of pluralism.

8. Most students of economics are not even faced with the basic concepts in philosophy of science. The same "as if" paradigm that represents one of the main arguments economics has developed against the accusation of lacking realism is often not presented to the students in the course of their studies.

9. It must be underlined that even if the opposite could also be true, heterodox economists, usually, show at least a partial knowledge and understanding of mainstream economics, as this approach is taught in any course of economics.

10. Concerning the difficulty of getting rid of old ideas and embracing new perspectives, we can refer to what Keynes wrote in the preface of his *General Theory*: "The difficulty lies, not in the new ideas, but in escaping from the old ones, which ramify, for those brought up as most of us have been, into every corner of our minds."

11. Ethics, in this framework, can only act in the way that a researcher could try to solve the kind of "cognitive dissonance" (Festinger 1957) that may arise in case the decisions taken in order to obtain a positive evaluation by their peers force them to go against their deep values and beliefs. See Frey (2003) for a nice account of how this argument applies to the publication of economics papers.

12. In many cases, the problem is further complicated by the fact that whatever the evaluation, it cannot be performed by looking only at the outcome of the activity because this same outcome can be influenced also by external factors that are beyond control. If this holds, we cannot exclude that "good" outcomes come out of faulty processes or that "good" processes end up producing poor performances. The research field is precisely one of the cases in which this last situation may arise, as far as doing research is by definition a complex activity that is always at risk of not succeeding, regardless of the amount or quality of individual and collective effort. Caution should then be used in assessing the quality of research only on the basis of partial indicators.

13. We know that in this way we may be moving on a sort of "slippery ground," as far as in the history of economic thought we have seen many times in the past when the intervention of society has represented a way to eliminate (or to marginalize) economic approaches that ran counter to the dominant interests (Lee 2009). However, we think that such an opening up of economics to society is almost unavoidable, in the present phase. It might also

represent a real substantial opportunity for change. Indeed, it seems quite difficult that economics can self-reform from within, for the reasons we have highlighted, and also given the present unbalance in the distribution of resources and power between different approaches: maybe an external push could represent an important element of change.

14. The European Charter for Researchers, among the "General Principles and Requirements applicable to Researchers," explicitly states that "Researchers should make every effort to ensure that their research is relevant to society" and that "Researchers should ensure that their research activities are made known to society at large in such a way that they can be understood by non-specialists, thereby improving the public's understanding of science. Direct engagement with the public will help researchers better understand public interest in priorities for science and technology and also the public's concerns" (http://eceuropa.eu/euraxess). If this holds for scientists in general, why should it not be applied also to economists?

References

Bazzoli, L. (2000). "Institutional Economics and the Specificity of Social Evolution. About the Contribution of J.R. Commons." In *Is Economics an Evolutionary Science?* Eds. F. Louca and M. Perlman. Cheltenham: Edward Elgar.

Boulding, K. E. (1969). "Economics as a Moral Science." *American Economic Review* 58: 1–12.

Caplow, T., and R. J. McGee. (2001). *The Academic Marketplace.* New Brunswick: Transaction Publishers.

Choi, K. (2002). "How to Publish in Top Journals." Retrieved from http://www.roie.org/howi.htm.

Colander, D. (1989). "Research on the Economics Profession." *Journal of Economic Perspectives* 3: 137–148.

Colander, D., H. Föllmer, A. Haas, M. Goldberg, K. Juselius, A. Kirman, T. Lux, and B. Sloth. (2009). "The Financial Crisis and the Systemic Failure of Academic Economics." Middlebury College Economics Discussion Paper No. 09-01.

Collins, R. (2002). "On the Acrimoniousness of Intellectual Disputes." *Common Knowledge* 8: 47–69.

Commons, J. R. (1990). *Institutional Economics: Its Place in Political Economy.* New Brunswick: Transaction Publishers.

Dobusch, L., and J. Kapeller. (2009). "Why is Economics Not an Evolutionary Science? New Answers to Veblen's Old Question." *Journal of Economic Issues* 43: 867–898.

Dow, S. C. (2000). "Prospects for the Progress of Heterodox Economics." *Journal of the History of Economic Thought* 22: 157–170.

Epley, N., and E. M. Caruso. (2004). "Egocentric Ethics." *Social Justice Research* 17: 171–187.

Epley, N., and D. Dunning. (2000). "Feeling 'Holier Than Thou': Are Self-Serving Assessments Produced by Errors in Self- or Social Prediction?" *Journal of Personality and Social Psychology* 79: 861–875.

Festinger, L. (1957). *A Theory of Cognitive Dissonance*. Stanford: Stanford University Press.

Frank, R. H., T. Gilovich, and D. T. Regan. (1993). "Does Studying Economics Inhibit Cooperation?" *Journal of Economic Perspectives* 7: 159–171.

Frey, B. S. (2009). "Economists in the PITS?" Institute for Empirical Research in Economics Working Paper No. 406, University of Zurich.

——. (2003). "Publishing as Prostitution?—Choosing Between One's Own Ideas and Academic Success." *Public Choice* 116: 205–223.

——. (2000). "Does Economics have an Effect? Towards an Economics of Economics." Institute for Empirical Research in Economics Working Paper No. 36, University of Zurich.

Gibbons, M. (1998). "Science's New Social Contract With Society." *Nature* 402: 11–18.

Gilpin, R. (2000). *The Challenge of Global Capitalism*. Princeton: Princeton University Press.

Jacobs, F. (2005). "Reasonable Partiality in Professional Ethics: The Moral Division of Labour." *Ethical Theory and Moral Practice* 8: 141–154.

Kitcher, P. (2001). *Science, Truth and Democracy*. New York: Oxford University Press.

Knorr Cetina, K., and A. Preda (eds.). (2005). *The Sociology of Financial Markets*. Oxford: Oxford University Press.

Kuznets, S. (1965). *Economic Growth and Structure*. New York: Norton.

Lee, F. S. (2009). *A History of Heterodox Economics: Challenging the Mainstream in the Twentieth Century*. London: Routledge.

——. (2008). "A Case for Ranking Heterodox Journals and Departments." *On the Horizon* 16: 241–251.

Locke, J. (1970). "The Second Treatise of Government." In *Locke's Two Treatises of Government* (second edition). Ed. P. Laslett. Cambridge: Cambridge University Press.

MacKenzie, D. (2006). *An Engine, Not a Camera. How Financial Models Shape Markets*. Cambridge: MIT Press.

Mandelbrot, B. (2004). *The (Mis)Behavior of Markets: A Fractal View of Risk, Ruin, and Reward*. New York: Basic Books.

Merton, R. K. (1973). *The Sociology of Science. Theoretical and Empirical Investigations*. Chicago: Chicago University Press.

Messick, D. M., and M. H. Bazerman. (1996). "Ethical Leadership and the Psychology of Decision Making." *Sloan Management Review* 37(2): 9–22.

Mokyr, J. (2002). *The Gifts of Athena. Historical Origins of the Knowledge Economy.* Princeton: Princeton University Press.

Mulkay, M. (1979). *Science and the Sociology of Knowledge.* London: Allen & Unwin.

Nowotny, H. (2008). *Insatiable Curiosity. Innovation in a Fragile Future.* Cambridge: MIT Press.

Novarese, M., and C. Zimmerman (2008). "Heterodox Economics and Dissemination of Research Through the Internet: The Experience of RePEc and NEP." *On the Horizon* 16: 198–204.

Polanyi, M. (1951). *The Logic of Liberty. Reflections and Rejoinders.* Chicago: University of Chicago Press.

Popper, K. R. (2002). *Conjectures and Refutations: The Growth of Scientific Knowledge.* London: Routledge.

Ricolfi, L. (2009). "Domande agli scienziati." *La Stampa* April 12.

Sartori, G. (2008). "Le previsioni fallite." *Il Corriere della Sera* October 16.

Scitovsky, T. (1976). *The Joyless Economy: The Psychology of Human Satisfaction.* Oxford: Oxford University Press.

Sent, E-M. (2006). "Pluralism in Economics." In *Scientific Pluralism.* Eds. S. Kellert, H. Longino, and K. Waters. Minnesota: Minnesota Studies in the Philosophy of Science.

Solow, R. (2001). "L'économie entre empirisme et mathématisation." *Le Monde* January 3.

Simon, H. A. (1991). "Organizations and Markets." *Journal of Economic Perspectives* 5: 25–44.

——. (1957). "Rational Choice and the Structure of the Environment." In *Models of Man.* New York: Wiley.

Taleb, N. (2009). *The Black Swan.* New York: Random House.

Index

for